S0-AUX-325

Gellhorn-Antitrust Law & Econ. 3rd Ed.—1

Nutshell Series
Hornbook Series
and
Black Letter Series
of
WEST PUBLISHING COMPANY
P.O. Box 64526
St. Paul, Minnesota 55164–0526

———

Accounting

FARIS' ACCOUNTING AND LAW IN A NUTSHELL, 377 pages, 1984. Softcover. (Text)

Administrative Law

GELLHORN AND BOYER'S ADMINISTRATIVE LAW AND PROCESS IN A NUTSHELL, Second Edition, 445 pages, 1981. Softcover. (Text)

Admiralty

MARAIST'S ADMIRALTY IN A NUTSHELL, Second Edition, 379 pages, 1988. Softcover. (Text)

SCHOENBAUM'S HORNBOOK ON ADMIRALTY AND MARITIME LAW, Student Edition, 692 pages, 1987 with 1989 pocket part. (Text)

Agency—Partnership

REUSCHLEIN AND GREGORY'S HORNBOOK ON THE LAW OF AGENCY AND PARTNERSHIP, Second Edition, Approximately 650 pages, 1990. (Text)

STEFFEN'S AGENCY-PARTNERSHIP IN A NUTSHELL, 364 pages, 1977. Softcover. (Text)

American Indian Law

CANBY'S AMERICAN INDIAN LAW IN A NUTSHELL, Second Edition, 336 pages, 1988. Softcover. (Text)

Antitrust—see also Regulated Industries, Trade Regulation

GELLHORN'S ANTITRUST LAW AND ECONOMICS IN A NUT-SHELL, Third Edition, 472 pages, 1986. Softcover. (Text)

HOVENKAMP'S BLACK LETTER ON ANTITRUST, 323 pages, 1986. Softcover. (Review)

HOVENKAMP'S HORNBOOK ON ECONOMICS AND FEDERAL ANTI-TRUST LAW, Student Edition, 414 pages, 1985. (Text)

SULLIVAN'S HORNBOOK OF THE LAW OF ANTITRUST, 886 pages, 1977. (Text)

Appellate Advocacy—see Trial and Appellate Advocacy

Art Law

DUBOFF'S ART LAW IN A NUT-SHELL, 335 pages, 1984. Softcover. (Text)

Banking Law

LOVETT'S BANKING AND FINAN-CIAL INSTITUTIONS LAW IN A NUTSHELL, Second Edition, 464 pages, 1988. Softcover. (Text)

Civil Procedure—see also Federal Jurisdiction and Procedure

CLERMONT'S BLACK LETTER ON CIVIL PROCEDURE, Second Edition, 332 pages, 1988. Softcover. (Review)

FRIEDENTHAL, KANE AND MILL-ER'S HORNBOOK ON CIVIL PRO-CEDURE, 876 pages, 1985. (Text)

KANE'S CIVIL PROCEDURE IN A NUTSHELL, Second Edition, 306 pages, 1986. Softcover. (Text)

KOFFLER AND REPPY'S HORN-BOOK ON COMMON LAW PLEAD-ING, 663 pages, 1969. (Text)

SIEGEL'S HORNBOOK ON NEW YORK PRACTICE, 1011 pages, 1978, with 1987 pocket part. (Text)

Commercial Law

BAILEY AND HAGEDORN'S SE-CURED TRANSACTIONS IN A NUT-SHELL, Third Edition, 390 pages, 1988. Softcover. (Text)

HENSON'S HORNBOOK ON SE-CURED TRANSACTIONS UNDER THE U.C.C., Second Edition, 504 pages, 1979, with 1979 pocket part. (Text)

NICKLES' BLACK LETTER ON

Commercial Law—Continued

COMMERCIAL PAPER, 450 pages, 1988. Softcover. (Review)

SPEIDEL'S BLACK LETTER ON SALES AND SALES FINANCING, 363 pages, 1984. Softcover. (Review)

STOCKTON'S SALES IN A NUTSHELL, Second Edition, 370 pages, 1981. Softcover. (Text)

STONE'S UNIFORM COMMERCIAL CODE IN A NUTSHELL, Third Edition, 580 pages, 1989. Softcover. (Text)

WEBER AND SPEIDEL'S COMMERCIAL PAPER IN A NUTSHELL, Third Edition, 404 pages, 1982. Softcover. (Text)

WHITE AND SUMMERS' HORNBOOK ON THE UNIFORM COMMERCIAL CODE, Third Edition, Student Edition, 1386 pages, 1988. (Text)

Community Property

MENNELL AND BOYKOFF'S COMMUNITY PROPERTY IN A NUTSHELL, Second Edition, 432 pages, 1988. Softcover. (Text)

Comparative Law

GLENDON, GORDON AND OSAKWE'S COMPARATIVE LEGAL TRADITIONS IN A NUTSHELL.

402 pages, 1982. Softcover. (Text)

Conflict of Laws

HAY'S BLACK LETTER ON CONFLICT OF LAWS, 330 pages, 1989. Softcover. (Review)

SCOLES AND HAY'S HORNBOOK ON CONFLICT OF LAWS, Student Edition, 1085 pages, 1982, with 1988–89 pocket part. (Text)

SEIGEL'S CONFLICTS IN A NUTSHELL, 470 pages, 1982. Softcover. (Text)

Constitutional Law—Civil Rights

BARRON AND DIENES' BLACK LETTER ON CONSTITUTIONAL LAW, Second Edition, 310 pages, 1987. Softcover. (Review)

BARRON AND DIENES' CONSTITUTIONAL LAW IN A NUTSHELL, 389 pages, 1986. Softcover. (Text)

ENGDAHL'S CONSTITUTIONAL FEDERALISM IN A NUTSHELL, Second Edition, 411 pages, 1987. Softcover. (Text)

MARKS AND COOPER'S STATE CONSTITUTIONAL LAW IN A NUTSHELL, 329 pages, 1988. Softcover. (Text)

NOWAK, ROTUNDA AND

Constitutional Law—Civil Rights—Continued

YOUNG'S HORNBOOK ON CONSTITUTIONAL LAW, Third Edition, 1191 pages, 1986 with 1988 pocket part. (Text)

VIEIRA'S CONSTITUTIONAL CIVIL RIGHTS IN A NUTSHELL, Second Edition, approximately 320 pages, 1990. Softcover. (Text)

WILLIAMS' CONSTITUTIONAL ANALYSIS IN A NUTSHELL, 388 pages, 1979. Softcover. (Text)

Consumer Law—see also Commercial Law

EPSTEIN AND NICKLES' CONSUMER LAW IN A NUTSHELL, Second Edition, 418 pages, 1981. Softcover. (Text)

Contracts

CALAMARI, AND PERILLO'S BLACK LETTER ON CONTRACTS, 397 pages, 1983. Softcover. (Review)

CALAMARI AND PERILLO'S HORNBOOK ON CONTRACTS, Third Edition, 1049 pages, 1987. (Text)

CORBIN'S TEXT ON CONTRACTS, One Volume Student Edition, 1224 pages, 1952. (Text)

FRIEDMAN'S CONTRACT REME-

DIES IN A NUTSHELL, 323 pages, 1981. Softcover. (Text)

KEYES' GOVERNMENT CONTRACTS IN A NUTSHELL, 423 pages, 1979. Softcover. (Text)

SCHABER AND ROHWER'S CONTRACTS IN A NUTSHELL, Second Edition, 425 pages, 1984. Softcover. (Text)

Copyright—see Patent and Copyright Law

Corporations

HAMILTON'S BLACK LETTER ON CORPORATIONS, Second Edition, 513 pages, 1986. Softcover. (Review)

HAMILTON'S THE LAW OF CORPORATIONS IN A NUTSHELL, Second Edition, 515 pages, 1987. Softcover. (Text)

HENN AND ALEXANDER'S HORNBOOK ON LAWS OF CORPORATIONS, Third Edition, Student Edition, 1371 pages, 1983, with 1986 pocket part. (Text)

Corrections

KRANTZ' THE LAW OF CORRECTIONS AND PRISONERS' RIGHTS IN A NUTSHELL, Third Edition, 407 pages, 1988. Softcover. (Text)

POPPER'S POST-CONVICTION REMEDIES IN A NUTSHELL, 360

Corrections—Continued

pages, 1978. Softcover. (Text)

Creditors' Rights

EPSTEIN'S DEBTOR-CREDITOR RELATIONS IN A NUTSHELL, Third Edition, 383 pages, 1986. Softcover. (Text)

NICKLES AND EPSTEIN'S BLACK LETTER ON CREDITORS' RIGHTS AND BANKRUPTCY, 576 pages, 1989. (Review)

Criminal Law and Criminal Procedure—see also Corrections, Juvenile Justice

ISRAEL AND LaFAVE'S CRIMINAL PROCEDURE—CONSTITUTIONAL LIMITATIONS IN A NUTSHELL, Fourth Edition, 461 pages, 1988. Softcover. (Text)

LaFAVE AND ISRAEL'S HORNBOOK ON CRIMINAL PROCEDURE, Student Edition, 1142 pages, 1985, with 1989 pocket part. (Text)

LaFAVE AND SCOTT'S HORNBOOK ON CRIMINAL LAW, Second Edition, 918 pages, 1986. (Text)

LOEWY'S CRIMINAL LAW IN A NUTSHELL, Second Edition, 321 pages, 1987. Softcover. (Text)

LOW'S BLACK LETTER ON CRIMI-

NAL LAW, 433 pages, 1984. Softcover. (Review)

Decedents' Estates—see Trusts and Estates

Domestic Relations

CLARK'S HORNBOOK ON DOMESTIC RELATIONS, Second Edition, Student Edition, 1050 pages, 1988. (Text)

KRAUSE'S BLACK LETTER ON FAMILY LAW, 314 pages, 1988. Softcover. (Review)

KRAUSE'S FAMILY LAW IN A NUTSHELL, Second Edition, 444 pages, 1986. Softcover. (Text)

Education Law

ALEXANDER AND ALEXANDER'S THE LAW OF SCHOOLS, STUDENTS AND TEACHERS IN A NUTSHELL, 409 pages, 1984. Softcover. (Text)

Employment Discrimination—see also Women and the Law

PLAYER'S FEDERAL LAW OF EMPLOYMENT DISCRIMINATION IN A NUTSHELL, Second Edition, 402 pages, 1981. Softcover. (Text)

PLAYER'S HORNBOOK ON EMPLOYMENT DISCRIMINATION LAW, Student Edition, 708 pages, 1988. (Text)

Energy and Natural Resources Law—see also Oil and Gas

Environmental Law—see also Energy and Natural Resources Law; Sea, Law of

FINDLEY AND FARBER'S ENVIRONMENTAL LAW IN A NUTSHELL, Second Edition, 367 pages, 1988. Softcover. (Text)

RODGERS' HORNBOOK ON ENVIRONMENTAL LAW, 956 pages, 1977, with 1984 pocket part. (Text)

Equity—see Remedies

Estate Planning—see also Trusts and Estates; Taxation—Estate and Gift

LYNN'S AN INTRODUCTION TO ESTATE PLANNING IN A NUTSHELL, Third Edition, 370 pages, 1983. Softcover. (Text)

Evidence

BROUN AND BLAKEY'S BLACK LETTER ON EVIDENCE, 269 pages, 1984. Softcover. (Review)

GRAHAM'S FEDERAL RULES OF EVIDENCE IN A NUTSHELL, Second Edition, 473 pages, 1987. Softcover. (Text)

LILLY'S AN INTRODUCTION TO THE LAW OF EVIDENCE, Second Edition, 585 pages, 1987. (Text)

MCCORMICK'S HORNBOOK ON EVIDENCE, Third Edition, Student Edition, 1156 pages, 1984, with 1987 pocket part. (Text)

ROTHSTEIN'S EVIDENCE IN A NUTSHELL: STATE AND FEDERAL RULES, Second Edition, 514 pages, 1981. Softcover. (Text)

Federal Jurisdiction and Procedure

CURRIE'S FEDERAL JURISDICTION IN A NUTSHELL, Second Edition, 258 pages, 1981. Softcover. (Text)

REDISH'S BLACK LETTER ON FEDERAL JURISDICTION, 219 pages, 1985. Softcover. (Review)

WRIGHT'S HORNBOOK ON FEDERAL COURTS, Fourth Edition, Student Edition, 870 pages, 1983. (Text)

Future Interests—see Trusts and Estates

Health Law—see Medicine, Law and

Human Rights—see International Law

VI

Immigration Law

WEISSBRODT'S IMMIGRATION LAW AND PROCEDURE IN A NUTSHELL, (Second Edition, 438 pages, 1989, Softcover. (Text)

Indian Law—see American Indian Law

Insurance Law

DOBBYN'S INSURANCE LAW IN A NUTSHELL, Second Edition, 316 pages, 1989. Softcover. (Text)

KEETON AND WIDISS' INSURANCE LAW, Student Edition, 1359 pages, 1988. (Text)

International Law—see also Sea, Law of

BUERGENTHAL'S INTERNATIONAL HUMAN RIGHTS IN A NUTSHELL, 283 pages, 1988. Softcover. (Text)

BUERGENTHAL AND MAIER'S PUBLIC INTERNATIONAL LAW IN A NUTSHELL, Second Edition, approximately 255 pages, 1990. Softcover. (Text)

FOLSOM, GORDON AND SPANOGLE'S INTERNATIONAL BUSINESS TRANSACTIONS IN A NUTSHELL, Third Edition, 509 pages, 1988. Softcover. (Text)

Interviewing and Counseling

SHAFFER AND ELKINS' LEGAL INTERVIEWING AND COUNSELING IN A NUTSHELL, Second Edition, 487 pages, 1987. Softcover. (Text)

Introduction to Law—see Legal Method and Legal System

Introduction to Law Study

HEGLAND'S INTRODUCTION TO THE STUDY AND PRACTICE OF LAW IN A NUTSHELL, 418 pages, 1983. Softcover (Text)

KINYON'S INTRODUCTION TO LAW STUDY AND LAW EXAMINATIONS IN A NUTSHELL, 389 pages, 1971. Softcover. (Text)

Juvenile Justice

FOX'S JUVENILE COURTS IN A NUTSHELL, Third Edition, 291 pages, 1984. Softcover. (Text)

Labor and Employment Law—see also Employment Discrimination, Social Legislation

LESLIE'S LABOR LAW IN A NUTSHELL, Second Edition, 397 pages, 1986. Softcover. (Text)

NOLAN'S LABOR ARBITRATION LAW AND PRACTICE IN A NUT-

Labor and Employment Law—
Continued

SHELL, 358 pages, 1979. Soft-cover. (Text)

Land Finance—Property Security—see Real Estate Transactions

Land Use

HAGMAN AND JUERGEN-SMEYER'S HORNBOOK ON URBAN PLANNING AND LAND DEVELOP-MENT CONTROL LAW, Second Edition, Student Edition, 680 pages, 1986. (Text)

WRIGHT AND WRIGHT'S LAND USE IN A NUTSHELL, Second Edition, 356 pages, 1985. Softcover. (Text)

Legal Method and Legal System—see also Legal Research, Legal Writing

KEMPIN'S HISTORICAL INTRO-DUCTION TO ANGLO-AMERICAN LAW IN A NUTSHELL, Second Edition, 280 pages, 1973. Softcover. (Text)

REYNOLDS' JUDICIAL PROCESS IN A NUTSHELL, 292 pages, 1980. Softcover. (Text)

Legal Research

COHEN'S LEGAL RESEARCH IN A NUTSHELL, Fourth Edition, 452 pages, 1985. Softcover.

(Text)

COHEN, BERRING AND OLSON'S HOW TO FIND THE LAW, Ninth Edition, approximately 700 pages, 1989. (Coursebook)

Legal Writing

SQUIRES AND ROMBAUER'S LE-GAL WRITING IN A NUTSHELL, 294 pages, 1982. Softcover. (Text)

TEPLY'S LEGAL WRITING, ANAL-YSIS AND ORAL ARGUMENT, 576 pages, 1990. Softcover. (Coursebook)

Legislation

DAVIES' LEGISLATIVE LAW AND PROCESS IN A NUTSHELL, Sec-ond Edition, 346 pages, 1986. Softcover. (Text)

Local Government

MCCARTHY'S LOCAL GOVERN-MENT LAW IN A NUTSHELL, Sec-ond Edition, 404 pages, 1983. Softcover. (Text)

REYNOLDS' HORNBOOK ON LO-CAL GOVERNMENT LAW, 860 pages, 1982, with 1987 pocket part. (Text)

Mass Communication Law

ZUCKMAN, GAYNES, CARTER AND DEE'S MASS COMMUNICA-TIONS LAW IN A NUTSHELL, Third Edition, 538 pages, 1988. Softcover. (Text)

Medicine, Law and

HALL AND ELLMAN'S HEALTH CARE LAW AND ETHICS IN A NUTSHELL, Approximately 389 pages, 1990. Softcover (Text)

KING'S THE LAW OF MEDICAL MALPRACTICE IN A NUTSHELL, Second Edition, 342 pages, 1986. Softcover. (Text)

Military Law

SHANOR AND TERRELL'S MILITARY LAW IN A NUTSHELL, 378 pages, 1980. Softcover. (Text)

Mortgages—see Real Estate Transactions

Natural Resources Law—see Energy and Natural Resources Law, Environmental Law

Office Practice—see also Interviewing and Counseling

HEGLAND'S TRIAL AND PRACTICE SKILLS IN A NUTSHELL, 346 pages, 1978. Softcover (Text)

Oil and Gas

HEMINGWAY'S HORNBOOK ON OIL AND GAS, Second Edition, Student Edition, 543 pages, 1983, with 1989 pocket part. (Text)

LOWE'S OIL AND GAS LAW IN A

NUTSHELL, Second Edition, 465 pages, 1988. Softcover. (Text)

Partnership—see Agency—Partnership

Patent and Copyright Law

MILLER AND DAVIS' INTELLECTUAL PROPERTY—PATENTS, TRADEMARKS AND COPYRIGHT IN A NUTSHELL, 428 pages, 1983. Softcover. (Text)

Products Liability

PHILLIPS' PRODUCTS LIABILITY IN A NUTSHELL, Third Edition, 307 pages, 1988. Softcover. (Text)

Professional Responsibility

ARONSON AND WECKSTEIN'S PROFESSIONAL RESPONSIBILITY IN A NUTSHELL, 399 pages, 1980. Softcover. (Text)

ROTUNDA'S BLACK LETTER ON PROFESSIONAL RESPONSIBILITY, Second Edition, 414 pages, 1988. Softcover. (Review)

WOLFRAM'S HORNBOOK ON MODERN LEGAL ETHICS, Student Edition, 1120 pages, 1986. (Text)

Property—see also Real Estate Transactions, Land Use, Trusts and Estates

BERNHARDT'S BLACK LETTER ON

Property—Continued

PROPERTY, 318 pages, 1983. Softcover. (Review)

BERNHARDT'S REAL PROPERTY IN A NUTSHELL, Second Edition, 448 pages, 1981. Softcover. (Text)

BURKE'S PERSONAL PROPERTY IN A NUTSHELL, 322 pages, 1983. Softcover. (Text)

CUNNINGHAM, STOEBUCK AND WHITMAN'S HORNBOOK ON THE LAW OF PROPERTY, Student Edition, 916 pages, 1984, with 1987 pocket part. (Text)

HILL'S LANDLORD AND TENANT LAW IN A NUTSHELL, Second Edition, 311 pages, 1986. Softcover. (Text)

Real Estate Transactions

BRUCE'S REAL ESTATE FINANCE IN A NUTSHELL, Second Edition, 262 pages, 1985. Softcover. (Text)

NELSON AND WHITMAN'S BLACK LETTER ON LAND TRANSACTIONS AND FINANCE, Second Edition, 466 pages, 1988. Softcover. (Review)

NELSON AND WHITMAN'S HORNBOOK ON REAL ESTATE FINANCE LAW, Second Edition, 941 pages, 1985 with 1989 pocket part. (Text)

Regulated Industries—see also Mass Communication Law, Banking Law

GELLHORN AND PIERCE'S REGULATED INDUSTRIES IN A NUTSHELL, Second Edition, 389 pages, 1987. Softcover. (Text)

Remedies

DOBBS' HORNBOOK ON REMEDIES, 1067 pages, 1973. (Text)

DOBBYN'S INJUNCTIONS IN A NUTSHELL, 264 pages, 1974. Softcover. (Text)

FRIEDMAN'S CONTRACT REMEDIES IN A NUTSHELL, 323 pages, 1981. Softcover. (Text)

McCORMICK'S HORNBOOK ON DAMAGES, 811 pages, 1935. (Text)

O'CONNELL'S REMEDIES IN A NUTSHELL, Second Edition, 320 pages, 1985. Softcover. (Text)

Sea, Law of

SOHN AND GUSTAFSON'S THE LAW OF THE SEA IN A NUTSHELL, 264 pages, 1984. Softcover. (Text)

Securities Regulation

HAZEN'S HORNBOOK ON THE LAW OF SECURITIES REGULATION, Student Edition, 739 pages, 1985, with 1988 pocket

Securities Regulation—Continued

part. (Text)

RATNER'S SECURITIES REGULATION IN A NUTSHELL, Third Edition, 316 pages, 1988. Softcover. (Text)

Social Legislation

HOOD AND HARDY'S WORKERS' COMPENSATION AND EMPLOYEE PROTECTION IN A NUTSHELL, 274 pages, 1984. Softcover. (Text)

LAFRANCE'S WELFARE LAW: STRUCTURE AND ENTITLEMENT IN A NUTSHELL, 455 pages, 1979. Softcover. (Text)

Sports Law

SCHUBERT, SMITH AND TRENTADUE'S SPORTS LAW, 395 pages, 1986. (Text)

Taxation—Corporate

WEIDENBRUCH AND BURKE'S FEDERAL INCOME TAXATION OF CORPORATIONS AND STOCKHOLDERS IN A NUTSHELL, Third Edition, 309 pages, 1989. Softcover. (Text)

Taxation—Estate & Gift—see also Estate Planning, Trusts and Estates

MCNULTY'S FEDERAL ESTATE AND GIFT TAXATION IN A NUTSHELL, Fourth Edition, 496 pages, 1989. Softcover. (Text)

Taxation—Individual

HUDSON AND LIND'S BLACK LETTER ON FEDERAL INCOME TAXATION, Second Edition, 396 pages, 1987. Softcover. (Review)

MCNULTY'S FEDERAL INCOME TAXATION OF INDIVIDUALS IN A NUTSHELL, Fourth Edition, 503 pages, 1988. Softcover. (Text)

POSIN'S HORNBOOK ON FEDERAL INCOME TAXATION, Student Edition, 491 pages, 1983, with 1989 pocket part. (Text)

ROSE AND CHOMMIE'S HORNBOOK ON FEDERAL INCOME TAXATION, Third Edition, 923 pages, 1988, with 1989 pocket part. (Text)

Taxation—International

DOERNBERG'S INTERNATIONAL TAXATION IN A NUTSHELL, 325 pages, 1989. Softcover. (Text)

Taxation—State & Local

GELFAND AND SALSICH'S STATE AND LOCAL TAXATION AND FINANCE IN A NUTSHELL, 309 pages, 1986. Softcover. (Text)

Torts—see also Products Liability

KIONKA'S BLACK LETTER ON TORTS, 339 pages, 1988. Softcover. (Review)

KIONKA'S TORTS IN A NUTSHELL: INJURIES TO PERSONS AND PROPERTY, 434 pages, 1977. Softcover. (Text)

MALONE'S TORTS IN A NUTSHELL: INJURIES TO FAMILY, SOCIAL AND TRADE RELATIONS, 358 pages, 1979. Softcover. (Text)

PROSSER AND KEETON'S HORNBOOK ON TORTS, Fifth Edition, Student Edition, 1286 pages, 1984 with 1988 pocket part. (Text)

Trade Regulation—see also Antitrust, Regulated Industries

MCMANIS' UNFAIR TRADE PRACTICES IN A NUTSHELL, Second Edition, 464 pages, 1988. Softcover. (Text)

SCHECHTER'S BLACK LETTER ON UNFAIR TRADE PRACTICES, 272 pages, 1986. Softcover. (Review)

Trial and Appellate Advocacy—see also Civil Procedure

BERGMAN'S TRIAL ADVOCACY IN A NUTSHELL, Second Edition, 354 pages, 1989. Softcover. (Text)

GOLDBERG'S THE FIRST TRIAL (WHERE DO I SIT? WHAT DO I SAY?) IN A NUTSHELL, 396 pages, 1982. Softcover. (Text)

HEGLAND'S TRIAL AND PRACTICE SKILLS IN A NUTSHELL, 346 pages, 1978. Softcover. (Text)

HORNSTEIN'S APPELLATE ADVOCACY IN A NUTSHELL, 325 pages, 1984. Softcover. (Text)

JEANS' HANDBOOK ON TRIAL ADVOCACY, Student Edition, 473 pages, 1975. Softcover. (Text)

Trusts and Estates

ATKINSON'S HORNBOOK ON WILLS, Second Edition, 975 pages, 1953. (Text)

AVERILL'S UNIFORM PROBATE CODE IN A NUTSHELL, Second Edition, 454 pages, 1987. Softcover. (Text)

BOGERT'S HORNBOOK ON TRUSTS, Sixth Edition, Student Edition, 794 pages, 1987. (Text)

MCGOVERN, KURTZ AND REIN'S HORNBOOK ON WILLS, TRUSTS

Advisory Board

JOHN A. BAUMAN
Professor of Law, University of California, Los Angeles

CURTIS J. BERGER
Professor of Law, Columbia University

JESSE H. CHOPER
Dean and Professor of Law,
University of California, Berkeley

DAVID P. CURRIE
Professor of Law, University of Chicago

YALE KAMISAR
Professor of Law, University of Michigan

MARY KAY KANE
Professor of Law, University of California,
Hastings College of the Law

WAYNE R. LaFAVE
Professor of Law, University of Illinois

RICHARD C. MAXWELL
Professor of Law, Duke University

ARTHUR R. MILLER
Professor of Law, Harvard University

ROBERT A. STEIN
Dean and Professor of Law, University of Minnesota

JAMES J. WHITE
Professor of Law, University of Michigan

CHARLES ALAN WRIGHT
Professor of Law, University of Texas

XIV

ANTITRUST LAW
AND
ECONOMICS
IN A NUTSHELL

THIRD EDITION

By

ERNEST GELLHORN

Attorney—Jones, Day, Reavis & Pogue
former T. Munford Boyd Professor of Law,
University of Virginia; Dean, Case Western
Reserve University

ST. PAUL, MINN.
WEST PUBLISHING CO.
1986

Nutshell Series, In a Nutshell, the Nutshell Logo are registered trademarks of West Publishing Co. Registered in
U.S. Patent and Trademark Office.

COPYRIGHT © 1976, 1981 By WEST PUBLISHING CO.
COPYRIGHT © 1986 By WEST PUBLISHING CO.
All rights reserved
Printed in the United States of America

Library of Congress Cataloging in Publication Data

Gellhorn, Ernest.
    Antitrust law and economics in a nutshell.

    (Nutshell series)
    Includes index.
    1. Antitrust law—United States.   2. Antitrust law—
Economic aspects—United States.   I. Title.   II. Series.
KF1652.G44   1986   343.73'072   86–19040
                             347.30372

ISBN 0–314–30072–4
2nd Reprint—1990

PREFACE

Justice Holmes once characterized the Sherman Act as "humbug based on economic ignorance and incompetence." * This description seemed particularly apt when case-law applications of the antitrust laws relied more on antiquated concepts of title applied in property or sales law than on the economic consequences of challenged transactions. See, e.g., United States v. Arnold, Schwinn & Co., 388 U.S. 365 (1967). Thus, the aim of the first edition of this basic text explaining antitrust law was to make a contribution toward redressing the imbalance between rational antitrust doctrine and economic ignorance. It sought to integrate economic understanding into the study of antitrust law by concentrating on basic and generally agreed upon concepts.

The past ten years have seen a remarkable growth of sophisticated antitrust scholarship and a widespread effort to integrate economic theory into antitrust. A listing of major texts integrating law and economics is indicative. Judges Robert H. Bork of Yale (*The Antitrust Paradox,* 1978), and Richard A. Posner of Chicago (*Antitrust Law,* 1976)

* 1 *Holmes-Pollock Letters* 163 (Howe ed. 1941).

have studied antitrust issues "through the lens of price theory" and generally concluded that case-law applications reflect inconsistent policy purposes and primative economic understanding. They have outlined an alternative "consumer welfare" approach to antitrust theory and doctrine. See also H. Hovenkamp, *Economic and Federal Antitrust Law* (1985) (hornbook focusing on economic analysis). While also favoring economic efficiency as the primary test for antitrust policy, Professors Phillip Areeda and Donald F. Turner of Harvard have published seven volumes of their treatise *(Antitrust Law)* that supports dispersion of persistent monopoly power not based on economies of scale and reflects concern over possible barriers to entry. Their centrist and comprehensive restatement of antitrust law has become an influential guide for the courts. Professor Laurence A. Sullivan of California-Berkeley has written a hornbook *(Antitrust* 1977) that openly favors judicial reliance on the sociopolitical underpinnings of antitrust and questions the rigorous application of economics to antitrust—at least to the exclusion of noneconomic considerations. Despite their differences, each accepts the importance of economics—and in particular, of price theory—to antitrust.

These and other writings have had a substantial impact. Probably the most significant example is Continental T.V., Inc. v. GTE Sylvania Inc., 433

U.S. 36 (1977), in which the Supreme Court over-ruled the per se rule announced in *Schwinn*, supra, because its economic basis and rationale had been shown to be unsound. Similar developments are occurring in merger and tie-in cases, in the definitions of price-fixing, in the interpretation of antimonopoly doctrines, and in other areas of antitrust. Yet it would be premature to conclude that all forces point in one direction, that economic understanding has penetrated all courts or enforcement agencies, or that a new unified approach has now been adopted. In point of fact, antitrust law is at most in transition, possibly toward higher ground. This requires even more of the student and practitioner. They must, for example, now be aware of more than antitrust case-law. Historical and political forces continue to be important. The procedural context of a case may be decisive. Legal doctrine has substantial independent weight and frequently provides direction, at least of inertia. Yet substantial attention must now also be given to economic theory and practice. Increasingly, courts and agencies are closely examining market concepts and effects in deciding antitrust issues.

This basic text therefore continues its economic focus in introducing the antitrust newcomer to the law's framework and operation. But its main message is unchanged: it seeks to explain and examine antitrust critically from a legal perspective.

PREFACE

Where helpful for gaining an understanding of antitrust case-law, economic analysis is applied to evaluate antitrust law. Frequently, simplifying assumptions are made and technical justifications are excluded. Admittedly, neither is irrelevant and this text can only serve as a beginning. Nor does this text expose or espouse exotic new economic ideas or theories; it focuses on generally accepted economic doctrine and applies widely accepted concepts to antitrust. Where differing views are reflected in thoughtful antitrust cases or comments—or among generally respected schools of economics—I have sought to present those positions with clarifying comments. Nonetheless, the principal task of the book remains: it is a critical examination of basic antitrust law.

There is one primary distinction between the second and third editions. It is the substantial yet often subtle change occurring in antitrust economics. The initial contribution of economic analysis, as illustrated in prior editions, was in its use of price theory to focus on whether a practice could limit output and raise price. Thus, price theory was relied upon to show that primitive antitrust ideas regarding monopoly leverage, the concentration doctrine or other techniques for "expanding monopoly power"—i.e., the antitrust of the 1940s through 1960s—were flawed; the emphasis instead was placed on property rights, free riders, and allocative efficiency. The focus of antitrust economics has once again been sharpened. In recent years antitrust economics has often turned to learning more about developing ideas of organization theory, transaction costs, and contestable markets. As these alternative explanations of business practices or market models have gained in understanding and acceptance, the traditional presumption of antitrust commentators and courts that markets not following Adam Smith's perfect competition model are anticompetitive has been weakened. As illustrated somewhat by air transportation, the crucial feature of a contestable market is its vulnerability to hit-and-run entry or exit. Transaction cost economics demonstrates that the primary purpose of firm organization and other market arrangements, such as tie-ins or joint sales agencies, may be to economize on costs. There is, in other words, no preset correct market form. If the results of competition—namely, lower prices, maximal output, intense innovation—are the objectives of antitrust, then antitrust laws should encourage a wide variety of market structures or firms.

These newer economic concepts are also having an impact on the courts. To be sure, the results are not always consistent (or economically coherent. Thus, the Supreme Court has approved price-fixing where it is necessary to make production more efficient (*Broadcast Music, Inc.*) and a group boycott where the group does not possess market power or exclusive access (*Northwest Wholesale Stationers*). These decisions reflect an increasing economic sophistication in the Supreme Court and a sound concern with efficiency and consumer welfare. On the other hand, maximum price fixing continues to be per se illegal (*Maricopa County*) and a monopolist has been held to violate the antitrust laws when it refuses to share a market with its sole competitor (*Aspen Skiing*). These decisions seem questionable. Education of courts and policy makers, like students, is a continuous process. At times it also seems very slow. Antitrust continues to be in transition. The rules seem, as a result, particularly uncertain. A careful analysis of the economic theory and of the case law is more important than ever.

ERNEST GELLHORN

Washington, D.C.
May, 1986

OUTLINE

OUTLINE

OUTLINE

*

TABLE OF CASES

References are to Pages

A

TABLE OF CASES

B

C

TABLE OF CASES

F

G

M

N

O

P

TABLE OF CASES

T

TABLE OF CASES

TABLE OF CASES

W

Y

*

ANTITRUST LAW
AND
ECONOMICS
IN A NUTSHELL

*

CHAPTER I

RESTRAINTS OF TRADE AT COMMON LAW

The antitrust laws are designed to control the exercise of private economic power by preventing monopoly, punishing cartels, and otherwise protecting competition. See Standard Oil Co. v. FTC, 340 U.S. 231, 249 (1951). Competition is relied upon as the principal mechanism of control. It is generally agreed that the primary goal of antitrust is to increase consumer welfare by assuring that markets remain open to entry and that output can expand—thus to maximize national wealth. Whether antitrust also serves to promote equality of business opportunity, the just distribution of goods, or other social or political goals is a matter of intense debate.

An examination of the origins of the antitrust laws is helpful in understanding and interpreting them. Their historical lineage can be traced from common law actions which were developed to limit restraints of trade and, in a more limited fashion, to proscribe monopoly power and middleman profits.

The common law of trade restraints is, as usual, untidy and unclear. Some courts have read it as permitting only those restrictive covenants in a contract which are limited in time and space and reasonably related to its central purpose—such as a five year limit imposed on the seller of a bakery not to compete with the buyer who purchased the seller's good will (i.e., his going business) as well as his bakeshop. Others have taken a more expansive view and even upheld unlimited territorial divisions. For example, an agreement by three luggage manufacturers to divide their sales territories so that each would be free to sell his goods without competition from the others (in his assigned territory) was enforceable because it left the trade open to any third party. In other words, it is neither instructive nor accurate to reconcile all cases or to force the law into any particular mold. The common law is only a metaphor; there are as many common laws as there are independent judicial systems, and the "common law of trade restraints" is no exception.

Nevertheless, a review of some leading early rulings and of the conflicting interests they sought to reconcile is useful as a forerunner for modern antitrust statutes and decisions. The authors of the Sherman Antitrust Act said that they were setting forth "the rule of the common law which prevails in England and this country," 20 Cong. Rec. 1167 (1889) (Senator Sherman), and the Act's terminology is borrowed from the common law. Early as well as current decisions applying the antitrust laws often rely on common law precedents. See National Soc'y of Prof. Engineers v.

United States, 435 U.S. 679 (1978). The "rule of
reason," first applied in 1711, is still the basic
standard for deciding close cases under the antitrust laws. (Its meaning has changed over time
and is, undoubtedly, still changing.) The ancient
property law rules against restraints on alienation
continue to govern resale price maintenance.
Whether so much honor should be paid to precedent, however, is not clear.

A. CONTRACTS IN RESTRAINT OF TRADE

The guilds of feudal England were a complex
system regulating relations among master, journeyman and apprentice. Periods of service, wages
and prices were defined, usually according to custom or statute. Occasionally a master would seek
to extend the usual term by preventing his servant
from becoming a full-fledged master at the end of
his term or by otherwise protecting himself from
competition. Although it is still unclear whether
John Dyer [1] was a journeyman, apprentice or master,[2] in the first known case, Dyer's Case, Y.B.
Pasch. 2 Hen. V, f. 5, pl. 26 (1414), the court
angrily denied an attempted collection on a bond
for John Dyer's breach of his agreement not to

1. The original reports spell "Dyer" as "Dier."

2. It is possible that the defendant gave his promise not to
compete as a master in connection with the sale of his business
(and hence was victimized after "having just met with great
loss," as Lord Parker assumed three centuries later), but the
short duration of the restraint suggests that he was in fact
oppressed by an over-reaching master.

"use his art of a dyer's craft within the town . . . for half a year." Not only was the condition restraining the dyer void as against the common law, but the court said it would have fined or imprisoned the plaintiff had he been in court. It seems, then, that the common law of trade restraints originated not with notions of competition and protection of the free market, but rather in support of "fair" commercial activity and of crumbling guild customs.

Subsequent cases reflect the conflict more clearly. Courts were inclined to approve contracts with restrictive trade covenants for the same reasons they upheld other contracts which were entered into freely and supported by consideration. Enforcement enhanced property values, increased trade, and satisfied the parties' expectations. And courts were not arbiters of how owners could dispose of their property. Yet courts were also not inclined to validate agreements depriving the promisor of his ability to use his skills and earn a livelihood. Nor did they want the public deprived of the advantages of competition. Nonetheless, until the eighteenth century, freedom of contract generally held sway; courts were not in a position to determine the adequacy of the terms of a contract or their fairness. But then a solicitude for wage earners and a philosophic acceptance of the need to assure that a free market in fact existed (coincidental with the industrial revolution) slowly became the dominant theme.

The clash between these competing principles first came to a head in the now celebrated case of Mitchel v. Reynolds, 1 P.Wms. 181, 24 Eng.Rep. 347 (1711), where the plaintiff leased a bakeshop for five years on condition that the assignor of the lease (also a baker) would not practice his baker's art in the parish for the term of the lease. Stated simply, the purchaser of the lease was buying not only the use of the bakeshop but also the trade that went with it, and he was unwilling to promise to pay for the lease if its value to him could be readily destroyed. Hence he demanded and received the defendant's restrictive promise. But when sued on his bond, the defendant presented, in essence, the argument that carried the day in *Dyer's Case:* namely, he had served his time as an apprentice and had been admitted to the guild; no private person could lawfully prevent him from working his trade. What was significant was not the court's rejection of this plea, but rather Lord Parker's opinion which systematically classified all restraints of trade and set forth doctrinal principles (still applied) to distinguish good restraints from bad.

His basic distinction was between general (invalid) and particular (valid) restraints. General restraints were condemned because they are entered into for the purpose of limiting competition. Viewed as a Mephistophelean pact (general restraints are "of no benefit to either party, and only oppressive"), the court justified its rule: the person

agreeing not to use his trade had to be protected
from himself; the public was entitled to intercede
in the bargain before he became a welfare charge
or deprived the public of the benefits of his competitive labors.   Moreover, not all particular restraints were valid. They had to be supported by
"good consideration" (which explained why the
contract in *Dyer's Case* was void). These "partial"
or "ancillary" restraints, as they became known,
were upheld if limited in time and restricted to a
geographical place. *Mitchel v. Reynolds* originated
the "rule of reason"—was the restraint reasonable?—which will become a familiar term throughout this text.

Whether a trade restraint was ancillary depended upon whether the covenant could be said to
be subordinate to the main lawful purpose of the
transaction; or was it the object of the contract
and therefore a "naked covenant not to compete."
As subsequent decisions explained, the interests of
the parties and the public were to be protected.
The courts, therefore, inquired: For what *purpose*
was the restraint imposed? What was the *effect* of
the agreement? (Could the promisor readily practice his trade elsewhere—and could the public receive the benefit of his competition somewhere?)
Not surprisingly, restrictive covenants in employment contracts were scrutinized more closely than
covenants connected to a sale of a business. As
courts became more sophisticated they also asked
whether the lawful objective could be obtained in

some less restrictive way. (Was it necessary to bind an employee's right to his trade in order to protect confidential business secrets?)

As the philosophy of laissez faire became more firmly entrenched, many exceptions to the rule of reason developed. Courts first suggested that what was reasonable could best be judged by the parties themselves, a doctrine familiar to students of contract law (and the peppercorn theory of consideration). It followed, then, that courts could presume that the terms were reasonable and not against the public interest; and this presumption became conclusive when courts refused to admit contrary evidence of market conditions. Ultimately the exceptions engulfed the rule, at least in England, where price-fixing agreements were often enforced and the House of Lords went so far as to uphold a worldwide covenant not to compete. See Mogul Steamship Co. v. McGregor Gow & Co. [1892] A.C. 25 (1891); Nordenfeldt v. Maxim Nordenfeldt Guns & Ammunition Co. [1894] A.C. 535.

The "common law" was not so receptive to trade restraints in the United States. In United States v. Addyston Pipe & Steel Co., 85 Fed. 271 (6th Cir. 1898), modified & aff'd, 175 U.S. 211 (1899), then Circuit Judge William Howard Taft traced its development here and concluded that the basic division between ancillary and nonancillary restraints had been followed. He also concluded, however, that apart from reasonable ancillary restraints, the common law had condemned all other restraints of trade. "Where the sole object of both parties in making the contract . . . is merely to restrain competition, and enhance or maintain prices, it would seem that there was nothing to justify or excuse the restraint, that it would necessarily have a tendency to monopoly, and therefore would be void." Contrary to the English rule, the American reasonableness/unreasonableness test did not apply to price-fixing, concerted refusals to deal, territorial divisions or similarly restrictive agreements, whether or not they could otherwise be classified as ancillary.[3] This view of the common law was adopted by the Supreme Court when it first interpreted the Sherman Act.

As this discussion indicates, the concept of restraint of trade (and what is reasonable or unreasonable) is neither an absolute nor an unvarying standard. Every bargain which reserves business to the bargainers and excludes others is a restraint of trade. But it would be a *reductio ad absurdum* to conclude that agreements essential to the creation of trade were also illegal restraints of trade. Yet some bargains may preclude a great deal of trade or competition, and their cost to competition (and society) may outweigh any possible benefit. The important policy question, therefore, is not whether the restraint is ancillary, but rather

---

3. Subsequent scholarly analysis concludes that Judge Taft in fact misread the case law in that price-fixing and other directly restrictive covenants were generally measured by the reasonableness test (if ancillary).

whether it further limits competition or protects an existing property value.

A routine sales transaction illustrates the issue. *A* agrees to supply goods to *B* (thus satisfying *B*'s needs for these goods for one week). Even as a simple one-shot sales transaction the agreement excludes *A*'s competitors, *C* and others, from making the same sale to *B* during this week. This "cost," however, is well recognized and accepted as a necessary counterpart to the benefits of *A*'s sale to *B*. However, what if *B* agrees to buy from *A* not just a one week supply but all of *B*'s requirements of these goods for the next 20 years? This elongated agreement effectively removes *B*'s needs from the demand market as far as *C* and other competitors of *A* are concerned. Few sellers can wait 20 years for the next sale. And where *B* is the dominant or possibly only current buyer of the commodity which *A* and *C* (and others) sell, the agreement inevitably restrains trade, and possibly unreasonably.

The point is that the line between ordinary business transactions and agreements which are viewed as restraints of trade is elusive and unmarked. Frequently one merges into the other. At the extremes the rule is readily seen and applied. Thus a seller's covenant not to compete with his purchaser for a limited period of time in a narrowly defined community in connection with the sale of a business and its highly personalized good will is generally upheld. Without it, the seller of a small business frequently would be unable to obtain a favorable (or possibly any) price for his business. Or the effect of the restraint may be *de minimus* and of no public interest. At the other end of the spectrum, agreements seeking to fix the price at which all sellers of the commodity sell their product, or to divide sales territories so that each seller has an exclusive area free of competition in that territory, seem clearly to restrain trade—and unreasonably. The difficulty, of course, is that many (most?) agreements fall between these polar positions and the courts have had to draw the line somewhere.

The rule of reason, then, is essentially a rule of construction.

B. MONOPOLY AND CONSPIRACY

The common law also addressed monopolistic practices. Some monopolies were privileged, others illegal. Grants of monopoly explicitly sanctioned by courts, custom or Parliament were not questioned. Thus courts recognized limited patents for inventors, approved customary monopolies held by towns and guilds, and acquiesced in Parliamentary grants. Eventually all other monopolies were held to be void.

This development can be traced to the now famous Case of Monopolies (Darcy v. Allein), 11 Co. Rep. 84b, 77 Eng.Rep. 1260 (K.B.1602). It appears that Queen Elizabeth I had granted Darcy, her groom, the sole right to import playing cards into

England. When Allein, a London haberdasher, made and sold some playing cards, Darcy challenged this infringement of his monopoly. The Court of King's Bench, however, unanimously held the monopoly void and dismissed the suit. "Letters patent" from the Crown encroached on the privileges and freedoms of her subjects to engage in trade. The ruling was justified on several grounds: monopoly harms actual and potential competitors, deprives others of the opportunity to practice a trade, and injures the public through higher prices and poorer quality. Since the Crown could, of course, intentionally do no wrong, the court rationalized its position by saying that the Queen had been deceived in making the grant.

The Court's position was further vindicated when Parliament enacted the Statute of Monopolies of 1624 (21 Jac. 1, c. 3) voiding "all" monopolies (with the several exceptions already noted). Before this result is read too broadly, note should be taken that the legislation was based not so much on a preference for competition as on a constitutional objection to the Crown's assumption of power to grant monopolies and to the arbitrary basis on which they were granted.[4] Whatever the rea-

4. One note of irony. Just a few years after Darcy's playing card monopoly was judged void, the very same monopoly was given—by Parliament—under the Statute of Monopolies to the Company of Card Players. The more things change the more they stay the same.

For a modern development in monopolization of picture card commerce, see Topps Chewing Gum, Inc., 67 F.T.C. 744 (1965) (leading bubble gum company held not to have monopolized

son (and the rapid erosion of the mercantile system probably contributed as much as anything), the common law courts became increasingly hostile to monopolies. Nineteenth century legislation furthered this trend and abolished the legal basis of most monopolies.

This antipathy toward quasi-public monopolies was incorporated into the common law of the colonies. Opposition to all grants of monopolistic privilege not explicitly sanctioned by the legislature became an established part of the American tradition although few reported cases actually faced the issue. This antimonopoly view was most frequently expressed in state constitutions and statutes. See M. Horwitz, *The Transformation of American Law, 1780–1860,* 109–39 (1977). Yet neither the English nor American common law actually ruled that private monopoly (i.e., garnered by competitive effort or agreement) was illegal, except in dicta.

However, the common law doctrine of conspiracy condemned combinations to gain any unlawful objective, even if accomplished by otherwise lawful acts.[5] In this context, unlawful covered anything

although it had 5-year exclusive contracts with nearly all major league baseball players to use their pictures on cards promoting confectionary products). See also Fleer Corp. v. Topps Chewing Gum, Inc., 658 F.2d 139 (3d Cir.1981) (exclusive promotional contract with major league baseball players upheld because other makers of bubble gum were free to compete for that contract).

5. To compound the confusion, the common law conspiracy doctrine also reached "unlawful" means used to accomplish otherwise proper objectives.

obviously contrary to public policy including, possibly, monopoly. But the doctrine never gained wide currency in commercial competition. It was once applied vigorously in this country against labor union activities. Otherwise it usually appeared only as an additional ground for rejecting an agreement already condemned as an unreasonable restraint of trade.[6]

Finally, there were a series of market interference offenses indictable under common law and also by statute. They sought to prevent middlemen from cornering markets or otherwise raising prices. They reflected the view, not completely abandoned in antitrust law today, that middlemen performed no useful function. These offenses, which had such quaint names as "forestalling" (buying goods before they reached the general market) and "regrating" (buying with the intent to resell in the same market)[7] never achieved significance in the United States.

The common law often provided (and still provides) a defense to the enforcement of contracts with "oppressive" terms. As an instrument of public policy it was severely limited. Restrictive covenants could be tested only when one party sought to enforce them against another who, in

6. Occasional state laws prohibited corporate combinations seeking to eliminate competition.

7. Also, "engrossing" (buying in bulk with the object of enhancing the price), "forbearing" (like forestalling but with intent to sell at a higher price), and—best of all—"badgering" (buying corn victuals in one place and reselling them elsewhere at a profit).

turn, was willing to contest the covenant. Then
the court could declare it void and unenforceable if
it did not meet the reasonableness test. But the
common law rule did not necessarily stop others
from working under or observing such agreements;
their acceptance depended upon the parties' satis-
faction with the bargain rather than competitive
norms. Nor did the common law reach noncon-
tractual restraints, such as a trust or holding company—or the acquisition of market power through
merger, selective price cutting, etc. Although supported by notions of the free market and the desire
to encourage competition, the common law doctrines were at most only a short step in that
direction.

CHAPTER II

THE ANTITRUST STATUTES

Dissatisfaction with the common law's protectionism and, more importantly, rising concern over abusive practices by corporate giants in the second half of the 19th century led to legislation restricting the power of the railroads and "trusts." Congress' initial response, the passage of the Interstate Commerce Act of 1887 and the Sherman Antitrust Act of 1890, did not, however, satisfy public concern. Continuing abuses and undulating business cycles as well as disappointing judicial interpretations of the new antitrust act created further pressures, until the antitrust issue dominated the Presidential election of 1912 and led to the adoption, in 1914, of the Clayton and Federal Trade Commission Acts.

A. THE DEMAND FOR REGULATION

The common law view of the market place was that the public was protected as long as the legal right to trade—primarily the freedom to enter and to compete—was guaranteed. The inadequacy of this safeguard first became apparent as railroads were believed to have taken advantage of their privileged position. The capital requirements of railroad construction made competitive service to sparsely settled territories impossible; nor was the right to build railroads freely available (even with the power of eminent domain) in densely populated areas. Freed from the spur of competition, railroad rates and service were thought to be characterized by discrimination among shippers and localities, traffic and earning pools, and secret rebates to powerful shippers or buyers. The concern was that railroads artificially inflated their rates where they had monopolies and used these profits unfairly to cut prices on competitive routes.

Several states responded by establishing regulatory agencies to oversee rates and service; and when the constitutionality of such regulation was challenged in court it was held that railroads were a business "affected with a public interest" subject to state regulation. Munn v. Illinois, 94 U.S. 113 (1876). But state jurisdiction was necessarily limited and constitutionally ineffective for interstate commerce. See Wabash, St. L. & Pac. Ry. v. Illinois, 118 U.S. 557 (1886). As a consequence, Congress created the Interstate Commerce Commission in 1887. The Commission was responsible for assuring just and reasonable rates and prohibiting undue discrimination. It sought, in other words, to substitute government regulation for the temper of competitive markets.

If the felt inadequacy of the common law first became apparent because of trade abuses engaged in by railroads, its limitations were more forcefully exposed by the tactics of the Standard Oil Company and other "trusts" [1] controlling a number of major industries—including fuel oil, sugar, cotton and linseed oil, lead, and whiskey. The trusts were attacked in litigation from several angles. The primary challenge was that the participating companies had acted ultra vires (beyond their charters) by entering into trust arrangements. A second argument was that trust practices constituted unreasonable trade restraints that created unlawful monopolies. However, these attacks took time, were costly, and did not always prevail.

The opponents of the trusts challenged them on several policy grounds. First, and probably foremost, was the concern that more and more business was being dominated by fewer and fewer enterprises each year. The trusts seemed to absorb new enterprises even faster than the industrial expansion created them. Second, the process of consolidation often was achieved by predatory tactics: competitors were ruined by below cost pricing or business espionage, and then markets were monopolized. The public perceived that the trusts gained their power with coercive threats of "sell or be ruined," and their record made clear that they

1. Trusts were a legal innovation created by Standard's attorneys from the theory of stockholders' voting trusts (themselves originally employed to safeguard corporate control, especially in railroad reorganizations). Technically a trust was an arrangement through which owners of stock in several companies transferred their securities to a set of trustees; in return the owners received certificates entitling them to a specified share in the pooled earnings of the jointly managed companies. In time the trust label applied to all forms of suspect business combinations.

had both the means and the will to carry out the
threats. These methods outraged smaller businesses and enraged the agrarian West.[2] A third
and related objection involved the use of outra-
geously unfair methods by trusts to achieve unreasonable ends. Investors were defrauded by
watered stocks; workers were discarded as worn
out tools by indiscriminate and harsh plant clos-
ings; liberty was threatened by bribes of public
officials; civil peace and property were threatened
by arson; and fair competition was disturbed by
bogus companies and harassing lawsuits. Frequent depressions or severe business cycles and
scandalous financial transactions, invariably involving trusts or railroads, further shocked the
public and destroyed its confidence in unregulated
markets. The atmosphere is difficult to recapture:
the public was naive; the tactics of the trusts were
ruthless.

It is not surprising, then, that the trust had few
defenders. The public clamor for action was loud
and clear: it wanted the law to destroy the power

2. The Standard Oil Company, for example, obtained its fuel
oil monopoly by first driving the price of kerosene to a penny or
two a gallon in isolated markets, well below cost; then when all
competitors had been forced to sell or close down, Standard
would raise the price far above the previous market level and
extort monopoly profits. For another reading of Standard Oil's
practices—at least as demonstrated in the trial record—see
McGee, *Predatory Price Cutting: The Standard Oil (N.J.) Case*, 1
J.Law & Econ. 137 (1958). But see F. Scherer, *Industrial
Market Structure and Economic Performance* 336–37 (2d ed.
1980). Whatever the actual facts, they were perceived at the
time as described in the text.

of the trusts. By 1888 both major parties had
received the message and their platforms contained strongly worded antimonopoly planks.
Though the public's mandate was clear it was not
specific. Little direction and thought had focused
on how to limit the power of the trusts without
destroying business and jobs at the same time.
State ownership drew scant support. Economists
generally thought prohibition futile since trusts
were the "natural" results of competition—else
why would they have occurred in the first place.
Lawyers favored a different tack and took their
direction from the common law. Generally they
recommended statutory prohibition of monopolies
and other combinations to which the common law
would deny enforcement. The Congress, perhaps
unwittingly, found a common ground in these
seemingly inconsistent positions. It constructed a
statute along common law principles barring ex-
cesses such as combinations in restraint of trade
and monopolizing activity, while, at the same time,
permitting fair competition and healthy combinations.

B. THE SHERMAN ACT

1. THE STATUTE

Perhaps like all legislative watersheds, the debates and events surrounding the passage of the
Sherman Act contain something for everyone.
Even a close examination does not answer whether
the Act's fire was aimed primarily at halting the

trend toward concentration of American industry
by the trusts, stopping the abusive pressure tactics
employed by Standard Oil and other trusts, or
dissolving the pervasive cartels which converted
competitive markets into monopoly territories.
Probably the most sensible answer is that it was
directed at all three.[3]

Still there are some consistent strands that may
prove useful while examining both the statute and
subsequent case developments. The Act's author
assured Congress that it "does not announce a new
principle of law, but applies old and well recognized principles of the common law." 21 Cong.Rec.
2456 (1890) (Senator Sherman). Yet what the common law held was never particularly clear and, in
any case, was not intimately familiar to the legislators of the 51st Congress. (In fact the relationship
between the Sherman Act and various common
law standards was one of the earliest questions
explored by courts in first applying the Act.) The
critical statutory concepts—"restraint of trade"

   3. Judge Robert Bork, for example, asserts that "[t]he legislative history of the Sherman Act . . . displays the clear and
exclusive policy intention of promoting consumer welfare"—
which he later defines as the improvement of allocative efficiency without a substantial impairment of productive efficiency.
R. Bork, *The Antitrust Paradox,* 61, 90–91, 104, 108, 405 (1978).
Others have pointed to different legislative aims. See, e.g., H.
Thorelli, *The Federal Antitrust Policy* (1954). One can find
support in the debates for almost any view for "[t]he great
bother is that the bill which was arduously debated was never
passed, and that the bill which was passed was never really
discussed." W. Hamilton & I. Till, *Antitrust in Action* (Mono-
graph 16, Temporary National Economic Committee), 76th
Cong., 3d Sess. 11 (1940).

and "monopolize"—included generic words of art and therefore were not the subject of extensive or critical analysis in the debates.

In general, the legislators expressed a clear preference for free enterprise and unrestricted competition; they were also concerned with excessive private power. But when it came to hard choices between approving or condemning restraints (or monopoly) which might possibly enhance or limit competition, the legislation and its history are silent. What emerges, rather, is that Congress had invested the federal courts with a new jurisdiction: they were to create a common law of federal antitrust within the general aim of—but apparently not confined by—the prior common law.[4]

The major substantive provisions of most antitrust laws are few and brief. The Sherman Antitrust Act of 1890, 15 U.S.C.A. §§ 1–7,[5] is no exception. Its two main provisions are:

§ 1: Every contract, combination in the form of trust or otherwise, or conspiracy, in restraint of trade or commerce among the several States, or with foreign nations, is hereby declared to be

4. When asked why Congress should make monopoly illegal if it was already prohibited at common law, one supporter of the Act answered: "Because there is not any common law of the United States." 21 Cong.Rec. 3152 (1890) (Senator Hoar).

5. With the enactment of the Antitrust Procedures and Penalties Act, offenses under the Sherman Act, which had been misdemeanors, became felonies subject to 3 years of imprisonment and fines of up to $100,000 for individuals and $1 million for corporations. 88 Stat. 1706 (1974). The principal antitrust statutes are reproduced in the Appendix.

illegal [and is a felony punishable by fine and/or imprisonment]. . . .

§ 2: Every person who shall monopolize, or attempt to monopolize, or combine or conspire with any other person or persons, to monopolize any part of the trade or commerce among the several States, or with foreign nations, shall be deemed guilty of a felony [and is similarly punishable]. . . .

Several general observations about the Act serve as a guide to understanding it. Note how the basic thrust of the two sections differs. Section 1 requires duality of action. One person cannot contract, combine or conspire by himself; the essence of the offense is the act of joining together. Section 2, on the other hand, applies to unilateral conduct: "every person who . . . ." Consequently the case law under Section 1 is often concerned with finding some agreement, as opposed to that of Section 2 where the prime concern is a structural condition (monopoly).

Section 1 focuses on restrictive agreements (wrongful purposes or effects) while Section 2 examines the aggrandizement or misuse of monopoly power (exclusionary actions). True, both sections seek ultimately the same end—curtailment of practices resulting in market control—but Section 2 is generally limited by a threshold finding of monopoly power. Even though the two sections approach the monopoly problem differently, it is clear that the means by which markets are controlled or competition dampened is a matter of indifference. Ultimately it is irrelevant whether a trade restraint was accomplished by a contract or by some looser form of agreement, or even by the sheer aggregation of market power.

Finally, the approach of the Sherman Act is proscriptive (thou shall not) rather than prescriptive (thou shall). The Act is not authority for positive administrative regulation of business conduct. On the other hand, its negative prohibitions are more stringent than the common law's mere refusal to enforce offensive contracts. And the proscription is powerful: trade restraints and monopolization are punishable as crimes; equity's broad powers are available to service antitrust policy; and private enforcement through treble damages supplements government enforcement (now through Section 4 of the Clayton Act). The legal risks of illegal restraints and monopoly actions are significant, especially in contrast with those of the common law where there was only a chance—and a remote one at that—that questioned actions would be challenged as unenforceable. Yet despite this stringency, the limits of permissible and illegal conduct are only vaguely defined.

In sum, the primary effect of the Sherman Act, especially when contrasted with that of the common law, was to bring the administration and enforcement of antitrust law within executive responsibility. Of course the final responsibility to determine the broad and ill-defined standard lay with the courts. Yet the law also did not limit the courts to prior case law in making that determination.

2.   EARLY INTERPRETATIONS

The initial judicial reaction to the Sherman Act can only be described as extreme. First the Act's coverage was emasculated by an unrealistically narrow reading; and then the Court applied the Act so rigidly as to render it unworkable unless broad exceptions were allowed. Finally the Court adopted a flexible "rule of reason," reading the statute as condemning only unreasonable conduct. But a clear standard was not provided. Thus, even this reading was widely criticized as being too hospitable to anticompetitive conduct on the one hand, or as allowing judicial discretion to rule the economy on the other. A brief review of the major cases illustrates this analysis.

It was not until 1895, five years after the Sherman Act was passed that the Supreme Court had to decide the meaning of the Sherman Act. The decision was a forerunner of future difficulties. In United States v. E.C. Knight Co., 156 U.S. 1 (1895), the Court refused to apply the Sherman Act to the sugar trust, holding that the law did not extend to restraints affecting merely the manufacture of commodities. "Commerce succeeds to manufacture, and is not a part of it." Consequently, insofar as the trust's monopoly of sugar refining was concentrated in Pennsylvania, it had not been shown to involve a *direct* restraint on interstate commerce within the Sherman Act's jurisdiction. If followed, this decision would have interred the Act before it had ever been applied, at least insofar as manufacturing monopolies were concerned.[6]

Another way to destroy legislation is to over-interpret it, to allow it no opportunity to adjust to practical necessities. Whether this was the original judicial design,[7] the Supreme Court's early interpretation of Section 1 ("Every contract . . . in restraint of trade") threatened to have this effect. In a series of closely divided opinions, beginning with United States v. Trans-Missouri Freight Ass'n, 166 U.S. 290 (1897), the Court condemned price-fixing agreements and territorial divisions because Section 1 condemned every restraint of trade without exception as unlawful. Subsequent cases quickly retreated from this absolute position in dicta, first limiting the condemnation to "direct" and "immediate" restraints with no purpose of promoting the legitimate business of either participant (Hopkins v. United States, 171 U.S. 578 (1898)), and then concluding that re-

6. The rule of *E.C. Knight* was expressly overturned in Mandeville Is. Farms, Inc. v. American Crystal Sugar Co., 334 U.S. 219 (1948). While it is still an essential element of a case under the antitrust laws to show that the challenged conduct is in or affects interstate commerce, the reach of the Sherman Act has now been interpreted as being coextensive with Congress' constitutional power under the Commerce Clause. See United States v. South-Eastern Underwriters Ass'n 322 U.S. 533, 558 (1944); see also pp. 37–40 infra.

7. A further analysis of the substantive bases of these early decisions is provided at pp. 165–69 infra.

straints lawful at common law (or some of them) were not in the category of restraints prohibited by the Sherman Act. United States v. Joint Traffic Ass'n, 171 U.S. 505 (1898).

This doctrinal dispute, of course, did not have much effect on popular support for antitrust enforcement. Antimonopoly agitation had pretty much run its course with the 1890 legislation. The public was apparently quite willing to accept these quixotic judicial approaches and executive indifference.[8] All this changed with President Theodore Roosevelt's succession to the Presidency—and even more so with his successor's (William Howard Taft's) administration. Amidst great public excitement generated by Roosevelt, the Supreme Court, in Northern Securities Co. v. United States, 193 U.S. 197 (1904), ruled that holding companies were not exempt from the Sherman Act and that the arrangement placing two competing railroads under one entity (in fact, a profit-pooling agreement) was an illegal restraint of trade.

Fueled by this successful challenge to the trust building efforts of two famous financiers, James J. Hill and J.P. Morgan, and sparked by the President's tempestuous reaction to his new Justice's

8. One study has shown, for example, that three-fourths of the 23 government cases prosecuted during the first 12 years of the Sherman Act were brought by U.S. attorneys in the field, not by the Justice Department; and of the 6 brought by the Justice Department, 4 were directed against labor unions and the other 2 (directed against the beef trust and a massive railroad merger) came at the end of the period.

(Oliver Wendell Holmes, Jr.) dissent,[9] the public reacted sharply to the Court's opinion in Standard Oil Co. of New Jersey v. United States, 221 U.S. 1 (1911). Although the decision ordered the dissolution of the oil trust into approximately 30 companies, the Court also ruled that only those restraints whose character or effect were unreasonably anticompetitive were outlawed by the Sherman Act. Some critics worried that the natural inclination of conservative federal judges would quickly reduce the Act to insignificance again; nor did inconsistent and generally lackluster enforcement by the Department of Justice inspire confidence. Others contended that if the Sherman Act now prohibited only unreasonable restraints, businessmen should be advised in advance which restraints were lawful and which were unreasonable. During the 1912 Presidential campaign public debate again focused on the scope and direction of government oversight of the economy—including new antitrust laws. After the victory of Wilson's "New Freedom," Congress created the Federal Trade Commission and enacted the Clayton Act. These laws also represent the last major passage of antitrust laws in the United States.

9. Holmes' once cordial relationship with Roosevelt was shattered as a consequence. As Max Lerner recounts, "Roosevelt was furious. 'I could carve out of a banana,' " he is reported (perhaps apocryphally) to have cried, " 'a justice with more backbone than that.' " *The Mind and Faith of Justice Holmes,* xxxiii (M. Lerner ed.1943). Lerner, however, does not report Holmes' supposed rejoinder: "Some banana! Some backbone!"

C. THE CLAYTON AND FEDERAL TRADE COMMISSION ACTS

In retrospect it seems that, typical of American politics, Woodrow Wilson won the election but most of the opposition's arguments were enacted into law. Wilson had contended that effective antitrust enforcement required specific enumeration of unlawful business practices. Business should be informed what the law expected; courts should not be free to emasculate the law through interpretation. Under the "rule of reason" businessmen were without guidance, and courts had no specific mandate to enforce. Wilson therefore proposed legislation enumerating precisely which acts were illegal (in what was to become the Clayton Act), and in order to assure business compliance criminal penalties were suggested. He also urged the creation of an administrative agency, an interstate trade commission, to investigate and publicize (but not otherwise prosecute) trade abuses as well as to advise businessmen which practices were lawful and which were not. The commission was to promote fair competitive activity.

But as these proposals traveled through Congress, Wilson became persuaded by Louis Brandeis (his closest adviser on antitrust and not yet a Supreme Court justice) that neither approach was practicable. Detailing prohibited practices might be somewhat effective, but only if criminal penalties were not assessed. Otherwise it was likely that the new law would be construed very narrowly; and, in any case, Congress was unwilling to provide for criminal penalties unless the trade abuse was universally condemned (and therefore already reachable by the Sherman Act). Another failing of clarity was that it might in fact invite business abuse; businesses would either avoid the act's coverage by seeking the same ends through unprohibited means or by playing the game of legal brinksmanship (i.e., engaging in questionable practices near the now clear line of illegality). No legislation could anticipate all restrictive practices.[10] In either case the proposed act seemed ineffective. The resulting consensus, therefore, believed that a general condemnation of undesirable trade practices was more likely to be effective, especially since it could be responsive to changing conditions and techniques. And in response to the growing concern over judicial hostility to antitrust enforcement, it was decided that an administrative agency should also be entrusted with enforcement responsibilities.

10. As the Conference Committee Report on the Clayton and FTC Acts stated:

It is impossible to frame definitions which embrace all unfair practices. There is no limit to human inventiveness in this field . . . . If Congress were to adopt the method of definition, it would undertake an endless task.

63rd Cong., 2d Sess. H.R.Rep. No. 1142, 18–29 (1914).

1. THE CLAYTON ACT

The Clayton Act of 1914 declared four restrictive or monopolistic acts illegal but not criminal: price discrimination—sales of a product at different prices to similarly situated buyers (§ 2); tying and exclusive dealing contracts—sales on condition that the buyer stop dealing with the seller's competitors (§ 3); corporate mergers—acquisitions of competing companies (§ 7); and interlocking directorates—common board members among competing companies (§ 8). In each instance, the prohibition was qualified (under somewhat different tests) by the general condition that the specified practice was illegal only "where the effect . . . may be substantially to lessen competition" or "tend to create a monopoly in any line of commerce." Never a paragon of clarity, Section 2, dealing with price discrimination, was rewritten but not improved upon by the Robinson-Patman Act of 1936; it is now a model of obfuscation and confusion. Jurisdictional holes in Section 7, the antimerger law, were patched and its prohibitions were expanded by the Celler-Kefauver Act of 1950.

2. THE FEDERAL TRADE COMMISSION ACT

Section 5 of the FTC Act of 1914 (as amended in 1938),[11] that Act's sole substantive provision, pro-

11. The Magnuson-Moss Warranty—FTC Improvements Act, 88 Stat. 2193 (1975), extended the Trade Commission's jurisdiction to matters "affecting" commerce. It also authorized addi-

vides: "unfair methods of competition in or affecting commerce, and unfair or deceptive acts or practices in or affecting commerce are hereby declared unlawful." Again no criminal penalties are attached; in fact, the Trade Commission was limited to issuing prospective decrees. The FTC shares, with the Department of Justice, enforcement of the Clayton Act. (The Department of Justice cannot, however, enforce the FTC Act.) As a practical matter, the Commission also has jurisdiction over violations of the Sherman Act because courts have ruled that Section 5's condemnation of unfair methods of competition includes Sherman Act offenses. FTC v. Cement Institute, 333 U.S. 683, 694 (1948).

D. EXEMPTIONS

Congress' attention to the antitrust laws since 1914 has focused principally on writing exceptions into the Sherman Act's coverage. As a result, several industries and activities are now insulated from the reach of the antitrust laws.

Among the broadest exemptions are those granted labor unions and collective bargaining agreements. The Clayton Act sought to exempt unions from the antitrust laws, and this position was

tional remedies, but they are limited to consumer protection actions relying on the FTC's authority to prosecute unfair or deceptive acts or practices. Since 1980, the FTC's authority to proceed under its powers to proscribe unfair acts or practices has been limited in its oversight of commercial advertising. FTC Improvements Act of 1980, 94 Stat. 374 (1980).

fortified by the Norris-LaGuardia Act of 1932. Unions seek to improve the wages, hours and working conditions of workers by monopolizing the supply of labor and policing concerted refusals to deal, and absent an exemption the antitrust laws would threaten the existence of unions. It was held in Apex Hosiery Co. v. Leader, 310 U.S. 469 (1940), that union monopolization of the labor supply does not violate the antitrust laws. This case was followed a year later by a celebrated pronouncement in United States v. Hutcheson, 312 U.S. 219 (1941), that union actions are exempt from antitrust scrutiny whenever the union acts in its self-interest and does not combine with nonlabor groups to accomplish its ends.

Unions seldom act alone to benefit workers; however, they benefit workers by entering into collective bargaining agreements with employers. Whether to accord an exemption to a particular subject of collective bargaining has vexed the courts. In Allen Bradley Co. v. Local Union No. 3, Int'l Broth. of Elec. Workers, 325 U.S. 797 (1945), a union bargaining agreement with electrical contractors to use only union-made equipment was not exempted when it was part of a larger scheme of bid-rigging and concerted refusals to deal by firms. A union act is not exempt when it aids and abets a businessmen's conspiracy.

The precise limits of the exemption for collective bargaining are difficult to find. Where a meat cutters' union and an employer agree on the hours at which meat can be sold in a Chicago supermarket employing the union's members, that agreement does not violate the Sherman Act because the subject matter of the agreement is "intimately related" to workers' hours and working conditions and the union's interest is "direct and immediate" (i.e., absent a restriction on marketing hours, union members would be forced to work night hours or would suffer employment losses). However, where a bargaining agreement obligates the union to impose a wage rate on firms not signatory to the agreement, the Sherman Act is violated upon a showing of predatory intent. Compare Local Union No. 189, Amalgamated Meat Cutters and Butcher Workmen v. Jewel Tea Co., 381 U.S. 676 (1965), with United Mine Workers of America v. Pennington, 381 U.S. 657 (1965).

In Connell Constr. Co. v. Plumbers & Steamfitters Local Union No. 100, 421 U.S. 616 (1975), the Court synthesized earlier cases and declared that there are two labor antitrust exemptions. A "statutory" exemption protects only union acts taken alone, and is not available to collective bargaining agreements. A "nonstatutory" exemption, stemming from an accommodation between Congressional policies favoring collective bargaining and favoring free competition in business markets, exempts bargaining agreement provisions which seek to remove wages, hours and working conditions from competition, but offers no exemption to agreements which restrain competition in business markets and which have anticompetitive effects not following "naturally from the elimination of competition over wages and working conditions."

The labor exemption is a subtle and untidy area not readily summarized. Among the primary issues determining whether the antitrust laws apply are: (1) whether an employer-employee relationship exists and the union is acting in its capacity as a representative of labor; (2) whether there is a combination by a union with a nonlabor group; (3) whether the union is acting in its self-interest; and (4) whether the means chosen by the union to implement its self-interest are more restrictive than necessary to achieve its goals. Thus, in H.A. Artists Assocs. v. Actors' Equity Ass'n, 451 U.S. 704 (1981), a system that required union actors to deal only with "franchised" agents was upheld as necessary to defend the union's wage structure and as designed to promote the union's self-interest. However, the fees charged for the franchises were not exempt (and were held unlawful) because they were not necessary in regulating the agents.

Public utilities, such as energy suppliers, broadcasters and common carriers, are also often exempt from antitrust enforcement, although the contour of each precise exemption varies. The approach here is somewhat distinct from other exceptions. The responsibility for assuring that the consumer receives the benefits of competition generally is assigned to an administrative agency with regulatory oversight and the antitrust exemption is justified by that regulation. In addition, many of these exempted industries involve natural monopolies or similar exceptions to the competitive market model and, as a consequence, the premise of the antitrust laws (that competition will assure the consumer quality goods and services at the lowest price) is inapplicable.

Whether this or other assumptions on which the particular antitrust exemptions are founded are correct, or whether the regulatory commissions perform their role adequately, is a matter of serious debate and concern—but beyond the scope of this text. It should be noted, however, that this is an area of ferment and change as major industries are being deregulated (see United States v. American Tel. & Tel. Co., 552 F.Supp. 131 (D.D.C.1982), aff'd, 460 U.S. 1001 (1983) (divestiture of various Bell local operating companies); Airline Deregulation Act of 1978, 92 Stat. 1705, 49 U.S.C.A. § 1374) and thus increasingly subject to antitrust review. Despite such changes, many exemptions still exist. For example, immunity from the antitrust laws has been granted to several special markets and activities, such as agricultural and fishery marketing associations, the banking and insurance industries, and export trade associations. See Foreign Trade Antitrust Improvements Act of 1982, 15 U.S. C.A. §§ 6a, 45(a)(3) (limits antitrust law coverage to effects within United States; export limitations that have an impact only on competition in foreign markets do not trigger Sherman or Clayton Act coverage).

Although these exemptions from antitrust coverage are not examined here, it should not be assumed that they are unimportant. In fact Professors Kaysen and Turner once estimated that almost one-fifth of the nation's national income originates in sectors of the economy beyond the reach of the antitrust laws. C. Kaysen & D. Turner, *Antitrust Policy* 42 (1959).

There are, in addition, many areas not covered by the antitrust laws. Some examples are government contracts and activities approved by state law. Illustrations of the former include situations where small business interests, minority preferences, or defense policies are paramount. In general the Sherman Act regulates only private conduct. Thus where state regulation supplants the competitive market and regulates it intensively, the antitrust laws do not apply. Compare Parker v. Brown, 317 U.S. 341 (1943), with Cantor v. Detroit Edison Co., 428 U.S. 579 (1976). After a decade of increasing confusion, the Court has now ruled that sovereign compulsion is not necessary for the state action doctrine to apply; it is enough if the policy is clearly articulated and supplemented by active state supervision. Town of Hallie v. Eau Claire, 105 S.Ct. 1713 (1985). See also Fisher v. Berkeley, 106 S.Ct. 1045 (1986) (rent control ordinance not preempted by Section 1 of the Sherman Act; unilateral action by the city does not meet the conspiracy requirement).

A related issue involves the scope and coverage of the antitrust laws themselves. Here judicial interpretations as well as statutes have carved out exceptions. For example, the Sherman and Clayton Acts apply only to transactions affecting interstate commerce; thus local arrangements wholly unrelated to interstate commerce are unsupervised by federal law. Non-commercial activity is also shielded from antitrust attack. This latter limitation sometimes involves extreme interpretations, such as baseball's freedom from antitrust scrutiny on the ground that it is a "sport" and therefore is not interstate "commerce" as defined in the Sherman Act. See, e.g., Flood v. Kuhn, 407 U.S. 258 (1972). But see Goldfarb v. Virginia State Bar Ass'n, 421 U.S. 773 (1975) (lawyers' price-fixing covered by the Sherman Act). The anomaly is clear when one notes that the same judicial treatment is denied all other professional sports. The statutory creation and judicial interpretation of protected havens from the antitrust laws are, in general, not analytically satisfying.

E. JURISDICTION: INTERSTATE AND FOREIGN COMMERCE

The federal antitrust laws are also limited by the power of Congress to regulate interstate commerce. Although there are minor differences which sometimes affect the coverage of various statutes, in general the antitrust laws apply to most significant commercial activity. The courts have wholly abandoned the dry conceptualism (see the *Knight* decision noted p. 24 supra) which once ruled that manufacturing was not "commerce." Today almost any activity, no matter how localized, which has "interstate incidents" is reached by the antitrust laws. See, e.g., McLain v. Real Estate Bd. of New Orleans, Inc., 444 U.S. 232 (1980) (real estate brokerage has an appreciable effect on interstate commerce in residential financing and title insurance). For example, in United States v. Employing Plasterers Ass'n, 347 U.S. 186 (1954) the Court applied the flow of commerce concept to uphold a complaint concerning restraints on plastering work in the Chicago area because they could adversely affect the otherwise continuing flow of plastering materials from out-of-state origins to Illinois job sites. See also United States v. Pennsylvania Refuse Removal Ass'n, 242 F.Supp. 794 (E.D.Pa.1965), aff'd, 357 F.2d 806 (3d Cir.1966), cert. denied, 384 U.S. 961 (1966) (conspiracy among Pennsylvania garbage collectors within the jurisdiction of the Sherman Act because some refuse was eventually disposed of in New Jersey).

Technically, there are two distinct tests for applying the interstate commerce requirement. One is whether the activity is "in" or "in the flow of" interstate commerce; the other is whether interstate commerce has been "affected." These requirements have not been applied rigorously, however, and courts have readily found some impact on interstate commerce even though a precise point at which the restraint occurs is not specified. See Mandeville Is. Farms v. American Crystal Sugar Co., 334 U.S. 219, 238 (1948). Trade practices are "purely local" and beyond the reach of the Sherman Act only if they are not within the flow of interstate commerce themselves and have no significant impact on that flow. See Hospital Building Co. v. Trustees of Rex Hospital, 425 U.S. 738, 743 (1976). Compare Gulf Oil Corp. v. Copp Paving Inc., 419 U.S. 186, 195, 202 (1974) applying a more restrictive test under the Clayton and Robinson-Patman Acts.

The fact that certain trade practices may not be reached by the federal antitrust laws does not mean that they are beyond legal control. Not only do tort actions often lie for unfair competitive acts, but almost every state also has a statute which emulates to some degree the federal law and applies to intrastate activity.

On the other side of the coin, the general prohibition in Section 1 of the Sherman Act against trade restraints applies not only to trade among the several states but also to trade "with foreign nations." Consequently, the Act and its penalties condemn restrictive agreements between domestic and foreign firms, foreign companies dealing in American markets, foreign companies run jointly with United States firms, United States companies and their foreign subsidiaries, etc. The resulting problems of jurisdiction over the person and subject matter and the scope of relief are too intricate for simple summation. The critical factor, however, is whether the questioned activity has had an impact upon United States commerce; in addition, questions of comity must also be considered. See generally, Timberlane Lumber Co. v. Bank of America, 549 F.2d 597 (9th Cir.1976).

F. ENFORCEMENT

Vigorous antitrust enforcement is a relative newcomer to the judicial battleground, and its arrival has often been signaled by easy rather than significant victories. After the initial skirmishes that lasted through 1910, antitrust languished in desuetude. Both the Justice Department and the FTC concentrated more on promoting "fair" competition, particularly through trade associations and other "sentinels" of fair competition, than on patrolling it by wiping out restrictive practices and attacking monopoly power. And during the early depression years of the 1930's, the emphasis was admittedly on restricting output and raising prices under government sponsored cartels. Only with the collapse of the New Deal's NRA in 1935 and the succession of Thurmond Arnold to the Antitrust Division did enthusiastic enforcement occur. Since then, except for a significant pause during the Second World War, emphatic antitrust enforcement has generally continued unabated, and it is now a serious force affecting business practices and the economic organization of American industry. Some, such as economists John Kenneth Galbraith and Lester Thurow, assert that antitrust is meaningless at best and probably counterproductive, a position accepted (on other grounds) by critics on the "right" side of the economic-political spectrum. For now, however, it is sufficient to note that antitrust enforcement is in the mainstream of serious and sometimes heated public debate. Ultimately, of course, the allocation of resources and the distribution of wealth are at stake.

The thrust of antitrust has shifted subtly over the years. The founders of antitrust directed their energies at the flagrantly anticompetitive activities of various trusts. They were concerned, actually and literally, with "antitrust" law. The harms they sought to correct were acknowledged by all and involved no commitment to any particular political persuasion or economic theory. Starting perhaps with the Clayton and FTC Acts of 1914 and certainly during the 1920's, the emphasis has shifted toward positive maintenance of competition—by eliminating unfair competition. This trend has increased sharply since World War II. It is now often presumed that any impairment of competition is harmful, sometimes seemingly without regard to allocative effects or efficiency designs. And the cases sometimes speak of other political and social designs: that antitrust serves societal goals favoring the dispersal of economic power, easy entry into business opportunities, and

ethical values of nondiscrimination. These strains
are not without their limits, however. The statutes only proscribe; they do not prescribe. Critical
observers have cautioned that such a use of the
antitrust laws undermines their purpose and is not
controlled by any rational principles. Business
views are also not without political power. And
courts are not insensitive to their own limitations
and to the demands of practicality.

During the past decade both the enforcement
agencies and courts have reflected a concern that
unbridled antitrust enforcement may inhibit competition and unduly favor market-place losers. Economic analysis and perceived requirements of consumers have been applied to shift antitrust
doctrine from an assumption of anticompetitive
effects to a requirement that the government or
private plaintiff demonstrate likely harms to competition.

A wide range of penalties are available for pun-
ishment of antitrust violations. The Sherman Act
(and isolated provisions of other statutes) is supported by criminal as well as civil penalties. Most
other statutes carry only civil sanctions, but these
may include injunctive relief and the three "D's"—
dissolution, divestiture and divorcement—designed
to neutralize and deny defendants the tainted
fruits of illegal practices. In general, criminal
enforcement is only rarely sought; it is limited in
practice to outrageous and clearly illegal conduct.
Consent decrees and orders are devices frequently

used by the Justice Department and Trade Commission; they constitute judicial or agency approval of settlements, and are as enforceable as any other court (agency) orders. As compromises they are not authoritative and do not necessarily reflect the state of the law.

Government enforcement is supplemented by private actions. Both the Sherman Act and the Clayton Act allow injured parties an action for treble damages (the additional award seeks to encourage these "private attorney general" prosecutions) and attorney's fees. The private plaintiff must show injury to his business or property by an activity of the defendant that violates an antitrust law. See Brunswick Corp. v. Pueblo Bowl-O-Mat, Inc., 429 U.S. 477 (1977) (injury from intensification of competition through merger was not "by reason of anything forbidden in the antitrust laws"); Reiter v. Sonotone Corp., 442 U.S. 330 (1979) (consumers paying more for goods for personal use held to be injured in their "property").

Government suits and judgments also aid private suits by extending the term of the statute of limitations on private suits and by constituting evidence of a prima facie case. In recent decades the private caseload has become a significant factor in the overall picture of antitrust enforcement.

Finally, state antitrust statutes often parallel the federal acts and rely on their interpretation. State attorneys general were granted the right in 1976 to sue in their sovereign capacity as "parens patriae" for treble damages for injuries to their general economy under the antitrust laws. Hart-Scott-Rodino Antitrust Improvements Act of 1976, 90 Stat. 1383, 1394, 15 U.S.C. A. §§ 15c–15h. See also Hawaii v. Standard Oil of Calif., 405 U.S. 251 (1972) (pre-Hart-Scott-Rodino action upholding state suit for injunctive relief as parens patriae but denying treble damages).

CHAPTER III

ANTITRUST ECONOMICS (IN A NUTSHELL)

The objective of antitrust law is to assure a competitive economy, based upon the belief that through competition producers will strive to satisfy consumer wants at the lowest price with the sacrifice of the fewest resources. Competition among producers allows consumers to bid for goods and services, and thus matches their desires with society's opportunity costs.

To express this in economic terms, competition maximizes consumer welfare by increasing both allocative efficiency (making what consumers want as shown by their willingness to pay) and productive efficiency (producing goods or services at the lowest cost thus using the fewest resources), and by encouraging progressiveness (rewarding invention). Competition maximizes total consumer wealth but it does not necessarily result in optimal income distribution. Thus, by emphasizing competition, antitrust is concerned with maximizing the size of the consumers' economic pie; how that pie is distributed is a matter left for other forces to decide (i.e., the market or other legislation).

In seeking to create or preserve a climate conducive to a competitive economy, the antitrust laws rely upon the operation of the "market" system (free enterprise) to decide what shall be produced, how resources shall be allocated in the production process, and to whom the various products will be distributed. The market system relies on the consumer to decide (by his willingness or refusal to buy) what and how much shall be produced, and on competition among producers to determine (through the production of the appropriate quality product at the lowest price) who will manufacture it.

Yet the economic case for a free and open market does not necessarily imply that the market will continue to function properly when confronted by efforts to substitute private rule (e.g., agreements among competitors to fix prices above the competitive price) for the more or less automatic adjustment mechanisms provided by competition. The antitrust laws are a legislative acknowledgement of an imperfect system—in reality some markets are not competitive. Their purpose is to assure that the gap between the ideal of competition and the reality of private rule does not become dangerously wide. Choices other than reliance on a competitive economy to protect consumer welfare are, of course, possible. Before the development of an industrial society (and particularly in feudal times), status or tradition governed production, resource allocation, and distribution. Today, in some sectors of our economy and in large areas of the world, these economic decisions are resolved

through central planning—which usually stems
from governmental direction and control. Central
planning substitutes the political and governmental process for that of the free market. However,
the same questions of who produces and consumes
what goods and in what manner must still be
resolved.

Because antitrust cases involve basic economic
issues, the great disputes that set trends and establish primary principles revolve around inferences
drawn from economic analysis. Microeconomics—
the study of the behavior of individual economic
units (the consumer, firm, and industry)—therefore
falls within the antitrust lawyer's province. The
hiring of an expert economic consultant or witness
will not discharge the responsibility; the specialist
in antitrust law must possess an understanding of
basic price theory. To understand antitrust thoroughly, it is essential to have a working knowledge
of the economic theory of competition, monopoly,
monopolistic competition, and oligopoly. Newer
theories of strategic or opportunistic behavior and
of contestable markets are also affecting antitrust
analysis.

These theories suggest relationships among industry variables and serve as a starting point for
policy analysis. Their chief value is their ability to
help clarify thought, to aid in understanding efficient resource allocation, and to bring a conceptual
basis to a typically untidy area of the law. This
chapter focuses on basic principles of economic

theory which bear directly on antitrust policy. It is not intended as a substitute for the study of economics. Rather, the emphasis here is on the central core.[1]

A. SOME BASIC EXPLANATIONS AND BEHAVIORAL ASSUMPTIONS

1. THE DEMAND SCHEDULE

When economists refer to "demand" or "the demand function," they are identifying a *demand schedule*—a statement of the different quantities of a particular good or service that a consumer would purchase at each of several different (alternative) price levels. Because the amount of an item that a person will purchase cannot be determined without also considering its price, demand cannot be identified as a set, specific quantity. Rather, it is a *range* of alternative quantities which constitutes the demand for a particular product. It is this relationship between the various possible prices and the quantities demanded at each of these prices that constitutes the demand schedule.

The demand schedule or demand curve for any good can also be illustrated on a simple, two-dimensional price/quantity graph as follows:

1. Economics is a discipline which has more than its share of contending schools of thought. Every effort will be made in this text to avoid taking sides and to confine the analysis to microeconomic concepts, an area of general agreement. The disagreements lie essentially in the application of theory and in the interpretation of empirical evidence. The contending views will be summarized in later chapters where relevant.

FIGURE 1: DEMAND CURVE

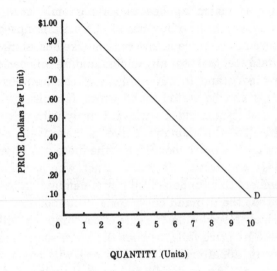

Notice that the demand curve slopes downward, reflecting the law of diminishing value. Simply stated, this rule holds that the more one has of any good, the lower the (personal substitution) value it possesses for him. The value which a consumer will attach to successive units of a particular commodity diminishes as his total consumption of that commodity increases (the consumption of all other commodities being held constant). For example, even the most ice cream-addicted child will begin to experience diminishing marginal utility after his fifth chocolate soda in the same afternoon.

Notice as well that the reverse is also true, namely, the higher the relative price for the good, the lower its rate of consumption. This simple statement, which applies to all economic goods, that one will seek to buy less as the price is raised (or more as the price is lowered), is a key economic postulate central to an understanding of basic price theory and to our analysis of the antitrust laws. It can be stated many ways: technically— the quantity demanded varies inversely with price; graphically—the demand curve is negatively or downwardly sloped; popularly—the more you have the less you want. It matters not whether one remembers this fundamental law of demand on the basis that the demand curve for all commodities is negatively sloped, that the rate of consumption will increase as price falls, or that the more sodas one drinks in an afternoon the less one will pay for another, as long as the central point is understood.

The basic theorem is substantiated by observed behavior; it is a law of demand because it describes a general truth about consumers' desires and about market behavior.[2] In recent years, for example, consumption of electricity and gasoline shifted drastically in response to price changes, and long-

2. Sometimes it is argued that consumer behavior defies this proposition, that consumers in fact occasionally buy more of some goods where the price rises. Three examples are usually offered: where the good is sought for speculative purposes; where the demand is for prestige goods; and where price is an index of quality. For a cogent explanation of why these examples further support or at least do not detract from the theory, see R. Lipsey & P. Steiner, *Economics* 161–63 (6th ed. 1981).

established automobile purchasing habits were radically modified because of increased gasoline prices and other pressures. A price decline increases the rate of consumption because more of the item will be consumed in current uses, because new uses will develop (which were valued at too low a level to have justified paying the former, higher rate), and because new users will appear from among consumers whose marginal utilities or incomes were too low. The reverse, of course, holds true for the case of higher prices. All of these factors explain why a change in the price of a commodity causes a change in the amount demanded.

2. PROFIT-MAXIMIZING BEHAVIOR BY FIRMS

The economic theory of the business firm assumes that each firm has but one primary goal, namely, to make as much money (more particularly, profit) as possible. That is, every firm seeks to maximize its profits. It follows, then, that a firm's ultimate objectives will not be influenced by who in the firm manages it (makes decisions) or the type of firm involved; the motive of generating profits is pervasive in all firms, whether they be corporate giants or individual proprietorships.[3] Businessmen may not consciously maximize their

3. Of course, taxes, legal restraints on corporate control, etc., may distort the methods by which this objective is achieved by the firm. But in making policy choices governing firm conduct, it is necessary first to understand the basic aim and operation of the firm where such conditions are not controlling.

profits, but competition among firms will drive
them to act as if they did. Firms fail or prosper
depending on how successful they are in approxi-
mating this result.

On this theory are based further predictions
about the firm's behavior. For example, in making production decisions, the firm will adhere to
the principle of substitution—that for a given set of
technical possibilities, efficient (profit-maximizing)
production will substitute cheaper factors (of labor,
land, or capital) for more expensive ones. Which
factors are "cheaper" will, of course, also depend
on their ability to produce the same output. It
also follows that a firm's methods of production
will tend to change with shifts in the relative
prices of factors involved. Therefore, if labor costs
increase relatively (or if material costs decline), a
firm will become capital intensive, and vice versa.
The theory of the firm *suggests* that in order to
achieve its goal of profit maximization the firm
will seek to organize its factors of production efficiently and put its resources to their most valuable
(highest valued) use. It only suggests this result,
however. Where the market is competitive, market pressures will force this result over time.

Efficient production generally means that a firm
will seek the lowest possible costs for a particular
rate of output. A profit-maximizing firm will increase production when the additional revenue exceeds the additional costs. That is, the firm will
expand its output as long as the marginal, or last,

unit adds more to revenues than it does to costs—
namely, as long as the marginal revenue exceeds
or equals marginal cost.[4] If the firm finds that
greater production increases profit, it will expand
output; if greater production decreases profit, output will be reduced. This rule of profit-maximizing behavior is readily illustrated as follows:

FIGURE 2: PROFIT MAXIMIZATION BY A FIRM [5]

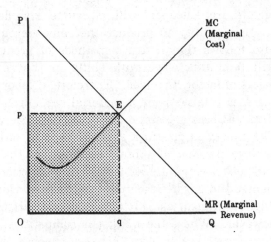

4. "Cost" as used here (and by economists), must include a
normal, competitive return on investment sufficient to attract
capital into the industry. See note 6, p. 54 infra.

5. In this and subsequent figures, "P" on the vertical line
stands for "price (per unit)," and "Q" on horizontal line stands
for "quantity (units)."

Thus, if it is profitable for a firm to produce at all, it will expand output whenever marginal revenue (*MR*) is greater than marginal cost (*MC*) and keep expanding output until marginal revenue equals marginal cost (or the intersection of *MC* and *MR* at equilibrium point *E*).[6] As is explained further below, the profit-maximizing price for this hypothetical firm in a competitive market is *p* which equates with output *q* (and generates total revenues reflected by the shaded square bounded by the lines drawn between points *p–E–q–O*, assuming a single price). Again, this explanation merely sets forth what common sense suggests. As a firm increases production, costs will first decline (the hook on *MC*), but as the firm's output reaches and then passes its most efficient production level, marginal costs will increase. And when these incremental per unit costs exceed the amount received for the last item produced, the firm will not further increase its production.

B. BASIC ECONOMIC MODELS

A traditional conclusion of economic theory is that the structure of an industry affects its behav-

6. This analysis is greatly simplified and stops short of exploring long-run versus short-run factors which would require consideration of fixed and variable costs, average and total costs, and long- and short-run variations. Obviously these distinctions and concepts are important, but they are not explored here (except in connection with the theory of monopolistic competition, see text p. 74 infra) Examination of these additional factors would confirm the basic principles and their introduction now seems likely to confuse rather than clarify.

ior and, ultimately, its performance. To clarify thought, it is helpful to examine several economic models. These structural models, though merely theoretical constructs, yield predictions about likely firm and market behavior.

They are presented as analytic models, however, not as complete explanations of the real world. More sophisticated and lengthier explanations of price theory should be consulted. This description is intentionally brief and limited. It is designed to *introduce* the beginning antitrust student and practitioner to the core economic concepts critical in antitrust. Actual markets are in fact located somewhere between the polar extremes of perfect competition and monopoly and are affected by many forces. Nevertheless, an understanding of these models is important because they assist in understanding how markets operate, in interpreting court decisions applying the antitrust laws, and in evaluating antitrust enforcement. Court opinions, with increasing frequency, also rely on these and related economic concepts.

1. PERFECT COMPETITION

Perfect competition describes a market where consumer interests are controlling. Producers respond to consumer tastes by producing what buyers want and, in competition with each other, at the lowest price. The market is efficient in the sense that no rearrangement of production or distribution will improve the position of any consumer or seller (without making someone else worse off). Societal wealth is maximized because resources are put to their highest valued use and output is optimal.

The following conditions which suggest the existence of perfect competition, are also useful in predicting whether competitive behavior is likely in a market:

(1) There are large numbers of buyers and sellers.

(2) The quantity of the market's products bought by any buyer or sold by any seller is so small relative to the total quantity traded that changes in these quantities leave market price unaffected.

(3) The product is homogeneous; there is no reason for any buyer to prefer a particular seller and vice versa.

(4) All buyers and sellers have perfect information about the prices in the market and the nature of the goods sold.

(5) There is complete freedom of entry into and exit out of the market.

Brief analysis explains why these market conditions are conducive to competition. With numerous sellers no one producer can charge more for his product than the cost (including a reasonable investment return) of making and selling it. If a higher price were charged, the buyer would simply turn to the seller's competitors. Easy entry and

exit are important because they make investment
attractive: a company that is frozen in a market
and cannot be sold is less attractive; and easy
entry limits the ability of firms in the market from
producing less and raising prices individually or
collectively.

An example illustrates the workings of a perfectly competitive market.[7] In a mythical industry
producing a standardized product known as a widget, there are 100 well-informed sellers and 500
well-informed buyers. No individual seller (or buyer) can affect the price of a widget, as each has a
trivial portion of the market. Except as the market is changing (to reflect changing costs, consumer
tastes, etc.) the price will be uniform. Since the
product is homogeneous, buyers will shift
purchases to sellers offering the best prices and
services. This pressure forces sellers to improve
their product and services while also providing
lower relative prices.

Graphically, the situation confronting any particular seller may be represented as follows:

7. See also R. Bork, *The Antitrust Paradox* 91–98 (1978).

FIGURE 3: OUTPUT OF A COMPETITIVE FIRM

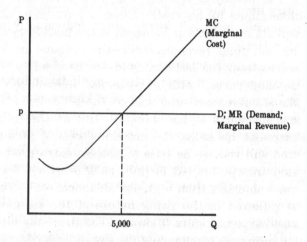

The *individual* seller is confronted with a level, *horizontal,* or *infinitely elastic demand curve* since 99 other firms sell widgets that are perfect substitutes for his widget.[8] The seller takes whatever price is set by the market and is therefore often called a price-taker. Regardless of the amount of his output that he puts on the market, the price will be *p.* Thus, if he raises his price above *p,* his sales will drop to zero. Nor does he have an incentive to charge less than the market price

8. The widget *industry* faces a *downwardly sloping demand curve* similar to that shown in Figure 1; however, because each firm sells such a small fraction of the amount demanded, the demand curve facing each seller appears to be virtually horizontal.

because all that he can produce can be sold at the prevailing price.

The output of a seller who is a price-taker is determined by his costs. Since a price-taker can sell all, or as little as he wants at the market price, his marginal revenue curve—the revenue he receives from the last unit sold—is identical to the demand curve; with a horizontal individual demand curve, each unit sold by the seller adds the same amount to his revenue. But as the seller increases his sales, the marginal costs of production will rise, as he tries to squeeze extra production from a limited facility, pays overtime, buys raw materials from a greater distance, etc.[9] This is reflected in the rising nature of the marginal cost curve in Figure 3, supra. The firm may alter its costs only by changing the size of its production run. As indicated earlier, the individual seller will operate where his marginal cost equals marginal revenue, here at 5,000 units, as this is the point at which profits are maximized.

We have, so far, described only the operation of one firm in a perfectly competitive market. The industry as a whole is the sum of its parts. Total output will be determined by what consumers will pay (the demand curve) at that price. Price is set

9. The theory of perfect competition also requires that costs eventually rise. Continually decreasing costs would lead a firm to increase output until it produced the entire industry output, in violation of the premise of many firms. This is the situation described as natural monopoly. See F. Scherer, *Industrial Market Structure and Economic Performance* 482 (2d ed. 1980); p. 74, n. 20 infra.

by the cost of producing that output by the lowest cost producers of that amount. If costs rise, so will price (but output will fall) as long as everything else remains the same—and vice versa.

To illustrate the aggregation of all firms in the widget industry, a second graph is useful:

FIGURE 4: OUTPUT OF A COMPETITIVE *INDUSTRY*

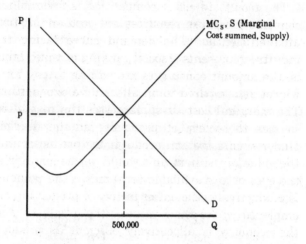

The *industry* marginal cost curve represents the sum of individual cost functions; it is also the industry supply schedule. The industry demand curve is *downwardly sloping* as there is no perfect substitute for widgets. The individual firms' demand curves were flat, indicating infinite price elasticity of demand (greater responsiveness of the amount demanded to a change in price), because the widgets of the other 99 firms were a perfect substitute. However, as there is no perfect substitute for widgets, the industry demand curve will reflect some inelasticity. Thus, a decrease in the price of widgets (e.g., due to new cost-cutting technology) will increase the quantity demanded; an increase in the industry price (e.g., due to a cartel controlling a factor of production) will cause a decrease in the quantity demanded.

The result of perfect competition is favorable to consumers because resources are used and distributed efficiently. The demand curve facing the industry represents a social ranking of wants, that is, the amount consumers are willing to pay for a widget as compared to an alternative expenditure. The marginal cost curve expresses the cost in resources to society of producing another widget. Under such a system, products are produced until the value of the next unit would not be justified in the eyes of any available consumer. The economy is productively efficient as factors of production are employed where their value is the greatest. And the economy is allocatively efficient as products are produced in the quantity consumers want.

The essential points bear repetition so that they are not missed.[10] In a perfectly competitive mar-

---

10. This discussion, it should be noted, once again makes no distinction between short- and long-run consequences—though, in fact, both are required to substantiate the conclusions stated in this paragraph. More comprehensive explanations are now set forth in most antitrust case books as well as any basic microeconomics text.

ket the individual firm is merely a quantity adjuster. All firms sell at marginal cost and earn only a normal return on investment. Each firm takes price as given to it by the market; no firm can affect the price by adjusting output or adjust output by raising or lowering price. Each firm pursues the goal of maximizing profits by adjusting its output (either increasing or decreasing the quantity sold) until its marginal cost equals the prevailing market price. In this circumstance the consumer is sovereign. The firms in a competitive market respond to rather than dictate changes in the market prices. Finally, the free-market system coerces efficiency from individual firms, and no firm realizes monopoly profits.

The theory of perfect competition is important even though it precisely describes few, if any, markets. Its insights are powerful in providing an understanding of how a competitive market works and the benefits it can confer. It also provides a standard against which market performance can be measured. The identified conditions of perfect competition (of numerous sellers/buyers, small market shares, product homogeneity, perfect information, and easy entry and exit) are similarly useful in suggesting where competitive behavior is likely. On the other hand, the absence of these conditions does not prevent a market from behaving competitively. And several examples of intensified competition in recent years even as these markets were becoming more concentrated (e.g., personal computers, soft drinks) come to mind. In other words, these conditions neither define perfect competition nor are a priori present where competitive rivalry is inevitable or likely.

2. MONOPOLY

In general terms, private monopoly presents the other side of the theoretical coin of perfect competition. A seller with substantial (i.e., total) market power restricts his output in order to raise his price and maximize his profits. Not only does this involve a wealth transfer from consumers to producers, it reduces output and may relieve the producer of pressures to innovate or otherwise be efficient.

Monopoly markets are also often described by three structural and functional factors, namely:

(1) A single seller occupies the entire market.

(2) The product it sells is unique.

(3) Substantial barriers bar entry by other firms into the industry and exit is difficult.

Again, however, the existence of some of these conditions is useful only in predicting where monopoly pricing (and output) is likely since it may not in fact occur and since markets with substantially different conditions may also exhibit monopoly practices. In other words, despite suggestions to the contrary, these conditions do not define or determine whether monopoly effects will exist.[11]

Perhaps the single most distinctive feature of a monopoly (or imperfectly competitive) market is the existence of barriers to entry. Without such constraints, other firms are likely to enter and take sales away if the monopolist seeks to raise price or lower quality from the competitive norm. The principal illustration of an entry barrier is a legal constraint such as a patent. Others include essential raw materials or distribution channels that make entry unlikely because of a relative cost disadvantage of those currently outside the market.

By definition, monopoly describes the situation where one seller produces the output of an entire industry or market—and the *downwardly sloping* industry demand curve is ipso facto identical with that seller's demand curve. If all widget manufacturers in our discussion of perfect competition had merged into one firm, it would be in such a monopoly position.

As a consequence of being faced by the downwardly sloping market demand curve rather than the competitive firm's flat demand curve, the mo-

11. As a practical matter, both economists and lawyers often define monopoly simply in terms of effects. That is, they suspect a market is monopolized if a firm consistently makes supra-normal profits, if its costs are greater than costs at the most efficient scale of production, or if selling expenditures are excessive or technological progress is inadequate. These effects flow from the use of monopoly power.

nopolist does not maximize his profits at the competitive output of 500,000 units. The reason is simple. For the competitive seller marginal revenue is the same at all output levels, and always equal to market price. How much he produces has no impact on price and is determined by the shape of his marginal cost curve. The monopolist, on the other hand, finds marginal revenue always less than price because his demand curve is downwardly sloping. If only a single price is charged, every expansion of output requires a price reduction (reducing his average revenue) and therefore, the last unit sold produces less revenue than the preceding sale. The central point is that a monopolist who cannot discriminate in his prices among customers and who expands output will have to accept a lower price, not just on the additional units but on all units sold. Additional sales can be obtained only by lowering the price charged on the monopolist's entire output.

As a result, the monopolist faces a choice on production and price. The choice is between a higher selling price (with fewer sales) and a lower price (with greater sales). In making this choice, the monopolist will maximize profits at less than the competitive output level—namely, where marginal revenue equals marginal cost. Thus, contrary to the competitive result, the monopolist will maximize profits by restricting output and setting price above marginal cost.

The description of the monopoly market can also be understood by reference to the market demand curve which was plotted in Figure 1, p. 49 supra. Viewing that curve as the market demand for widgets, the monopolist has the same curve for his firm's demand. Knowing this demand, he can determine the price which would maximize his profits by determining his marginal revenue (i.e., the revenue earned from each additional widget sold). The seller can determine his total revenue from each price, then the marginal revenue for each additional unit sold, and finally, assuming that he could manufacture widgets at a cost of ten cents each, the profit from each additional unit sold:

TABLE 1—DEMAND SCHEDULE, MARGINAL
REVENUE AND ECONOMIC PROFIT

Price	Amount Demanded	Total Revenue	Marginal Revenue	Marginal Cost	Total Cost	Economic Profit
$1.00	1	$1.00	$1.00	$.10	$ .10	$ .90
.90	2	1.80	+.80	.10	.20	1.60
.80	3	2.40	+.60	.10	.30	2.10
.70	4	2.80	+.40	.10	.40	2.40
.60	5	3.00	+.20	.10	.50	2.50
.50	6	3.00	0	.10	.60	2.40
.40	7	2.80	−.20	.10	.70	2.10
.30	8	2.40	−.40	.10	.80	1.60
.20	9	1.80	−.60	.10	.90	.90
.10	10	1.00	−.80	.10	1.00	0

As is evident from this table, the seller's most profitable position is to sell five units at $.60. At this point his economic profit is $2.50, a return on investment that he cannot improve upon. That is, the seller maximizes his profits at a price of $.60 because there would be no additional profit from selling an additional unit.

Another way of seeing why the monopolist exercises his pricing/output option in this way is to draw a graph of the monopolist's demand (or average revenue) and marginal revenue curves:

FIGURE 5: PRICING BY A MONOPOLIST [12]

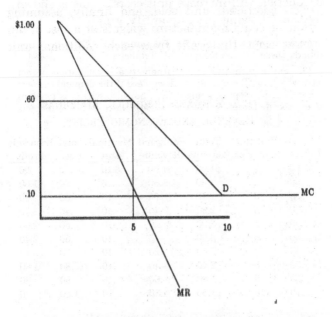

12. Actually, the monopolist would like to increase output slightly since his profit-maximizing position is where marginal revenue and marginal cost intersect. See Figure 6, p. 69 infra. This could be achieved if widgets were sold in partial units (and

As stated earlier, the marginal revenue line is always less than price because the monopolist has to lower his price on *all* units in order to sell an extra (last, or marginal) unit.[13]

To describe a more realistic picture of the situation facing the monopolist, then, one need only alter Figure 5 to show an increasing marginal cost curve. Both the competitive industry (as shown in Figure 4, supra) and the monopolist generally face increasing marginal costs because an increase in production will increase unit costs. This is shown by the following price/quantity graph:

price were set at less than 10 cent intervals). The illustration rounds these figures for sake of simplicity.

13. For a technical and mathematical explanation of not only why the MR curve slopes downward if the demand curve is a downwardly sloping straight line, but also why it is twice as steep, see R. Lipsey & P. Steiner, *Economics* 242, 935 (6th ed. 1981).

FIGURE 6: PROFIT–MAXIMIZING MONOPOLIST
(increasing marginal cost)

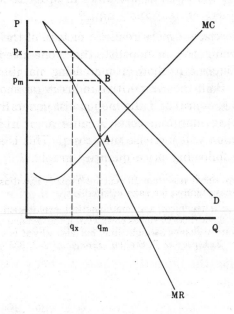

The monopolist maximizes his profit by producing an output quantity where his marginal revenue equals marginal cost (Point *A*, Figure 6; i.e., q_m will be drawn in, vertically, where MR intersects MC) and by charging whatever price his demand curve reveals is necessary to sell that output (Point *B*, Figure 6).[14] Stated more simply, the profit-maximizing monopolist, facing a downward sloping

14. The monopolist's output will equal that amount revealed by the intersection of the marginal revenue curve (MR) and the marginal cost line (MC). The output q_m will be sold at price p_m.

demand curve, will increase his output only as long
as his profitability increases.[15] The monopolist's
total net revenue no longer increases when marginal cost (MC) exceeds marginal revenue (MR) for
a unit because, by definition, the cost of producing
and selling this last unit of sales then exceeds the
revenue garnered by that sale. That is, it is sold at
a loss. And in order to maximize his profit, the
monopolist sets the price (p_m) at which the market
demand curve intersects this quantity (q_m). If, for
example, he sets price above this level, at say p_x,
consumers would buy only quantity q_x. While unit
price (p_x) and profit per unit would be higher, total
profits would be reduced. Similarly, if prices were
set below this level and quantity were unchanged,
he would not be charging "all the market could
bear." Remember, profits are *always* maximized
by selling the quantity indicated where marginal
costs equal marginal revenue.

Before closing this section, it is appropriate to
note that the theory of monopoly describes a seller
who is insulated from the loss of customers by
sellers of other identical or substitute products.
However, all products face some substitutes for the
services they provide, so that total monopoly power
never exists. Monopoly power is, in other words, a

15. For purposes of exposition, it is assumed that the monopolist's profit is his total revenue less his marginal cost. In fact,
the monopolist's profit is determined by his average total cost
curve. All that is in fact known when marginal cost equals
marginal revenue is that the monopolist does better at this
output level than at any other output, not whether his operation is particularly profitable.

variable or a matter of degree not an absolute; it is not the complete counterpart to perfect competition.

3. COMPETITION AND MONOPOLY COMPARED

The primary effects of monopoly, when compared to perfect competition, are reduced output, higher prices, and transfer of income from consumers to producers.[16] In short, should a perfectly competitive industry become monopolized, and all cost curves remain unaffected, price will rise (from p_c to p_m, Figure 7) and quantity produced will decline (from q_c to q_m, Figure 7). This is readily seen when the price/quantity graphs for the two industries are overlaid on one another:

---

16. Some economists have also suggested that monopolies can tolerate waste and inefficiency in their operations as they are not disciplined by competition. The resulting higher costs lead marginal cost to equal marginal revenue at an output even smaller than that produced by an efficient monopolist, thus producing further resource misallocation. See F. Scherer, supra at 464–71.

FIGURE 7: MONOPOLIZING A COMPETITIVE INDUSTRY [17]

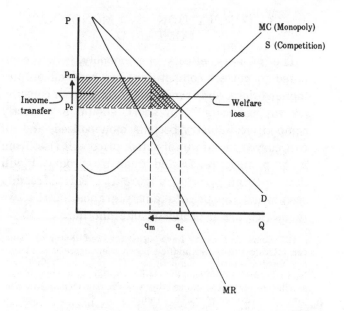

For example, when the industry is competitive, price will be at p_c and output at q_c. Should the industry become monopolized, output would be reduced to q_m and price raised to p_m. A transfer of income from consumers to producers would also occur which, if costs remain unchanged, will be reflected in increased profits for the monopolist as

17. This figure merely duplicates onto one graph Figures 4 and 6 supra.

generally illustrated by the diagonally-lined rectangle.[18]

In addition, monopoly pricing leads to a deadweight welfare loss, illustrated by the cross-hatched triangular area. It represents the loss in value to those consumers who at the competitive price would buy the product, but who at the monopoly price are deflected to "inferior" substitutes. The fact that the price charged by the monopolist exceeds the marginal cost in this region indicates that the value of the product to consumers who no longer purchase it exceeds society's cost of producing it. This loss to some customers is not recouped by the monopolist (or anyone else), for the monopolist obtains no revenue from output that he does not produce. Society is poorer as resources in the economy could be used more productively in the industry restricting output than in the industry producing the inferior substitute in which they are actually used. The area of this deadweight loss is

18. Once again note that this description simplifies the analysis and makes no distinction between average and marginal costs. The inclusion of average cost would alter the size and shape of the rectangle, but it would not dispute the basic point that income is being transferred from consumers to producers.

According to one commentator, the diagonally-lined rectangle is a rough approximation of the cost resulting from competition among firms to become a monopolist. Thus, the area of this rectangle may also represent a resource cost to society. See R. Posner, *Antitrust Law* 11–13 (1976).

an indicator of society's welfare loss due to monopolistic resource misallocation.[19]

While most emphasis is placed on the undesirable features of monopoly in comparison with competition, especially with respect to allocative and productive efficiency, it should be noted that monopoly is not universally condemned. Monopoly may, according to some theories, generate profits which support innovation; it may be inevitable and result in a reduction of price and an increase of output where it alone would bring economies of large scale production. It may also provide the product variety which consumers desire and which perfect competition might preclude.[20]

4. MONOPOLISTIC COMPETITION

Another theory seeks to deal with the problem of pricemaking in imperfect markets. Monopolistic

19. For a more complete examination of this effect, see F. Scherer, supra at 17–18, 459–64. It understates the total welfare loss because the costs of forming and maintaining the monopoly are not included. Landes, *An Introduction to the Economics of Antitrust* in R. Posner & F. Easterbrook, *Antitrust* 1069 (2d ed. 1981). On the other hand, according to the theory of "second best" the deadweight loss may be overstated. See R. Posner, supra at 13–14; P. Areeda *Antitrust Analysis* 39–40 (3d ed. 1981).

20. It should be noted, however, that by definition a monopoly profit is an unnecessary payment to a firm; it would have produced the same goods even at a competitive price. When it is necessary to allow a firm a market monopoly in order to realize economies of scale, a "natural monopoly" is said to exist. In such markets, government price regulation is frequently imposed to prevent the "natural monopolist" from pushing price above competitive levels. See generally 2 A. Kahn, *The Economics of Regulation* ch. 4 (1971).

competition seeks to reconcile the contending forces of perfect competition and monopoly, yet it is not necessarily the middle ground between the two. The important difference inherent in the theory of monopolistic competition lies in its recognition that each producer sells a somewhat differentiated, but substitutable, product. That is, this theory treats market behavior where there are many sellers, yet each seller's product is distinct and distinguishable by brand or other means of identification from those sold by others in the industry. This contrasts sharply with both competitive and monopolistic retailing where distinctive product packaging, labeling, advertising, and similar selling techniques are absent because they would not increase either price or output in the case of competition or demand in the case of monopoly.

Where there are many sellers in an industry with differentiated products, this theoretical model predicts that the sellers will concentrate on *non-price competition,* namely in advertising, product quality, and sales techniques, rather than price competition. It also forecasts that industry return on investment will reflect normal, competitive returns since the firms in the market "compete" by increasing selling costs and entry is possible; prices, on the other hand, will reflect monopoly conditions in that price will reflect these "extra" selling costs, output will be less than with pure competition, and average costs will be higher.

Proponents of this theory find examples in consumer industries such as breakfast cereals, deodorants, proprietary drugs (e.g., aspirin), and household bleach. In each instance, several firms sell virtually identical products or services which have been separately identified in the buyer's mind. The firms appear to obtain sales primarily from advertising and other aspects of nonprice competition. Monopolistic competition resembles monopoly in that sellers face a negatively sloped demand curve for their somewhat unique products. It also portrays aspects of competition, however, in that firms in the market face a substantial number of actual or potential competitors, and earn normal profits.

In this situation, where elements of both competition and monopoly exist, sellers are able to price their products above competitive levels because brand differentiation gives them a degree of monopoly power. That is, other similar products are not complete substitutes either because of physical differences or special features such as trademarks, distinctive styles, or advertising. On the other hand, sellers are not in the same position as monopolists because close substitutes exist for their products. For example, other antifreeze is recognized by consumers to be adequate as a replacement for Prestone, even though the latter has established (in this case, primarily by advertising) a strong consumer preference. Thus it is asserted that competitive pressures from close substitutes force sellers of branded products to respond with more advertising, sales promotions, product distinctions, or similar costly efforts that dissipate monopoly profits. The result is that firms in monopolistic competition do not get the rewards of monopoly (their return on investment is similar to that earned by firms in competitive industries), yet output and prices continue at a monopoly level. It seems, in other words, the worst of all possible worlds.

The theory of monopolistic competition is an important step in understanding monopolistic behavior. In particular, it demonstrates how monopolistic elements in an industry can lead to production at a point where output is restricted and costs are above those of the most efficient scale, even thought the industry firms only earn a "normal" return. As a description of actual behavior, however, the theory is largely inadequate. Its assumption that all firms in an industry have identical cost and demand curves is unrealistic. Also, it is substantiated by scant empirical evidence. Moreover, monopolistic competition can, in theory, provide substantial consumer benefits. Real and imagined product differences may benefit consumers in the form of greater product variety. Selling expenses by firms in such industries are likely to reduce buyer search costs. These benefits may exceed the costs of either less efficient production or image advertising, thereby in fact improving consumer welfare. Finally, it should be noted that there are alternative—but not necessarily mutually exclusive—explanations for non-price competition. The most prominent of these is the theory of oligopoly, namely that sellers tacitly coordinate their prices in order to earn supranormal profits. In this circumstance, product differentiation can provide an avenue for competitive activity.

5. OLIGOPOLY

Of even greater significance in antitrust than the preceding market model has been the theory of oligopoly. Although based on a variety of theories, the basic characteristic of each is the postulate that because there are only a *few sellers* in oligopoly markets, all sellers recognize that they are to a substantial degree interdependent. Therefore, each seller takes into account the reactions of rival sellers when making output and pricing decisions. This means that firms in oligopoly markets will not reduce prices to increase market share because they expect that action to be fruitless. Any gains will be cancelled immediately when rival sellers retaliate with similar price reductions.

As a consequence, oligopoly sellers concentrate, according to theory, on coordination and anticipation. What competition exists is in the form of indirect competition—by disguised price cuts (through improved product quality, credit terms, delivery service, or secret selective price reductions) and nonprice competition such as the introduction of differentiated products, advertising and sales promotions. Such competition is limited, however, so as not to invite retaliation or to increase average total costs (which would deny the oligopolist supranormal profits).[21]

The primary theoretical difference, then, between oligopoly on the one hand, and competition and monopoly (and even monopolistic competition) on the other hand, is that in oligopoly markets price and output decisions are made while anticipating the reactions of the identified rivals. Neither the competitive firm nor the monopolist considers the reactions of others; the competitive seller has no impact on his rivals and the monopolist has no close rivals. On the other hand, coordination among oligopolists is unlikely to be perfect; cost curves may differ, and more efficient firms have a strong incentive to engage in disguised price cutting in order to capture additional sales at or above their marginal cost but below the "market" price. Oligopoly theory does not assume that output and pricing decisions in oligopoly are identical to those in monopoly; the expectation rather is that each is somewhere between predicted competitive and monopoly levels.

Both oligopolists and monopolists are affected by the actions of other firms.[22] The oligopolist's price

21. In monopolistic competition, by contrast, rivalry forces profits to normal levels because there are many sellers, each of whom seeks to increase his market share at the expense of his rivals; hence such coordination is impossible.

22. For a similar description, see P. Asch, *Economic Theory and the Antitrust Dilemma* 49–52 (1970).

strategy will be determined not only by his costs but also by his estimate of his rivals' pricing strategy. The monopolist's prices are determined by his costs and the price of substitute goods which, in turn, sets his demand curve. The difference between the two, then, is that the actions of rival firms both affect the oligopolist and are affected by him; the situation is circular and therefore hard to predict.

The oligopoly analysis can be illustrated as follows: assume that three firms, Able, Baker and Charlie, are the only sellers of widgets. If they could coordinate their output and pricing decisions, they would raise price above a competitive level and earn monopoly profits. To do so, however, requires some understanding that one firm's price increase will not be undercut by the others, or the advantage will be lost for all. The difficulty is that each firm's "best" pricing/output decision cannot be defined in advance without some understanding of what rival firms will do. That is, Able's best (profit-maximizing) policy depends on how much Baker and Charlie produce and the price they set for their products. And, by the same analysis, neither Baker nor Charlie can know what to do until they know what Able's policy will be—or what the other will do. This is not the end of the matter, however. For now each of the firms must also anticipate what their rivals expect them to do. This process of guessing and outguessing one's rivals, of course, can go on and on, and for this reason oligopoly marketing strategy is often called a guessing game.

Left to their own devices, it seems clear that the firms, Able, Baker, and Charlie, would form a cartel (or to use the turn of the century term, a "trust") and collectively act as a monopolist. However, such formal agreements are unlawful per se and even punishable by criminal penalties under Section 1 of the Sherman Act as illegal price-fixing. The question, therefore, arises: can firms achieve similar ends without express or tacit agreements prohibited by the antitrust laws? Is it possible, in other words, that oligopolists can successfully estimate their rivals' actions, and vice versa, so that similar market coordination is achieved.

Observation of industries with a few large sellers occupying most of the market tells us that reality may not be as indeterminate as this description suggests. Pricing and output decisions are constantly made in fact in oligopolistically structured industries as they reach equilibrium. Just as problems of mutual interdependence are frequently encountered in military actions, poker games and football tactics, oligopolists engage in offensive and defensive maneuvers that appear to depend not only on their abilities but also on how they use the resources available to them. These decisions, of course, are made in the light of experience—namely, past performance, available resources, possible returns, the desire to minimize possible losses as well as maximize gains, etc.

Nonetheless, oligopoly analysis has to this point been without a unifying theory satisfactorily describing and predicting market outcomes (as is available generally in competition and monopoly). This shortcoming is not for lack of effort, as economists and others have devised numerous theories and tests of oligopoly ideas for over a century. See generally Weiss, "The Concentration-Profits Relationship and Antitrust," in *Industrial Concentration: The New Learning* 188–96 (H. Goldschmid, H. Mann & J. Weston eds. 1974).

Oligopoly theory has proceeded on two fronts in seeking to systematize such speculation. First, it has sought to develop a systematic analysis of possible alternatives facing the seller in an oligopoly market and to predict performance. The focus here is on rationalizing how a firm seeking to maximize profits would react when facing an oligopoly market. In general the theory has not addressed the more basic question of how the price was initially established. More recently, the insights of sophisticated mathematicians have been brought to bear on oligopoly theory in the introduction of the theory of games—the study of "rational" (optimizing) strategy in small group situations where the rivals are mutually dependent. But the various game theories also have their limitations for oligopoly analysis. They are based on zero-sum assumptions—i.e., that the payoff sums to zero—where a minimax strategy of minimizing losses is unbeatable. However, the nature

of oligopoly pricing is in fact more complex and
game theory "is ill-suited to the typical variable-
sum game of oligopolistic rivalry." F. Scherer,
*Industrial Market Structure and Economic Per-
formance* 161 (2d ed.1980).

The second process which has been used to understand oligopoly has been to observe the performance of firms in oligopoly markets and to
measure the results. This approach was pioneered
by Professor Joe S. Bain who studied the profit
rates of forty-two industries for the years 1936–40
and found that where the eight largest firms controlled seventy percent or more of the market,
average profits were considerably higher than
where markets were less concentrated. Bain, *Relation of Profit Rate to Industry Concentration:
American Manufacturing, 1936–40*, 65 Q.J.Econ.
293 (1951). The conclusion which this survey supported was that oligopolistically structured (i.e.,
highly concentrated) industries were acting inter-
dependently to restrict output and to raise prices
above average cost and thus to earn supranormal
returns. The basic findings were confirmed in
numerous subsequent studies. But more recent
analyses have argued forcefully that the Bain and
subsequent studies are flawed. The criticisms not
only focus on numerous technical deficiencies in
the studies correlating concentration with profits,
but also question the persistence of any such correlation over time. In fact, even accepting the statistical correlations as accurate reflections of indus-

try profits, it is argued that they are explainable on the hypothesis that firms of superior efficiency will generally expand their market share. Increasing concentration in an otherwise open market, then, may be simply the result of competitive efficiency with the "winners" in the market struggle gaining a larger proportion of the sales. This questioning of the statistical evidence of oligopoly is the center of debate and further investigation. See generally "The Concentration and Profits Issue" in *Industrial Concentration: The New Learning* 162–245 (H. Goldschmid, H. Mann & J. Weston eds. 1974). Other ideas challenge conventional economic theory and present views that industry structure does not necessarily determine market performance: see, e.g., W. Baumol, J. Panzar & R. Willig, *Contestable Markets and the Theory of Industry Structure* (1982); O. Williamson, *Markets and Hierarchies* (1975) (strategic behavior); O. Williamson, *The Economic Institutions of Capitalism* (1985) (transaction cost economics). The extent to which these views will affect antitrust law remains uncertain.[23]

A related development, that also builds on cartel (monopoly) theory is the recent focus on the mar-

23. Although the Supreme Court has not disavowed its stance of relying on evidence that increasingly concentrated industries are likely to result in diminished competitive vigor (e.g., United States v. U.S. Gypsum Co., 438 U.S. 422 (1978)), it has demonstrated a willingness to review statistical cases of "undue concentration" more rigorously. Compare United States v. Philadelphia Nat'l Bank, 374 U.S. 321 (1963), with United States v. General Dynamics Corp., 415 U.S. 486 (1974).

ket characteristics that make it easier for oligopolists to cooperate through express or tacit collusion.[24] Industries characterized by high
concentration (four firms producing at least half
and usually three-quarters of the industry output),
product homogeneity, frequent sales, similar cost
structures among firms, and high barriers to entry
are, according to this theory, more prone to collusion and more likely to approximate the performance of a collective monopoly.

CONCLUSION

This introduction to basic economic concepts and
the exploration of several primary theories is relevant to a study of antitrust for two reasons: (1)
they inform us in pursuing the antitrust goal—to
maximize consumer welfare by controlling the misuse of private economic power; and (2) they apply
where competition is the generally accepted
method of social control. Obviously, then, the enforcement of the antitrust laws requires an understanding of the competitive market system, how it
operates, its limitations, and why it seems worth
preserving. Only from this foundation can the
wisdom of a particular antitrust policy be assessed
by measuring the costs and benefits of specific

24. See, e.g., Posner, *A Statistical Study of Antitrust Enforcement,* 13 J.Law & Econ. 365 (1970); Hay & Kelly, *An
Empirical Survey of Price Fixing Conspiracies,* 17 J.Law & Econ.
13 (1974); Asch & Seneca, *Characteristics of Collusive Firms,* 23
J.Ind.Econ. 223 (1975); Fraas & Greer, *Market Structure and
Price Collusion: An Empirical Analysis,* 26 J.Ind.Econ. 21
(1977).

actions—or, alternatively, by considering whether
business practices or enforcement efforts deviate
from the competitive norm. In other words, famil-
iarity with the ideas considered here is only a first
step in understanding the antitrust laws or in
evaluating their application.

However, just as it is important to understand
the economic theory of antitrust, it is important to
realize the limitations of the theory. One apparent shortcoming is its inability to explain—absent
reprehensible behavior—substantial and persistent
monopoly in a market capable of supporting many
firms. The assertion that superior efficiency is at
the core of persistent monopoly does not adequately explain why the cost of a monopoly's superior
factors of production or management is not bid up
over time, thus dissipating the monopoly profit.
Similarly, the contrary assertion that barriers to
entry permit persistent monopoly effectively side-
steps the issue. A barrier to entry is an obstacle
that affects some firms and entrants but not
others; if a given obstacle affects all firms and
entrants in the same fashion, it is simply a condition affecting the rate of entry. Absent reprehensible behavior or legal barriers (such as patents), it
is difficult to see how an entrant's costs would
persistently exceed those of existing firms.

Economic theory also has difficulty explaining
the behavior of oligopolistic and monopolistically
competitive industries. Many equally plausible

and often conflicting theories of oligopoly and monopolistic competition exist, with arguable empirical support. Considering the number of economists who have toiled in this area, the failure to
produce an acceptable theory draws attention to
the limits of economic science. In such circumstances, where the efficient market organization is
difficult to perceive, some assumptions and normative judgments may be usefully employed to bridge
the gap left by incomplete theory and uncertain
empirical evidence.

Although economic theory has not provided us
with a definitive theory describing firm behavior in
most real world market structures, it has offered
highly useful bits and pieces of information about
firm behavior. These elements of economic theory
and empirical evidence frequently provide strong
evidence as to the efficiency implications of alternative antitrust policies, though in some instances
they admittedly provide only weak guidance. This
is not a basis, however, for arguing that enforcement authorities should only search for acknowledged and unenforced agreements to fix prices. (It
is the secret but enforced cartels that are likely to
injure consumers.) Enforcement authorities
should also direct their attention to industries with
above normal profits and with characteristics that
predispose them to coordinated price behavior.

It is sometimes argued that the antitrust laws
are designed to serve social and political objec-

tives.[25] Where such factors confirm economic goals, these additional arguments further support antitrust efforts to foster economic efficiency. Where they conflict with notions of efficiency, however, the soundness of this approach and the trade-offs involved must be carefully assessed. For example, should the exercise of monopoly power be condemned even though that power was acquired solely by competitive efforts which are otherwise applauded? To condemn monopoly in this circumstance may discourage vigorous competitive effort by large firms nearing monopoly size.

As this suggests, economics is not the end of the analysis. To be sure, in many circumstances an understanding of the economic impact of a challenged business practice is likely to suggest the appropriate judicial response. But not all—or, perhaps more accurately, not many—antitrust cases can be explained by so rigorous an analysis. The history of antitrust is often as important as the most lucid economic understanding. This does not mean, however, that rational antitrust enforcement should or even can serve the ends of both economic efficiency and other political programs (such as controlling inflation, solving energy needs,

25. E.g., Brown Shoe v. United States, 370 U.S. 294, 344 (1962) (protection of small, locally owned businesses); Northern Pac. Ry. v. United States, 356 U.S. 1, 4 (1958) (preservation of democratic, political, and social institutions; United States v. Aluminum Co. of America, 148 F.2d 416, 427 (2d Cir.1945) (initiative, thrift, and energy in industrial progress). See Pitofsky, *The Political Content of Antitrust,* 127 U.Pa.L.Rev. 105 (1979); Schwartz, *On the Uses of Economics: A Review of the Antitrust Treatises,* 128 U.Pa.L.Rev. 244 (1980).

or protecting the environment). See generally, R. Bork, *The Antitrust Paradox* 50–89 (1978).

The use of economic analysis in antitrust has not followed a straight path. During the 1960's, when the antitrust laws were being applied expansively, real market divergences from the model of perfect competition were prosecuted almost automatically. The reason was that enforcement agencies and courts almost automatically concluded that if the market was imperfect it could not be competitive; thus there was room for it to be improved.

However, other theories of organization, including transaction cost analysis and contestable market theory, now explain how other market structures or models could be beneficial. In a contestable market, firms need not be small, numerous or independent. Nor need they produce homogeneous products. The crucial feature of a contestable market is its vulnerability to hit-and-run entry and exit. Similarly, transaction cost analysis shows that the main purpose of various economic institutions—firms, joint ventures, distribution contracts, etc.—is to economize on costs. As these alternative explanations or models have gained acceptance, the presumption that any deviation from the model of perfect competition is anticompetitive and harmful has faded. Using new economic models to expand our understanding, courts are increasingly aware that there is no "right" form of market structure or firm organization.

Applying some of these concepts, the Supreme Court has held that an industry may organize and cooperate where this is likely to make production more efficient. Broadcast Music, Inc. v. Columbia Broadcasting System, Inc., 441 U.S. 1 (1979); see NCAA v. University of Okla., 468 U.S. 85, (1984). Indeed, it has now recognized that the market and firm are on the same continuum. Copperweld Corp. v. Independence Tube Corp., 467 U.S. 752, (1984). The result is that the courts are requiring direct proof that challenged practices are harmful to consumer welfare (i.e., allocative efficiency). See, e.g., United States v. Waste Management, Inc., 743 F.2d 976 (2d Cir.1984) (merger with almost 50 percent market share did not violate antitrust law because entry barriers were very low).

CHAPTER IV

THE MONOPOLY PROBLEM

Economic analysis is able to explain why a monopolist, unless otherwise constrained, will exercise his power to limit output and raise prices by producing only that quantity at which the revenue from the last unit sold covers that unit's cost of production, i.e., where marginal revenue and marginal cost intersect. See Figure 5, p. 67 supra. It also identifies the major difference between competition and monopoly, at least conceptually, as rivalry or its absence. But economic theory does not predict why or how monopoly power develops in an open market where entry is not blockaded with government assistance such as patents or occupational licenses. In fact, the growth of monopoly power except for desirable reasons (such as economies of scale limiting the number of firms) remains without theoretical support.

The absence of a viable theory to explain the acquisition of monopoly power has left its indelible imprint on antitrust interpretations of Section 2 of the Sherman Act which declares monopolization unlawful. Monopoly power is feared both because of its consequences and its potential for abuse. Restriction of output leads to higher prices and a transfer of income from customers to producers; this restriction of output, moreover, indicates that

91

the monopolist has used his power to exclude rivals from the market. Thus, the use of illegal marketing techniques to obtain a substantial market advantage is likewise condemned.

But evidence of such practices is rare and what is more, very difficult to prove.[1] Illegal trade practices cannot be inferred merely from the existence of monopoly power because the ultimate reward of monopoly—namely, profits above normal—is in essence what every vigorous competitor seeks. Moreover, a restricted output and higher price are not necessarily the fruits of predatory conduct. They may also be the rational acts of a profit-maximizing firm possessing market (i.e., a degree of monopoly) power. And it is a general and wise rule of law that conduct defined as criminal (especially if malum prohibitum, such as the Sherman Act) be limited to those practices which are avoida-

---

1. Despite assumptions to the contrary, evidence of predatory pricing (below the monopolist's cost) to achieve or sustain monopoly power is very rare. See Koller, *The Myth of Predatory Pricing: An Empirical Study*, 4 Antitrust L. & Econ.Rev. 105 (Summer 1971); McGee, *Predatory Price Cutting: The Standard Oil (N.J.) Case*, 1 J. of Law & Econ. 137 (1958). Simple analysis suggests why. The monopolist will not accept the losses resulting from below-cost prices unless he is assured that (1) he can outlast his rivals, and (2) he can recoup these losses and more after his rivals have been driven out. However, that will occur only if the monopolist can establish a barrier to entry by those attracted into the market after the prices have been raised. Without the aid of law (e.g., patent protection), however, such barriers are unlikely to be substantial or stable—and thus the prospect of future profits generally does not appear likely enough to accept the certainty of immediate losses. See Easterbrook, *Predatory Strategies and Counterstrategies*, 48 U.Chi.L. Rev. 263 (1981).

ble. Moreover, according to the theory of competition, monopoly profits can be relied upon to attract entry, to break down monopoly power and to restore competition. Since legal constraints cannot be directly enforced against all market participants, it is highly desirable that open markets be allowed to self-correct market abuses. Unless the monopolist is permitted to charge a monopoly price, such corrections cannot occur.

A. MONOPOLY POWER

Without market power, actual or probable, there is little reason to be concerned with the actions of a single firm.[2] Consequently, one of the two elements in the offense of monopolizing under Section 2 is "the possession of monopoly power in the relevant market." United States v. Grinnell Corp., 384 U.S. 563, 570 (1966). A firm without power cannot impose its choices on the market—either on its competitors or its customers. Such a firm has no alternative but to accept or take the market price; it has no ability to charge more than its competitors, and no reason to sell for less.

Market power, in economic terms, is the ability to act in a less than perfectly competitive manner with respect to raising prices and restricting output.[3] This sweeping definition is much too broad

2. But see the doctrine of attempts to monopolize discussed pp. 149–52 infra.

3. Returning to the preceding chapter, a firm's market power is reflected in the slope and shape of the demand curve facing it. (The more steeply (negatively) sloped or inelastic the

to be useful in antitrust, however. Almost every departure from the perfectly competitive market indicates that certain firms possess market power. Therefore, the first issue for antitrust law in the monopoly context is to determine what degree of market power becomes so excessive or at least so significant that its exercise should be subjected to scrutiny and control. Obviously the antitrust laws cannot be applied so as to move against all uses of market power. If such were the case no business could operate without substantial fear of subsequent examination in a criminal or private treble damage, as well as a civil suit. On the other hand, a narrow definition of market power could readily eviscerate the Sherman Act. The issue is an important one and should not be passed over lightly despite its inherent complexity.

Little direction was given to the courts for deciding when a firm becomes a monopolist within the antitrust laws. The Sherman Act and its monopolization provision in Section 2 ("Every person who shall monopolize . . . any part of the trade or commerce . . . .") make no mention of market power and provide no guidance for determining either how market power is to be measured or what minimal aggregation constitutes monopoly power within the meaning of the Act. It is not surprising, therefore, that judicial precedents seldom focus on the measurement of monopoly power.

demand curve, the greater the firm's market power.) See Figure 1, p. 49 supra.

In most applications of Section 2, attention centers on the uses and abuses of monopoly power, the court assuming, at least for analytical purposes, that the defendant's share of the product's sales in the appropriate geographic area is such as to meet the statutory threshold.

Three different approaches could be used to measure market power: performance, rivalry, and structure. First, and probably the most accurate, is the measurement of a firm's actual performance through examination of the degree to which it deviates from the competitive norm. The procedure involves determining how much a firm's prices depart from its marginal cost, or the amount that a firm's net profits exceed the industry average (if that average reflects similar risks in a competitive industry). Performance tests are not particularly satisfactory, however, and such measures are seldom used in antitrust cases: marginal cost estimates are difficult to derive and economic profit figures may not reflect actual market power where a firm fails to maximize profits. Moreover, the reliability of cost figures varies according to accounting conventions. And profit figures may also underestimate market power where the firm's costs are out of line.

The second test, focusing on competitive behavior, studies the sensitivity of the firm's sales or output to changes in its rivals' sales and prices. While this standard is in fact used under the broad designation of cross-elasticity of demand to ascertain which products compete with each other (and will be explored, pp. 103–05 infra), it suffers the drawback of severe difficulty in acquiring accurate data for use in specific cases and of the requirement that the comparable prices be competitive if the interchange is to demonstrate rivalry.

The third, and perhaps most widely used method, is the structural approach. This involves, in essence, simply counting the number of firms within a market and comparing the sales volume controlled by each firm; these market shares are then used as surrogates for market power (see pp. 115–21 infra), and it is inferred that a firm with a major share of the market has monopoly power. Structural tests also consider entry barriers and product differentiation among other things.

In sum, the measurement of market power is an inexact and often misunderstood process. Usually in a monopoly case the product and geographic markets are first defined. Next the sales of the defendant are compared with those of other sellers who compete with the defendant. Then this market share is used as a rough index of the defendant's market power, along with ease and likelihood of entry, availability of secondhand goods or other acceptable (but nonequivalent) substitutes, and similar factors which indicate whether the defendant has the ability to raise prices and reduce output.

We previously considered the concept of "market" in the sense of identifying the general conditions under which sellers and buyers exchange goods or services. The alternative market theories of perfect competition, monopoly, monopolistic competition and oligopoly were then developed to predict market behavior and consequences. Now the term is used in another sense: namely to define the boundaries that identify groups of sellers of goods. This involves a delineation of the product and geographic lines within which specific groups of goods, buyers, and sellers interact to establish price and output. While antitrust (and economic) analysis presses toward identifying links in the chain of available alternatives—so that lines can be drawn and markets identified—such distinctions are necessarily somewhat artificial; they are the inevitable result of having to make decisions based on imperfect data. Despite the frequency with which product and geographic markets are drawn in antitrust litigation, the process of exclusion is a matter of degree, and hence the basis of frequent disagreement. The aim is to select that set of alternatives (e.g., those available to buyers) and transactions which are sufficiently interrelated so that further subdivision is artificial. The goal is easy to state; the defining of the measurement criteria as well as the applying of such criteria is much more difficult.

[handwritten margin note: it does Not represent A true mkt"]

1. PRODUCT MARKET

Definition of the product market in which the seller operates is an effort to locate all substitutes available to buyers of the seller's products. That is, the defining process asks whether the seller's product competes with other products, whether these products limit his ability to raise price, and whether they should be included in the product market. If the definition is drawn too narrowly and substitutes are excluded, the defendant's ability to affect price and output will be overstated; if nonsubstitutes are included, the defendant's market share (and inferentially its market power) will be understated because some of the included products will have only an insignificant impact on his price-setting powers.

The question of whether various products are sufficiently close substitutes to be included within a market—an empirical question presumably subject to ready verification—has proved surprisingly difficult. Obviously corn is not a close substitute for virgin aluminum, but what of scrap aluminum? For many uses scrap is favored by aluminum fabricators. Other illustrations further demonstrate the problem. For example, is the sole manufacturer of cellophane in direct competition with producers of saran wrap, wax paper, or aluminum foil, or does the cellophane firm have a monopoly of a distinctive product? Is tea a good substitute for carbonated beverages? The makers of soft drinks contended that tea is a close enough substitute to require its inclusion in the same product market along with Coke and Pepsi. See Coca-Cola, Co., 91 F.T.C. 517, 634–35 (1978). But if both are included within the same market, then what of coffee, milk, water, liquor, etc.?

Notice the importance of such line drawing in determining the market power of a seller of carbonated beverages such as Coke. The seller of Coke may have only one rival soft drink seller (Pepsi) and have, as a consequence, apparent power to set a supra-competitive price for Coke; but if he also faces dozens of rivals in the larger beverage market he may have little power to control the price of beverages—and perhaps even of Coke if users would transfer their loyalties as soon as the price is changed. Depending on the product market selection, the Coke seller's market share will also fluctuate widely.

How does one decide, then, whether to include other beverages in the product market? One method is through asking consumers. But is it not already obvious that consumers will only tell us that they drink some of each, that each product has its distinctive characteristics and uses, and that the degree of substitutability will vary depending on the consumer's tastes, the time of day, the price of each product, the consumer's wealth, etc.?

The *Cellophane* case is not only the leading case outlining the dimensions of product market analysis, but it also illustrates how the judicially developed criteria are applied—and possibly sometimes misapplied. In United States v. E.I. du Pont de Nemours & Co., 351 U.S. 377 (1956) (*Cellophane*), the primary question before the Court was in which product market should du Pont's market power be measured. While the ultimate issue was whether du Pont had monopolized the cellophane market in violation of Section 2, since no effort was made to show that du Pont had attempted to monopolize, the government had the burden of proving that du Pont possessed a high degree of market power. The government relied on the fact that du Pont produced almost 75 percent of the cellophane sold in the United States as demonstrating, at least prima facie, du Pont's monopoly power. It also argued that other flexible wrapping materials were not sufficiently competitive to limit du Pont's control of the cellophane market price. Du Pont countered that cellophane was not a distinct product since it competed directly and closely with other flexible packaging materials such as aluminum foil, wax paper, saran wrap, polyethylene, etc. And with these goods included in the product market, du Pont's market share declined to less than 20 percent—well below the monopoly threshold. Note, du Pont did not deny that cellophane was a distinctive product; rather it contended that since cellophane was under severe competitive pressure from substitute flexible wrapping materials, it lacked the power to exclude competitors and its power over price was correspondingly limited.

The government proposed that before other products could be included in the cellophane product market they must be substantially fungible and sell at close to the price of cellophane. The Supreme Court rejected this narrow measure of physical and price identity, however, since the producers of many patented or branded products would have been monopolies under such a definition and would have been subjected to Section 2 scrutiny.[4] Instead it called for "an appraisal of the 'cross-elasticity' of demand in the trade" to determine whether the "commodities [are] reasonably interchangeable by consumers for the same purposes." Reasonable interchangeability, the Court said, has three components: "[the product] market is composed of products that have reasonable interchangeability for the purposes for which they are produced—*price, use* and *qualities* considered."

Applying the quality test—that is, determining whether the physical attributes of cellophane and other flexible wrappings were sufficiently similar—the Court was persuaded that cellophane generally possessed no qualities desired by consumers which were not possessed by a number of other products. Eighty percent of du Pont's cellophane was sold for packaging in the food industry. Commercially suitable packaging material for fresh vegetables, for example, must be transparent so that consumers can examine the quality of the

4. In fact, such a narrow interpretation might support the anomalous result that Section 2 could not be enforced since courts would be unwilling to impose the restrictive conduct requirements of Section 2 (see pp. 123–49 infra) on many firms selling patented or branded products.

produce, must have low permeability to gases so that the enclosed produce will not be contaminated from surrounding odors, and must have low moisture permeability so that produce freshness will be retained. Many of the flexible wrapping products other than cellophane (specifically, pliofilm, plain glassine, and saran) have these qualities. Therefore, the inclusion of other flexible wrappings with cellophane appeared reasonable.[5]

(END use?)

Similarly, the functional interchangeability test—that is, whether buyers were able to shift back and forth from cellophane to other flexible wrappings—supported du Pont's contention that cellophane belonged in a broader product market. Despite cellophane's advantages of transparency and strength, it had to meet competition in every one of its uses. The government did not challenge du Pont's statistics which showed that cellophane controlled less than half of any use (except cigarettes which were not argued to be a separate market) and that buyers frequently shifted their product loyalties.

These two tests of reasonable interchangeability—quality and end-use—are essentially subjective considerations, and the Court's conclusions are not without support. Less persuasive, however, was the Court's examination of price movement and responsiveness to indicate whether cellophane be-

5. The line was not perfect, however. Aluminum foil, for example, is completely opaque and could not serve as an alternative source of supply for packaging fresh produce, yet it was included in the larger product market.

longed in the larger flexible wrapping market. (This test seeks to measure the cross-elasticity of demand between products by looking primarily at the responsiveness of the sale of one product to price changes in the other.) The justification for this criterion was clearly explained: "If a slight decrease in the price of cellophane causes a considerable number of customers of other flexible wrappings to switch to cellophane, it would be an indication that a high cross-elasticity of demand exists between them; that the products compete in the same market." Id. at 400. In other words, if a buyer of cellophane will shift his purchases to wax paper in response to an increase in the price of cellophane, this price responsiveness indicates that wax paper competes with cellophane and that both belong to the same product market. In holding that other flexible wrappings competed with cellophane, the Court relied on the finding that some price-sensitive buyers did shift their purchases in response to price changes, and that for other users, who were not so sensitive, packaging constituted but an insignificant portion of their product's price.

The Supreme Court's analysis of cellophane's price elasticity seems inadequate on several grounds.[6] Buyer price responsiveness to changes

---

6. By focusing on substitute products the Court was considering direct competition of other products. Equally important in evaluating monopoly power is whether those making other products could switch to producing cellophane and did so whenever du Pont sought to raise its cellophane price. Competition from production can be as effective as that of consumption (i.e.,

in cellophane prices establishes that other flexi-
wrap products are close substitutes only if competitive prices were in fact being charged for cellophane. (In that situation, du Pont's cellophane
position is not that of a monopoly.) But if du Pont
were charging a monopoly price for cellophane, the
high cross-elasticity for cellophane may have signi-
fied only that du Pont could not have raised its
price still further without a substantial sales loss.
That is, despite the Supreme Court's contrary assumption, a finding of high cross-elasticity of demand may mean only that monopoly power has
already been exercised by raising price to the profit-maximizing point. Thus the high cross-elasticity
possibly was not a measure of the relevant product
market for monopoly determination. It may, however, be a useful measure of market power (and of
a separate product market) where price is shown to
be close to cost. The Court's reliance on evidence
of high cross-elasticity of demand to determine the
product market would have been correct if two
cellophane producers in a competitive market had
sought to merge and the question was whether the
merged cellophane company would now have monopoly power.[7] (See Chapter 9 infra.)

substitute products). See R. Posner, *Economic Analysis of Law*
222 (2d ed. 1977). In *Cellophane*, patents and barriers insulated
du Pont from such competitive inroads by other producers.

7. For a technical explanation noting that "a monopolist
always sells in the elastic region of his demand schedule" and
that evidence of high cross-elasticity of demand does not demonstrate whether products are close substitutes, see R. Posner,
Economic Analysis of Law 222 (2d ed. 1977). Areeda and
Turner further contend that the Court misread the facts in

The concept of cross-elasticity of demand is helpful in establishing whether two products are close substitutes only when both are sold at competitive prices. H. Hovenkamp, *Economics and Federal Antitrust Law* 65 (1985). However, the evidence in *Cellophane* indicated that du Pont had a higher than normal rate of return on cellophane. And there were no reasonable substitutes for cellophane in the cigarette market.

Perhaps the result in *Cellophane* is explainable on the practical ground that the Court was influenced by du Pont's exceptional record of research and innovation. That is, this hardly seemed the time or place to condemn monopoly.

In any case, when it subsequently applied the *Cellophane* test of reasonable interchangeability, the Court relied only on the elements of quality and end-use. For example, finding that accredited central station protective services constituted a distinct product, the Court, in United States v. Grinnell Corp., 384 U.S. 563 (1966), separated other fire and burglar alarm systems such as watchmen and local alarm systems from the product market because they were less reliable and hence less desirable to customers. Price responsiveness was not examined. Whether it will no longer be considered was not settled, however.

Cellophane and that high cross-elasticity of demand between cellophane and other flexible wrappings had not been established. 2 P. Areeda & D. Turner, *Antitrust Law* ¶ 531, at 398 (1978).

A recent challenge to IBM's defense of its market position in the sale of peripheral equipment further illustrates the problems that can arise. There IBM had been the dominant manufacturer of central processing units as well as of other hardware (i.e., peripheral equipment). Several firms, including Telex and Memorex, entered the peripheral field by copying IBM's equipment and by selling it below IBM's price. When IBM countered by reducing its prices and by introducing design changes—with the result that Telex began losing customers and then money—Telex sued. Telex Corp. v. International Business Machines Corp., 367 F.Supp. 258 (N.D.Okla.1973), aff'd in part and rev'd in part, 510 F.2d 894 (10th Cir.1975). The immediate question was what was the product market.

The District Court ruled that the market was limited to peripherals that could be plugged into IBM machines (i.e., IBM plug-compatible peripheral equipment) because IBM's own products defined the market in which it competed. Limited in this fashion, IBM obviously had a monopoly. The difficulty with this analysis, however, is that it overstates IBM's market share and relative market power at any point in time. As the developer of its computers and peripheral equipment, IBM necessarily began with a monopoly position, and by including only IBM compatible peripherals in the denominator of the equation and all IBM controlled peripheral installations in the numerator, even substantial peripheral sales by IBM competitors would not markedly change IBM's share for many years.

Thus on appeal the Tenth Circuit Court of Appeals expanded the defined market (and denominator) to *all* peripherals (including those not compatible with IBM computers, because makers of this hardware could shift their production from one kind of peripheral to another). It also noted that the demand created by makers of central computers affected the demand for hardware. Professor Sullivan, however, has pointed out the analytical difficulty with this approach. See L. Sullivan, *Antitrust* 65–66 (1977): that is, those using IBM computers could not switch to other (nonIBM) hardware, and suppliers of IBM peripherals in fact could not easily abandon their customers. That is to say, the Tenth Circuit's approach appeared to understate IBM's market power.

A more accurate assessment of IBM's power in the peripheral market in which it operates would add to these tests (appropriately discounted) an examination of its share of new installations annually among IBM plug-compatible units as well as among all hardware units. This measure of net new orders or installations more nearly reflects the relative market power of IBM, Telex, and others. A simple illustration further demonstrates the point. Assume IBM had sold 1,000 units at the time the first imitator appeared. It then has 100 percent of the market (and is a monopolist). But the new entrant, let us say, is extraordinarily successful and captures 75 of the 100 new IBM plug-compatible peripheral installations sold the next year. If the market is defined as all installations—new or old—the new competitor has only 75 of 1,100 total units or 6.8 percent. On the other hand, if the market is defined as new installations, the new firm has 75 of 100 units and its market share is 75 percent. Again neither figure is a complete indicator of IBM's position, although the second approach focusing on new installations seems a closer approximation of IBM's actual market power. Other factors that should be considered in determining IBM's market power (which here decrease the significance of the imitators' market position) include: the effect of the second hand market (as considered in *Alcoa,* p. 130 infra), the existence of other (nonIBM) peripheral equipment makers, IBM's history as a stable supplier and record as an innovator, and so forth.

2. GEOGRAPHIC MARKET

After wrestling with the difficulties of defining product markets, one might reasonably expect that the determination of geographic markets would be relatively easy. And often they are. Where products are sold nationwide and transportation costs are not significant, courts frequently define the geographic market as the entire nation. See, e.g., United States v. Aluminum Co. of America, 148 F.2d 416, 423 (2d Cir.1945). Or where a manufacturer and his rivals sell their product only in a limited geographic area and their customers have no ready access to an outside source of supply, the general rule has been to define the geographic market as that particular area and to include only the sales made within that market. See, e.g., Union Leader Corp. v. Newspapers of New England, Inc., 284 F.2d 582 (1st Cir.1960).

Where the seller's geographic market is less certain, however, attention is paid not only to actual sales patterns but also to price relationships and movements in different areas. A close correlation among prices and price movements, especially when supported by sales interchanges, will be a strong indication that a geographic market has been identified. Conversely, significant price differences and uncorrelated price changes may suggest that more than one geographic market exists, even where some sales interchanges occur. Transportation barriers are another principal basis for separating geographic markets. See United States v. Addyston Pipe & Steel Co., 85 Fed. 271 (6th Cir. 1898), modified & aff'd, 175 U.S. 211 (1899).

Thus the relevant geographic market in antitrust analysis is that "section of the country" where a firm can increase its price without attracting new sellers or without losing many customers to alternative suppliers outside that area. See Landes & Posner, *Market Power in Antitrust Cases,* 94 Harv.L.Rev. 937 (1981). But if either response occurs (when prices are raised above marginal cost), then a larger market should be drawn to include the sellers.

Application of these criteria in drawing geographic market boundaries does not necessarily assure accuracy. As was noted in the discussion of product markets, looking to current sales and buying practices can be either over- or under-inclusive. If the market is not monopolized, a reliance on actual sales ignores those suppliers operating on the fringe who "keep" the market price at competitive levels by their presence—that is, they would ship into the geographic area if the price rose. On the other hand, if the market is monopolized (and price exceeds marginal cost), the monopoly price may attract sellers from distant areas who otherwise would not have entered because of higher transportation and selling costs. That is, the sales figures within the geographic market would include sales of firms located there only because the market is monopolized. The significance of these related observations and the resulting anomaly is that geographic market definitions in monopoly cases tend to understate market shares where market price reaches monopoly levels while overstating a defendant's market power (shares) where it faces competitive rivals. Thus, geographic market-drawing tests that rely on actual sales patterns may tend to give erroneous results. However, this difficulty is probably better resolved by the evaluation of market shares (i.e., the weight given or

reliance placed on them) rather than in the determination of geographic market boundaries.

Another problem in locating geographic markets
is that markets can be identified from either the
supply or demand viewpoint. Consider, for example, a typical purchase of a new car in Peoria. To
the individual buyer the alternative sources of
supply are the various automobile salesrooms in
Peoria and the relevant sellers are the car dealers
located there. To the various auto manufacturers
who sell cars in Peoria, however, the transaction
(and possible price) takes on quite a different aspect. Their rivalry with other manufacturers competing for the consumer's new car dollar is nationwide—or if the product market includes small or
middle-sized cars, it may extend worldwide. Note
the significance of our answer. If the relevant
geographic market is Peoria, market shares for the
car manufacturer may differ markedly from their
national or international figures. And the issue
cannot be decided in the abstract. The answer, if
there be one, depends on the question being asked.
Is the issue whether an auto maker has monopolized the new car market for buyers or for sellers?
In either case, however, the question is where is
the locus of competition: for buyers it may well be
limited to Peoria (except perhaps for commercial or
fleet accounts); for sellers it is likely to be the
entire nation since interfirm rivalry is not confined
to any geographic area.

The Supreme Court was forced to consider these questions in United States v. Grinnell Corp., supra. The district court had ruled that a national market existed in accredited central station protective services even though seller rivalry for sale of fire and burglar alarm systems was admittedly confined to individual metropolitan areas and customers in one city could not realistically transfer their patronage to sellers located in other cities. Accepting this determination, the Supreme Court relied on the defendant's national planning and price schedule, relations with other large businesses on a nationwide basis, and similar factors to find a national market. However this conclusion cannot withstand close analysis because the recited facts neither define the locus of competition nor indicate the scope of interfirm rivalry. Whether an individual firm operates on a national or local basis does not define a geographic market. Perhaps this point is more readily understandable if one examines competition in a more familiar setting operating under similar circumstances. Retail grocery competition exists between local stores and chains as well as among large interstate chains. But competition between sellers and alternate sources of supply for buyers are invariably local—i.e., at the most, the geographic market extends over a metropolitan area. The same would seem to hold true in *Grinnell.*

The clear establishment of this point by two of the dissenters and the fact that Grinnell faced no

competition in at least 92 of the 115 cities in which
it operated (i.e., if geographic markets were defined
as the 115 metropolitan areas, Grinnell had 92
separate monopolies), compels one to consider why
the Court struggled so laboriously to find a national market. It seems, perhaps, that the exclusionary practices (e.g., restrictive agreements and acquisitions) which were the basis for the finding of
illegal monopolizing behavior could not be attached
to each (or many) of the separate markets. The
dissent reinforced this point in noting that the
remedy approved by the Court of local divestiture
to create localized competition in essence rebutted
the national geographic market conclusion.

In sum, the available precedents do not provide a
clear or coherent basis for drawing geographic
markets. Despite the critical nature of market
definition, monopoly case guidance is often of little
value; yet courts frequently rely on similar rulings
in merger decisions.

3. DEPARTMENT OF JUSTICE GUIDELINES

The Department of Justice's merger guidelines
issued in 1982 and revised in 1984 outline sophisticated new criteria that it expects to apply in determining whether mergers will be challenged. 49
Fed.Reg. 26,823 (1984). In particular, the Guidelines provide an intriguing approach to market
definition also relevant for monopolization cases.
Thus, they are worth close consideration.

A relevant product market is defined as "a group of products such that a . . . firm that was the only present and future seller ('monopolist') could profitably impose a 'small but significant and nontransitory' increase in price" (defined usually as a 5 percent increase for one year). The process of definition starts with the products made by the defendant. Next it adds those products that the firm's customer's view as good substitutes at "prevailing prices." [8] Finally, the guidelines ask whether a small but significant and nontransitory price increase will cause a substantial shift of buyers to substitute products; when that shift no longer occurs, a relevant product market has been identified.

The Department asks on the supply side whether "a firm has existing productive and distributive facilities that could easily and economically be used to produce and sell the relevant product within one year in response to a 'small but significant and nontransitory increase in the price.' " If so, they would be added to the product market. A similar approach is used in defining the relevant geographic market.

Finally, the guidelines state that close consideration will be given to a wide variety of factors, including shipping patterns or considerations, rela-

8. This is, of course, appropriate in merger cases where the relatively low market shares of the firms support the inference that current prices are competitive. It should not apply in monopoly cases unless the evidence supports the view that a monopoly price is not being charged. See pp. 369–74 supra.

tive price movements of likely substitute products, transportation and local distribution costs, and excess capacity of outside suppliers.

If followed, the effect of this economic approach to market definition is probably that substantially larger markets (and smaller market shares) will be drawn as compared to those previously applied by courts. By considering likely market responses to price changes and by including excess capacity in a defined market, this technique of market definition seems closely tailored to marketplace realities. On the other hand, these very additions are likely to increase the uncertainty of market definition. It is too early to tell whether the courts will accept the Justice Department's lead.

4. MARKET SHARE

Once the product and geographic markets are determined, the actual computation of market shares is often a simple or at least straight-forward task. It is accomplished by setting the defendant's production or sales as the numerator and then dividing that by the larger denominator constituting total production or sales in the defined area. See, e.g., American Tobacco Co. v. United States, 328 U.S. 781, 794–96 (1946).

However, as illustrated by Judge Learned Hand's celebrated decision in United States v. Aluminum Co. of America, 148 F.2d 416 (2d Cir.1945) (*Alcoa*), market share determination—even after the product and geographic market are defined—

can prove difficult and controversial. There it was generally conceded by the parties involved that ingot aluminum consumed in the United States was the appropriate market. Obviously this included all virgin ingot produced and sold on the open market. If this were all, Alcoa was conceded to be a monopolist, being the sole American producer. But what of secondary aluminum—that is, clippings, trimmings and second-hand ingot available from aluminum fabrications previously sold and processed as scrap—which was an almost perfect substitute for virgin ingot? Or what of virgin ingot not sold by Alcoa but instead used by Alcoa in its own fabrication facilities? Or imported virgin, both fabricated and secondary? The extent to which this additional aluminum was included in the market (denominator) could have dramatic effects on Alcoa's market share.[9] It, therefore, is instructive to note why Judge Hand included some of these sources of the metal and excluded others, especially since his opinion is still a leading antitrust case.

The first issue was whether to include in the market computation the ingot produced by Alcoa but not sold on the open market because it was consumed in Alcoa's own fabrication facilities. The trial court concluded that this captive production should not be included, because it was not available to buyers and hence, the court said, had

9. In this case that range was between 33 and 90 percent of the aluminum production market.

no effect on price or output. Judge Hand rejected this premise because "[a]ll ingot—with trifling exceptions—is used to fabricate intermediate, or end, products; and therefore all intermediate, or end, products which 'Alcoa' fabricates and sells, pro tanto reduce the demand for ingot itself."

While this analysis seems unexceptional—Alcoa's control of ingot aluminum supply is wholly unaffected by whether it is used for self fabrication or sold to other fabricators—it does not necessarily follow that captive production should always be included when totalling market shares. For example, in measuring a coal company's market power, it probably would not be appropriate to include all the production of those coal mines owned by automobile or steel companies whose entire output is consumed by them. While production from these mines may effectively reduce total demand for coal, this output is often not available to the market. Unless the auto and steel makers also have a sales force and the other capabilities necessary to sell coal, the production of these mines will not have the same market effect as that of coal produced by rival coal sellers—and hence to include all their production would understate the defendant coal company's power.

By a parity of reasoning one might also assume that secondary (scrap) aluminum, salvaged from the virgin which Alcoa and others produced in the first place, should also be included in the market. Secondary competed directly with virgin; custom-

ers normally accepted it as a suitable substitute
and paid the same price for it as they would for
virgin ingot. Again, Judge Hand reversed the trial
court, but this time because he believed it had
erred in including secondary in the market. Reasoning that " 'Alcoa' always knew that the future
supply of ingot would be made up in part of what it
produced at that time, . . . [he concluded that]
that consideration must have had its share in
determining how much to produce." While Alcoa
could only estimate the future impact of current
production, experience would aid it in making this
estimate and uncertainty would not forestall the
impact. "The competition of 'secondary' must
therefore be disregarded, as soon as we consider
the position of 'Alcoa' over a period of years; it was
as much within 'Alcoa's' control as was the production of the 'virgin' from which it had been derived." The difficulty with Hand's reasoning is
that he totally excluded secondary from the market, rather than just discounting it. Nor is this a
simple debating point. If secondary is included,
Alcoa's market share declines from 90 to 64 percent (because, being out of Alcoa's control, the
secondary would be included only in the denominator of the question). It was unclear then whether
the latter figure amounted to monopoly power.

In light of our earlier analysis of market power
definition, the total exclusion of secondary seems
questionable. Secondary and virgin aluminum
were admittedly almost identical substitutes, and

this is the essential reasoning behind product market groupings.[10] Nor is Hand's reference to Alcoa's original production of what later became secondary persuasive. Had another firm produced it instead, the competitive force of the secondary in the aluminum market would have been precisely the same. While this secondary supply was limited and therefore could not exert the same price check on Alcoa as could a competing producer, it nonetheless was a substantial restraining force on Alcoa's power to set aluminum prices.

More compelling is the court's inclusion of imported virgin aluminum in the market; it reduced Alcoa's market share by 10 percent. Under this approach it could also be argued that aluminum products fabricated abroad and imported into the United States—or, perhaps, even all foreign production regardless of where it was ultimately shipped—should also be included. However, substantial transportation and tariff barriers as well as constant low import volume, support the court's ruling on this point.[11]

10. The treatment of secondary aluminum in *Alcoa* is also contradicted by the concern expressed in *United Shoe* (discussed pp. 138–41 infra) about a monopolist's lease-only policy. That is, by refusing to sell shoe machinery equipment, the monopolizing manufacturer eliminates the competitive pressures otherwise presented by the second-hand market.

11. Moreover, it was Alcoa's obligation to prove that foreign production not imported into the United States was available and operated as a check on Alcoa's market power. It may have decided that the amount was insignificant. Or other barriers such as price might have prevented the importing of the foreign virgin aluminum used in foreign fabrications, thus limiting its impact—as in the case of captive coal, see p. 117 supra.

When so able a judge as Learned Hand makes several disputed calls in resolving the market share equation, one is alerted to the inherent limitations of any market share determination. Even the most carefully defined market—as in *Alcoa* — inevitably includes some firms or production whose impact on the defendant is insignificant, while excluding others having greater market force. Market shares are, in other words, only an indication of market power; they should mark the beginning point for further careful analysis, not the end of it; they are not synonymous with market power. And the courts have recognized this point, at least implicitly.[12] For example Judge Hand noted that although foreign imports accounted for 10 percent of United States consumption, they were at most a ceiling on Alcoa's market power since tariffs and transportation costs borne only by foreign competitors allowed Alcoa a margin for maneuver in its pricing policy.

Nor does the 90 percent figure in *Alcoa* appear to be the floor of monopoly power. Seventy five to 95 percent of the shoe machinery market was sufficient in United States v. United Shoe Machinery Corp., 110 F.Supp. 295, 307 (D.Mass.1953), aff'd

12. Compare United States v. Grinnell Corp., supra at 571 ("The existence of such [monopoly] power ordinarily may be inferred from the predominant share of the market."), with United States v. International Business Machines Corp., 60 F.R.D. 654, 658 (S.D.N.Y.1973) ("Market share is no holy talisman that alone determines whether a defendant has monopolized an industry."). See also United States v. General Dynamics Corp., 415 U.S. 486 (1974), discussed pp. 365–66 infra.

per curiam 347 U.S. 521 (1954), and only a much
lower percentage need be shown where the charge
is attempting to monopolize (see pp. 149–52 infra).
See also United States v. Grinnell Corp., supra at
571 (87 percent or a "predominant share of the
market"); American Tobacco Co. v. United States,
supra at 797 ("over two-thirds of the entire domestic field of cigarettes" and over "80 percent of the
field of comparable cigarettes").   But a market
share below 70 percent is unlikely to support a
finding of monopoly power.   Compare Moore v.
James H. Matthews & Co., 473 F.2d 328 (9th Cir.
1973) (65–70 percent) with Dimmitt Agri Indus.,
Inc. v. CPC Int'l Inc., 679 F.2d 516 (5th Cir.1982),
cert. denied, 460 U.S. 1082 (1983) (25 percent and
17 percent).   The percentage necessary to support
a showing of monopoly power is also affected by
clarity of the market boundaries and the persistence (or growth) of the market share over time. A
similar "sliding scale" approach has been applied
to determine how much abusive conduct is required to justify a finding of illegal monopolization.

B. MONOPOLIZATION: THE USES OF MONOPOLY POWER

Section 2 of the Sherman Act does not on its face
condemn the mere possession of monopoly power.
Size alone is not an antitrust offense, primarily
because it may be unavoidable as the result of
natural or legal monopoly or the consequence of
vigorous competitive activity, which the Sherman

Act seeks to encourage. Relying on the Sherman Act's prohibition of conduct which "monopolizes," the courts have focused instead on the monopolist's purpose and intent—that is, on its positive drive to seize or exert monopoly power.

Distinguishing monopolizing intent from the permissible business activity of a firm with massive market power is not simple, especially since an unlawful purpose is generally inferred from the conduct of the monopolist. Sound policy encourages all firms, regardless of size, to engage in vigorous rivalry in the understanding that through competition consumers are served with the desired quality of goods at the lowest price. On the other hand, allowing firms with market power to use any trade weapons available to firms without market power may result in the exclusion of competitors, the consolidation and persistence of monopoly power, and ultimately higher prices and reduced output. Thus it is strenuously debated whether a monopolist should be allowed to stimulate and meet demand, to bargain for its outlets in both monopolized and competitive markets as one unit, or to offer its goods on a lease-only basis—if the result is to make competitive entry more difficult. The debate occurs at two levels: (1) whether the conduct is in fact exclusionary; and (2) if it is, whether that justifies an inference of illegal purpose and intent. The area of current controversy is pricing and product innovation by firms with monopoly power. Should a monopolist be allowed to reduce its prices or redesign its products to meet (or beat) competition?

1. CLASSIC TEST

The earliest monopoly cases condemned railroad mergers even though the resulting market power was not shown to have been misused and in fact may have served a desirable economic purpose. In Northern Securities Co. v. United States, 193 U.S. 197 (1904), the Court relied upon the elimination of competition between previously competitive railroads (which were now consolidated under a holding company) as evidencing an illegal purpose and intent. Subsequent railroad cases applied this rule so rigidly that even consolidations between lines which did not overlap but which used common terminal points were condemned without considering the effect of the merger on competition. See United States v. Southern Pacific Co., 259 U.S. 214 (1922). These decisions, however, have traditionally been distinguished as limited to railroads which had special common law obligations because (at least then) they controlled a natural monopoly and shippers generally had no realistic alternatives.[13]

13. Relegated to antitrust antiquity, these cases had a brief revival when the Supreme Court excavated them to condemn by a narrow margin bank mergers under Section 1 of the Sherman Act. See United States v. First National Bank & Trust Co., 376 U.S. 665 (1964) (*Lexington Bank*). But the Bank Merger Act of 1966, 12 U.S.C.A. § 1828, exempted bank mergers from further attack under Section 1 of the Sherman Act (though not from Section 2).

Aside from the railroad merger cases, the early landmark cases were those attacking the marauding practices of John D. Rockefeller's oil giant and of the tobacco trust. See Standard Oil Co. of N.J. v. United States, 221 U.S. 1 (1911); United States v. American Tobacco Co., 221 U.S. 106 (1911).[14] There was no question that both defendants had monopoly power; Standard Oil controlled almost 90 percent of the nation's refining capacity, and the tobacco trust controlled 95 percent of cigarette sales. Nor was there much doubt, according to the Court, that each had engaged in patently unreasonable business practices which could not be justified as normal competitive activities. Standard Oil had coerced railroads into granting it preferential rates, had engaged in local price discrimination and business spying, and had committed other unsavory acts, all to force local competitors out of business. The tobacco trust's tactics, including its purchase of over 30 competing firms whose plants were immediately closed, were, in the words of the Court, "ruthlessly carried out"—again, all in support of the trust's monopoly position.

These cases, then, presented the Supreme Court with classic examples of aggressive unsavory business practices by monopolists. There was no sig-

14. Both cases also involved suits under Section 1 of the Sherman Act (which was the sole basis for attacking the railroad mergers) for conspiring to restrain trade and were the basis for the Supreme Court's first enunciation of the famous "rule of reason" which is explored in Chapter 5 infra.

nificant dispute about the defendants' market power, how they attained that power, or the uses to which it was put. What was at issue, however, was the legal status of these findings. On the one hand, the government argued that the Sherman Act should be interpreted literally (e.g., that Section 1 condemned *every* combination which restrains trade), and once it was established that the defendants had used their power to impose a restraint on trade, conviction under the Sherman Act was justified. In response, the defendants urged that the nature of the restraint—its purpose and impact—especially as revealed by the parties' intent, was determinative. Any other test, they argued, would put every successful business in jeopardy.

Accepting the defendants' view, in its famous "rule of reason," that the Sherman Act did not condemn reasonable business practices and was to be read as a charge to the courts to develop a common law of antitrust, the Court went on to spell out the primary reach of Section 2's prohibition of monopolization. The Court held that the latter was an adjunct to Section 1.[15] The legal standard under Section 2, as established in *Standard Oil* and *American Tobacco,* condemned monopoly power when it was abused as evidenced by

15. Section 1, by its terms, condemned only unreasonable trade restraints resulting from combination of two or more parties. It did not reach similar trade practices imposed by a single firm seeking monopoly power. That was the function, said the Court, of Section 2.

trade practices which would violate Section 1 if engaged in by two parties in combination.

The Court's analysis was not so directly stated, however. Instead, it considered the defendants' business methods to attain power "solely as an aid for discovering [their] intent and purpose." The Court contrasted the defendants' abusive market practices with what it called "normal methods of industrial development" which the Sherman Act, of course, did not condemn. The difference between lawful and unlawful activity by a business with monopoly power was the presence of a positive drive for monopolization. Whether this positive drive existed was determined by examining the intent and purpose of the defendants' acts, not their market shares or the market's structure. For example, in upholding most of the district court's drastic decree, the Court in *Standard Oil* relied on defendant's growth which occurred primarily from acquisitions of competitors, its pressure on railroads for illegal rebates, its reliance on espionage, and its practice of predatory pricing, as illustrating an illegal intent.

This initial approach to Section 2 of the Sherman Act is significant for many reasons. First, it establishes the minimum threshold for a violation of Section 2—a showing of monopoly power and of conduct involving a restraint of trade (such as would violate Section 1) which demonstrates illegal purpose and intent. The essence of the offense was not the defendants' particular acts—these merely evidence their intent—but rather their purpose or intent. Second, the Court did not question or condemn monopoly power alone. In considering defendants' positive drive for monopoly power, the Court seemingly ruled that market power acquired by "usual methods" was not unlawful. Third, the legal definition of illegal monopoly was necessarily distinct from the economic concept. The economic concept furnishes a tool for analysis and focuses on market power, i.e., the firm's ability to restrict output and raise price. From a legal standpoint, however, the size of a firm or its share of total output of a product appears to be significant in judging monopoly only when accompanied by exploitive or predatory practices affecting the ability of others to compete. The Court concluded that if the market place were open, competition would prevent the rise of monopoly power. Except where protected by law, monopolies would arise only because of deliberate or planned action. Antitrust therefore did not prohibit monopoly power (the economic concept); it punished only those acts that created or continued monopoly power. Thus, power plus intent was condemned. See P. Asch, *Economic Theory and the Antitrust Dilemma* 240 (1970).

The limits (or, as critics charged, the limitations) of this "classic" test were exposed in a line of subsequent cases. First in United States v. United Shoe Machinery Co., 247 U.S. 32 (1918), and then in United States v. United States Steel Corp., 251

U.S. 417 (1920), the Court upheld acquisitions of complementary and competing companies even though done with a seemingly obvious intent to obtain monopoly power. United Shoe Machinery's 50 acquisitions were considered separately (rather than cumulatively), and no single merger established the requisite intent. Likewise its lease-only policy was upheld as within its patent grant, as assuring users of adequate services and of merely continuing the practice of the constituent firms before the merger.

The steel consolidation controlled a much smaller market share—U.S. Steel controlled around 80–90 percent of domestic production at the time of its creation, but this amount had dropped to 41 percent at the time of trial. However, the formation of U.S. Steel involved a larger number of entities (about 180) of massive size in a basic industry. Nonetheless, the Court again found no violation of Section 2. The steel company's market share and supporting testimony convinced the district court and the Supreme Court that U.S. Steel no longer had monopoly power. This was further supported, the Court noted, by government evidence of pricing agreements between the company and its rivals; in a tour de force the Court asserted that such collusion would have been unnecessary if U.S. Steel possessed effective power. Having failed to establish U.S. Steel's monopoly power, the government's case collapsed because it had failed also to argue that the company had violated Section 2 in its "attempt to monopolize"; that would have required only evidence of a specific intent to achieve market power and a dangerous probability of success. See pp. 149–51 infra. In its analysis the Court seemed to concede the likelihood of illegal intent in U.S. Steel's formation and growth. But in now famous dictum it concluded: "[T]he law does not make mere size an offense, or the existence of unexerted power an offense. It, we repeat, requires overt acts . . . ." Id. at 451.

This dictum proved troublesome later, as we will find in discussing *Alcoa* shortly, but at the time it appeared to expand the rule of reason in Section 2. It is power plus overt acts that constitutes a violation, and here the overt acts were benign. U.S. Steel had "resorted to none of the brutalities or tyrannies" relied upon by Standard Oil or the tobacco trust. Id. at 440–41. To be sure, it had sought to make price-fixing arrangements with its competitors, but they were ineffective. In a strange logical twist, the Court apparently was saying that competition may have been damaged, but competitors were not harmed. That is, collusion might violate Section 1, but where it is ineffective it would not be a basis for a finding of illegal monopolization—at least where other monopolizing actions were not offensive. By implicitly approving U.S. Steel's price leadership and protection of smaller competitors, the Court also seemed to be providing a protective cover (at least under Section 2) for the quiet life of the monopolist.

However the particular facts of the steel consolidation are viewed, the damage to Section 2 had been done. If U.S. Steel was immune from attack under Section 2, few firms or industries with competent counsel were in danger. And after the rule of *United States Steel* was reaffirmed by the Court in United States v. International Harvester Co., 274 U.S. 693 (1927), it is not surprising that the Justice Department declined for a decade to attack consolidations of monopoly power under Section 2.

2. *ALCOA*

Between the decisions in *United States Steel* in 1920 and Learned Hand's landmark opinion in United States v. Aluminum Co. of America, 148 F.2d 416 (2d Cir.1945) (*Aloca*),[16] Section 2 of the Sherman Act was, in effect, a dead letter. But in *Alcoa* the court shifted the emphasis if not the foundation and reach of the anti-monopoly law. Rather than focusing on the defendant's abusive market practices (since none were shown), the court emphasized market structure and Alcoa's apparent market power.

Alcoa was formed in 1888 and obtained its dominance in the production of virgin aluminum through a legal (patent) monopoly which expired in

16. The Second Circuit acted as the court of last resort because the Supreme Court could not muster a quorum of six qualified justices to hear the case; in that circumstance the matter was referred for decision (under a specially drawn statute) to the court of appeals in the circuit from which it came. See 28 U.S.C.A. § 2109.

1909. It maintained that position until 1912 through a series of cartel arrangements limiting aluminum imports into the country, but it abandoned these under a consent decree that year. At the time suit was brought 25 years later, in 1937, Alcoa was still the sole domestic producer of virgin ingot, and the government charged that this position violated Section 2.

As explored earlier (see pp. 115–20 supra), the court determined that Alcoa's only competition was from imported virgin aluminum, and that its market share during the last five years before trial always exceeded 90 percent. Alcoa argued that despite this market share it was not a monopolist because, as the district court found, its lifetime profits had been only around 10 percent—hardly a monopolist's rewards. Hand refused to accept this figure as evidence that Alcoa had not exerted monopoly control: a firm's overall profit figures do not necessarily reflect profits earned on one line (virgin ingot); nor is it an excuse that a monopoly has not used its power to extract monopoly profits.

Aside from showing Alcoa's market power, the government argued that Alcoa violated Section 2 by virtue of its complete control over aluminum production. The origin of this power as well as the reasonableness of its exercise were accordingly immaterial; Section 2 condemns "every person who shall monopolize." [17] Alcoa responded that it had

17. The government also complained of Alcoa's purchase of patents and combination with foreign producers to restrain

not interfered with any attempts by others to enter the virgin aluminum market nor had it sought to eliminate smaller fabricators of aluminum products. Whatever monopoly power it had, Alcoa argued, was simply the result of natural growth, reasonably exercised. Thus if Alcoa were to be dissolved and transformed into several companies as sought by the government, the efficiency and future progress of the industry would be jeopardized at no benefit to consumers.

In an elegant yet ambiguous opinion, Judge Learned Hand rejected Alcoa's plea that it was a well behaved, natural monopoly—that power was "thrust upon it." Accepting the premise of this argument, that a busines which acquires a monopoly position "merely by virtue of his superior skill, foresight and industry" is not guilty of monopolization, Hand reasoned that Alcoa had nevertheless trespassed Section 2. Three interrelated arguments formed the core of Hand's analysis. First, since price-fixing among rivals is illegal per se (see pp. 175–85 infra), it would be illogical to approve comparable power in a single firm. Thus once a monopolist sets a price for its product and then sells it, the monopolist can be said to have acted unreasonably. Second, Alcoa had actively discouraged new entry into aluminum production by expanding its capacity more rapidly than warranted

competition in the United States, and of its cost squeeze of independent fabricators. The first charge failed of proof and the price squeeze, while unlawful, was not relied upon in finding Alcoa guilty.

by the demand for its output. Combined with substantial capital requirements, this program of accelerated development effectively foreclosed any entry opportunities and reserved the field to Alcoa. Third, the possibility that condemning Alcoa might impair industry efficiency and progress was no defense; Congress had sought to promote social and political as well as economic objectives in passage of the Sherman Act.

These arguments are, as Judge Robert Bork has shown, "thoroughly perverse." Price-setting by a monopolist is unavoidable, and the monopolist's position may merely be a reflection of internal efficiencies unavailable to a cartel fixing prices for several firms. Hand's proposed rule, therefore, is at bottom a simplistic attack on corporate size. Disapproving expansion of capacity to stimulate and meet customer demand also discourages efficiency-enhancing competitive activity by firms occupying most or all of the market. It may satisfy populist urges but does little for either the economy or consumers. Nor is there any reason to suppose that the social and political values relied on by Hand to favor smaller firms are a satisfactory basis for rational policy. They provide no policy guidance, for it is unclear whether or when these values should override an efficiency-based standard. It also is not established why courts should be assigned this value-choosing authority.

The true meaning of *Alcoa* continues to be disputed. On the one hand, the court stated that

Alcoa's existence—that is, its sheer size—offended Section 2 because it allowed Alcoa, as a consequence, to acquire monopoly profits and power of such magnitude that entry would be discouraged. With this view in mind the decision can be read as not applying the abuse theory (where an illegal intent to monopolize is inferred from predatory conduct) but instead adopting a structural test, where corporate size is the primary determinant. Read in this fashion, *Alcoa's* radical departure from *United States Steel* is obvious. A test of presumptive illegality, the government need only prove the defendant's monopoly position to establish a prima facie case, and then the burden would shift to the defendant to show that it had not abused its position or that the latter was unavoidable.

The drawback to this conclusion is that it places the successful firm in the almost untenable position of proving proper business justifications for every move, even though each could generally be given a different interpretation. It would penalize and therefore discourage vigorous competition by firms as they acquire substantial market positions. It seems anomalous for the antitrust laws to encourage oligopoly behavior. Moreover, Hand appears to have rejected this legal standard or at least did not rely upon it, because, as noted above, he also found that Alcoa had abused its monopoly by anticipating demand and maintaining excess productive capacity.

Even so, the *Alcoa* decision clearly established a new precedent. It moved the abuse theory to a different level, no longer requiring that the plaintiff prove predatory conduct violative of Section 1. As a consequence the term abuse now includes acts which, taken alone, would generally be considered "honestly industrial," but when considered in their totality showed "no motive except to exclude others and perpetuate its hold upon the ingot market." The proof of intent or purposive drive was less demanding; the prerequisite now is only a showing of deliberateness by the monopolist to maintain its monopoly position.[18] While the requisite degree of deliberateness is established if monopoly power is maintained by illegal means violating Section 1, more importantly it also exists where the defendant's acts are legal in themselves but nevertheless have an exclusionary effect on competitors or potential entrants. In other words, it is no longer necessary to show brutal or ruthless behavior to bring the monopolist within the Sherman Act's net. Yet power alone, while suspect, is not tantamount to a violation. Rather it is necessary to show in addition that the monopolist's actions were instrumental in maintaining its market position.

18. The court spoke generally of Alcoa's "intent," but this perfunctory test is without analytical content since it is satisfied by showing that the defendant has monopoly power. That is, the defendant is presumed to have intended the obvious consequences of his actions. It may, however, be relied on to absolve a temporary monopolist whose position is due solely to a head start from having first developed a new product.

Even this less expansive reading of *Alcoa* is not immune from criticism. Whether Alcoa's maintenance of excess capacity effectively deterred entry seems doubtful. Rather, Alcoa's head start and the size of the investment needed to begin production were probably more important deterrents. Nor does the court's broad suggestion that deliberateness may be established by any practice deterring competition seem sound. A monopolist then faces a Hobson's choice: if it responds to the threat of entry by pricing at competitive (marginal cost) levels, it violates Section 2; yet if it disregards potential entrants by charging a monopoly price, Hand's opinion suggests that it will be deemed to have acted unreasonably and, therefore, illegally. In this regard the opinion seems to invite a middle ground practice not dissimilar to oligopoly behavior (condemned Chapter 7 infra). It also seems likely that the court misapplied the "thrust upon" defense (which provides that a defendant who maintains his position "merely by virtue of his superior skill, foresight and industry" is not guilty of monopolization). Is it not *skill* to have "the advantage of experience," trade connections and "the elite of personnel"? What is *foresight* if it does not include "anticipat[ing] increases in the demand for ingot and be[ing] prepared to supply them" or "embrac[ing] each new opportunity as it opened"? And what does *industry* mean, if it does not cover Alcoa's investments "doubling and redoubling its capacity"? Each of these factors was relied upon to find that Alcoa deliberately main-

tained its monopoly power, yet each comes close to
establishing the primary defense also recognized in
Alcoa. Finally, it seems questionable as a matter
of public policy to condemn Alcoa for increasing its
capacity. In fact, Alcoa's monopoly has been criticized by economic observers for consistently failing
to embrace expansion opportunities, so that the
country was extremely short of aluminum productive capacity at the outset of both world wars.

3. POST–*ALCOA* DEVELOPMENTS

In the years since *Alcoa,* the standards set forth
by Judge Hand have been affirmed and occasionally clarified. But the basic structure remains unchanged. Thus, one year later, in American Tobacco Co. v. United States, 328 U.S. 781, 813–14
(1946), the Supreme Court specifically endorsed
Hand's opinion.

Two years after *American Tobacco,* in United
States v. Griffith, 334 U.S. 100, 107 (1948), the
Court in dicta appeared to adopt some of the
broadest statements of *Alcoa* when it asserted that
monopoly power, however acquired, "may itself
constitute an evil and stand condemned under § 2
even though it remains unexercised." The Court,
however, also relied on the defendants' use of their
monopoly power; that is, their practice of buying
film distribution rights for all their movie theaters
as a block was condemned. Since some of their
theaters had a monopoly and others did not, this
block purchasing was an abuse of Griffith's monop-

oly power inasmuch as it was used to gain an advantage in competitive markets.[19] In ruling that the defendants' combination of buying power was illegal when exercised by a monopolist, the Court further indicated that special duties are imposed on a monopolist.[20]

The history of antitrust litigation against United Shoe illustrates both the development of antitrust theory and its practical limitations. In 1918 the company successfully defended itself against a monopolization charge stemming from its acquisition of over 50 shoe machinery producers holding complementary patents. United States v. United Shoe Machinery Co., 247 U.S. 32 (1918). Since United Shoe was itself a product of the patent system, the Court accepted its argument that the combination was formed to achieve economies of vertical integration and to remove the serious danger of costly patent litigation hanging over the industry. Four years later, however, the Court prohibited (under Section 3 of the Clayton Act) United Shoe's use of tying clauses relating to supplies used in conjunction with its leases of shoe machinery equipment.

19. The soundness of *Griffith* is seriously questioned because monopoly profits can be extracted only at one level. Thus whether Griffith bargained with movie distributors as one or several units should not affect the terms at which they dealt— except, of course, that the savings of one negotiation for all Griffith theaters might be shared by lower prices to consumers, higher payments to distributors or increased profits for itself. See also United States v. Loew's, Inc., 371 U.S. 38 (1962).

20. Ironically, part of Griffith's troubles arose from its limited monopoly position. If it had had a monopoly in *all* towns, its block purchasing practice would not have been illegal.

United Shoe Machinery Corp. v. United States, 258
U.S. 451 (1922). Then in United States v. United
Shoe Machinery Corp., 110 F.Supp. 295 (D.Mass.
1953), aff'd per curiam, 347 U.S. 521 (1954), the
government again challenged United Shoe's monopoly. While United Shoe's dominance derived
primarily from its research and development, the
court found, in a celebrated opinion by Judge
Wyzanski, that the company's lease provisions on
its machines further enhanced its monopoly position. Entry by competitors was blockaded, the
court concluded, by the lease terms. Furthermore,
United Shoe's policy of repair without separate
charges was also said to deter independent service
organizations. Despite United Shoe's exemplary
record—"[p]robably few monopolies could produce
a record so free from any taint" of predatory practices—its lease policies were viewed as restricting
competition and therefore as having contributed to
its monopoly position. Accordingly, it had violated
Section 2.

Whether United Shoe's restrictive leasing policies were (or could be) effective to continue its
monopoly power is questionable. While each could
be said to be directed at raising entry barriers,
each also undoubtedly served other, nonexclusiona-
ry functions—such as metering machine usage, reducing customer capital outlays, etc. See D. Ar-
mentano, *Antitrust and Monopoly* 112–18 (1982).
Professor Williamson has explained that the lease
terms could have been designed to prevent oppor-

tunistic behavior by both United Shoe and its customers. Williamson, *Transaction-Cost Economics: The Governance of Contractual Relations,* 22 J.L. & Econ. 233 (1979). And to the extent that they restricted customer choice, the lease restrictions are likely to have required price concessions. Thus, it is argued that "customers of United would be unlikely to participate in a campaign to strengthen United's monopoly position without insisting on being compensated for the loss of alternative, and less costly (because competitive), sources of supply." R. Posner, *Antitrust Law* 203–04 (1976).

In any case, *United Shoe* seems similar to *Alcoa* on two counts. First, its analysis of monopolists' business practices—their effect and purpose—is questionable. Nevertheless, its ruling is reflective of the law today, at least until the Supreme Court speaks more authoritatively on the subject. See H. Hovenkamp, *Economics and Federal Antitrust Law* 143 (1985) ("No court has articulated a general theory of what the rule of reason in monopolization cases is, or how it should function.")

The second and simpler point is to note the close relationship between the two (*Alcoa* and *United Shoe*) decisions. That is, practices that do not alone violate the antitrust laws may, in conjunction with overwhelming market power, violate Section 2. Restrictive leasing by a nonmonopolist is not contrary to the antitrust laws. In the setting of a monopoly, however, such practices which are not inevitable (and were not thought to be related to efficiency) might aid the monopoly position; as a consequence, they are condemned. *United Shoe,* therefore, further reaffirms *Alcoa's* retreat from the abuse theory that required a showing of illegal intent in monopolization cases. It is now enough to show that the continued monopoly power resulted from exclusionary practices that were deliberate even though not otherwise illegal. Occasional cases have extended *United Shoe* and ruled that companies with dominant market power must conform to a more rigorous standard of conduct. Cf. Grand Caillou Packing Co., 65 F.T.C. 799 (1964) (The Peelers case), aff'd in part, sub nom., LaPeyre v. FTC, 366 F.2d 117 (5th Cir.1966) (unjustified discrimination between classes of users by a monopolist violates FTC Act, § 5); Reuben H. Donnelley Corp., 3 Trade Reg.Rep. ¶ 21,650 (Jan. 10, 1980) (duty not to be arbitrary), rev'd sub nom., Official Airline Guides, Inc. v. FTC, 630 F.2d 920 (2d Cir. 1980), cert. denied, 450 U.S. 917 (1981). To date, however, this authority is questionable. See Berkey Photo, Inc., v. Eastman Kodak Co., 603 F.2d 263, 273–79 (2d Cir.1979), cert. denied, 444 U.S. 1093 (1980). More reliable probably is the FTC decision in E.I. duPont de Nemours & Co., 96 F.T.C. 650 (1980) (the titanium dioxide case) where the Commission upheld aggressive marketing practices including the expansion of production capacity to capture all of the anticipated increase in demand. Although *Alcoa* was distinguished on several technical grounds (e.g., the purpose here was not to deter entry, the additions to capacity had not occurred over a long period of time and were carefully justified), *duPont (titanium dioxide)* reflects a very different view of the monopoly problem.

Nonetheless, the careful student of antitrust law should be aware of the case law tradition imposing stringent standards on a monopolist's business conduct. For example, Judge Wyzanski again examined the monopolization standard in United States v. Grinnell Corp., 236 F.Supp. 244 (D.R.I.1964), aff'd except as to the decree, 384 U.S. 563 (1966). The company's market position was held to be the result of business practices amounting to per se violations of Section 1 and of a series of acquisitions. The district court also speculated that

a day would come when the Supreme Court would announce that where one or more persons acting jointly had acquired so clear a dominance in a market as to have the power to exclude competition therefrom, there was a *rebuttable* presumption that such power had been criminally acquired and was a monopolizing [act] punishable under § 2.

The Supreme Court, by Justice Douglas, declined the invitation, however. Finding that

the record clearly shows that [defendants'] monopoly power was consciously acquired, we have no reason to reach the further position of the District Court that once monopoly power is shown to exist, the burden is on the defendant to show that their dominance is due to skill, acumen, and the like.

Subsequent cases have not taken this further step. Indeed, in *Grinnell* the Court defined the essential elements of monopolization as:

(1) the possession of monopoly power in the relevant market and

(2) the willful acquisition or maintenance of that power as distinguished from growth or development as a consequence of a superior product, business acumen or historic accident.

Its decision relied on the finding that Grinnell's monopoly "was achieved in large part by unlawful and exclusionary practices" such as the buying up of competitors. Coupled with the Court's seemingly deliberate failure to cite *Alcoa* on the monopolist's lawful role, the law of monopolization has remained particularly unclear.

This may explain why Section 2 has not been widely applied despite the apparent openness of the legal standard. Another limitation on Section 2 is judicial reluctance to disintegrate monopoly power. Government prosecutions have concentrated on proving a violation. Even when they have won this battle, they have failed to present plausible dissolution schemes and have thereby lost the war. Dissolution, for example, was not ordered in *Alcoa*, and the company is still the undisputed leader in the aluminum industry. The absence of many successful monopoly prosecutions has not meant that there are no developments to report. Indeed, this area of antitrust law has created intense scrutiny and occasional controversy.

4. RECENT APPLICATIONS

Three types of conduct have received the most attention in monopolization cases, predatory pricing, product innovation, and refusals to deal.

a. Predatory Pricing

While predatory pricing has long been condemned, there was little agreement on the standard for distinguishing legitimate from predatory pricing. On the one hand, it was recognized that the monopolist must be allowed to set his own prices—else the antitrust court would merely become a regulatory agency. Yet it was also widely accepted that a rich monopolist could, by pricing below its competitors' costs, drive them out of the market and entrench his position.

Relying on basic economic theory that competition drives prices to marginal costs (see pp. 61–62 supra), Professors Areeda and Turner developed a test for measuring when prices charged by a monopolist are likely to be predatory and thus should be condemned if not justified. Relying on the competitive market model, they argued that it is usually unreasonable for a competitive firm to drop its prices below short-run marginal costs unless it can expect to recover these costs by future

monopoly pricing. Thus they proposed that a price
lower than reasonably anticipated short-run marginal cost should be held to be predatory, while a
higher price should be held to be nonpredatory.
Because this marginal cost benchmark is difficult
to compute (and probably impossible to do so under
the constraints of litigation), they proposed an alternative measure, namely average variable cost—
i.e., dividing a firm's cost (less fixed charges) by the
number of units produced—for determining whether the challenged prices were below cost. See
Areeda & Turner, *Predatory Pricing and Practices
Under Section 2 of the Sherman Act,* 88 Harv.L.
Rev. 697 (1975), reformulated in 3 P. Areeda & D.
Turner, *Antitrust Law* ¶¶ 710–22 (1978).

The Areeda-Turner test has been widely com-
mented upon and inevitably criticized. One argument is that the average variable cost test "makes
predatory pricing easy to 'prove' in markets where
it is almost certain not to occur, but very difficult
to prove in markets that are conducive to predation." H. Hovenkamp, supra at 177. Another is
that this test is underinclusive and would insulate
"strategic entry deterrence" by prices that are not
below cost. Williamson, *Predatory Pricing: A Strategic and Welfare Analysis,* 87 Yale L.J. 284 (1977).
These discussions have influenced the courts where
the Areeda-Turner test has otherwise had a great
impact.

In general, courts have held that proof of pricing
below marginal or average variable costs is pre-

sumably predatory and thus the burden of proof is on the defendant to show that the price was promotional or that his costs were expected to fall. The judicial debate has focused on whether prices above this level—which is the usual case—can also be found to be predatory. The Ninth Circuit has ruled that prices above total cost can be found unlawful if the justification for such prices are based "on their tendency to eliminate rivals and create a market structure enabling the seller to recoup his losses." William Inglis & Sons Baking Co. v. ITT Continental Baking Co., 668 F.2d 1014, 1035 (9th Cir.1981). But this view was rejected in an influential decision by Judge Breyer because it would inhibit prices from moving in the right direction, was vague, and did not effectively distinguish between pricing practices designed to discipline from those designed to compete. Barry Wright Corp. v. ITT Grinnell Corp., 724 F.2d 227 (1st Cir.1983). Thus, in *Barry Wright* the court concluded that Section 2 did not prohibit prices that exceeded both incremental and average costs.[21]

21. Economic experts in the IBM monopolization case (dismissed in 1982, see In re IBM, 687 F.2d 591 (2d Cir.1982)) have offered the intriguing argument that firms regardless of size should be free to lower prices or redesign products so long as they earn a profit. F. Fisher, J. McGowan & J. Greenwood, *Folded, Spindled, and Mutilated: Economic Analysis and U.S. v. IBM* (1983). Pricing is predatory, they assert, only when prices are set so low that the firm loses money and can recoup only if it can raise prices without fear of entry by new competitors who will take its market away. See also Easterbrook, *Predatory Strategies and Counter-strategies,* 48 U.Chi.L.Rev. 263 (1981).

b. Product Innovation

After a period of debate and sometimes contradictory signals, the courts have similarly upheld the aggressive development of new products or innovations by companies with large shares of a market. In Berkey Photo Inc. v. Eastman Kodak Co., 603 F.2d 263, 296 (2d Cir.1979), cert. denied, 444 U.S. 1093 (1980), the court ruled that "any firm, even a monopolist, may generally bring its products to market whenever and however it chooses" even though it may thereby make it more difficult for smaller firms to compete or survive. Courts are reluctant to inhibit desirable conduct or substitute their judgment for that of the individual business or market. Perhaps reflecting a corollary reluctance to allow monopoly firms too much market freedom, the cases have noted that coercion (including reliance on monopoly market power) to gain market acceptance of a new product is unlawful. But it is unclear what evidence will establish such coercion.

c. Refusals to Deal

Finally, there is a line of authority holding that a refusal to deal by a monopolist may be a violation of Section 2. See Eastman Kodak Co. v. Southern Photo Materials Co., 273 U.S. 359 (1927); Otter Tail Power Co. v. United States, 410 U.S. 366 (1973). These cases, however, have generally been limited to situations where a firm had monopoly power at one level of a chain of distribution and had refused to deal with firms at the next level in order to gain a monopoly position at both levels. See MCI Communications Corp. v. American Tel. & Tel. Co., 708 F.2d 1081 (7th Cir.1983), cert. denied, 464 U.S. 891 (1983) (bottleneck doctrine). Thus it was somewhat of a surprise when the Supreme Court recently held that a monopolist's unwillingness to participate in a joint marketing scheme with its only competitors could amount to monopolization. In Aspen Skiing Co. v. Aspen Highlands Skiing Corp., 105 S.Ct. 2847 (1985), the Court held that the evidence supported a jury's determination that the refusal by the owner of three of four mountain slopes used for skiing in Aspen with the other owner and to continue their joint ski ticket reflected "a deliberate effort to discourage customers from doing business with its smaller rival." The Court emphasized that the defendant "was apparently motivated entirely by a decision to avoid providing any benefit to [the smaller rival] even though accepting [its] coupons would have entailed no cost" and would have greatly benefited potential customers. Perhaps the case should be read only as meaning that the evidence was sufficient to support a jury verdict—especially since the defendant did not challenge the market determination or jury instruction before the Court. Nonetheless, the implication that a monopolist can violate Section 2 for changing its distribution pattern and, indeed, that the monopolist can be required to cooperate with its competitors in a joint marketing arrangement (itself questionable under Section 1 as an illegal market division, see pp. 202–12) seems remarkable.[22] See also Olympia Equip. Leasing Co. v. Western Union Tel. Co., 768 F.2d 794 (7th Cir.1986) (Posner, J.).

C. ATTEMPTS TO MONOPOLIZE

In addition to monopolization and conspiracy to monopolize,[23] attempts to monopolize are recognized as felonies under Section 2. Few cases explore this avenue of enforcement. Justice Holmes provided the leading statement on attempts to monopolize in Swift & Co. v. United States, 196 U.S. 375 (1905). Drawing closely on the criminal law analogue, he concluded that attempted monopolization consisted of conduct that closely approaches

22. This apparent "reversal" of *Alcoa*, as well as the inordinate time it has taken for government monopoly cases to be tried, has led to proposals that persistent monopoly power alone be made illegal under a statutory "no fault" standard. The underlying assumption of these proposals is that monopoly which continues without government protection is probably due to illegal or undesirable conduct. See generally 1 *Report of the National Commission For The Review of Antitrust Laws And Procedures* 141 (1979) (recommending that Congress consider legislation "aimed at strengthening the ability of the Sherman Act to deal with persistent monopoly power"); 3 P. Areeda & D. Turner, *Antitrust Law* ¶ 623d (1978). But see H. Hovenkamp, *Economics and Federal Antitrust Law* § 5.3 (1985).

23. The Supreme Court recognized conspiracy to monopolize as a separate offense in American Tobacco Co. v. United States, 328 U.S. 781 (1946). It differs from single firm monopolization by not requiring proof of monopoly power and by requiring a showing of specific intent (as in attempts). See ABA Antitrust Section, *Antitrust Law Development* 145–46 (2d ed. 1984). For an analysis of issues involved in establishing conspiracy, see pp. 257–65 infra.

but does not quite attain completed monopolization, plus a wrongful intent to monopolize. Thus conduct amounts to an attempt to monopolize if it is demonstrated that there is a specific intent to monopolize and a dangerous probability that, if unchecked, such conduct will ripen into monopolization. Beyond these formulations lurk the difficult questions: what degree of market power must a defendant have before it can be charged with an attempt to monopolize; what conduct constitutes an attempt; and what of limited objectives—e.g., does an attempt include deterring additional entrants or driving only one competitor out of business? See generally, Cooper, *Attempts and Monopolization: A Mildly Expansionary Answer to the Prophylactic Riddle of Section Two,* 72 Mich.L.Rev. 373 (1974).

The Supreme Court cases do not resolve these questions and lower court decisions concerning them are in disarray. As the offense of monopolization expanded—in particular with Judge Hand's opinion in *Alcoa*—the role of attempt to monopolize has become particularly cloudy. Nor did the Supreme Court provide much guidance in Otter Tail Power Co. v. United States, 410 U.S. 366 (1973), even though the substantive charge involved an attempt to monopolize. In holding that a power company could not refuse to sell or deliver over its own subtransmission lines the power purchased by towns from its competitors, the Court merely summarily concluded that the "[u]se of monopoly power 'to destroy threatened competition' is a violation of the 'attempt to monopolize' clause of § 2 of the Sherman Act."

As with monopolization, the primary difficulty in developing a legal standard defining illegal attempts is the dichotomy between prohibiting undesirable business conduct likely to result in monopoly and the possibility of stifling rivalrous conduct. Since many, if not most, business practices support both inferences, actions to punish attempts necessarily involve close scrutiny of particular facts which do not lend themselves to succinct summary. Moreover, by definition, an attempt case involves prosecution of the unsuccessful monopolist,[24] which increases judicial caution. Subjective intent may be crucial, but courts have generally declined to accord substantial weight to inferences of such intent from objective conduct. As a consequence, the requirements that there be specific intent to monopolize and a dangerous probability of success (but without monopolizing in fact), has meant that the offense of attempt to monopolize is seldom meaningfully distinguished from monopolization itself.

One particular area of controversy is the degree to which it must be shown that the defendant was

24. While it has been held that a defendant can be convicted of both monopolization and an attempt to monopolize, United States v. General Elec. Co., 80 F.Supp. 989, 1016 (S.D.N.Y.1948), the more frequently held view is that the attempt merges into the offense of monopolization. See, e.g., American Tobacco Co. v. United States, 328 U.S. 781, 783 (1946).

likely to succeed. A few courts have said the element is not essential; evidence of the specific intent and predatory conduct are enough. Lessig v. Tidewater Oil Co., 327 F.2d 459 (9th Cir.1964), cert. denied, 377 U.S. 993 (1964). The majority, however, have read the dangerous probability of success test as requiring a showing of close proximity to actual monopolization. They have feared that any more restrictive rule will deter competitive conduct. And there is no reason to punish unsuccessful firms whose efforts did not harm consumers and who were already punished by the market.

CHAPTER V

HORIZONTAL RESTRAINTS: THE EVOLUTION OF STANDARDS

The primary role in the Sherman Act has not been in controlling single firm monopolies, but rather in dealing with various anticompetitive practices such as agreements among competitors to fix prices, to restrict output, to divide markets, or to exclude other competitors. These activities have been prosecuted under both Section 1 (as restraints of trade) and Section 2 (as conspiracies to monopolize). However, unlike charges of monopolization under Section 2, examinations of market-rigging practices under Section 1 usually have not focused on whether the defendants succeeded or failed to achieve monopoly power; instead, the judicial gaze has been directed, at least initially, toward the participants' conduct or actions, as distinct from their market power.

The assumptions underlying Section 1 are that the societal benefits from competition will be endangered if rivals are permitted to join together and to consolidate their market power. Competition is directly impaired by agreements to restrict output and raise prices above competitive levels. Similarly deleterious effects can be indirectly achieved through exclusion of rivals from a market. While courts readily assume the existence of these undesirable results, careful analysis of actual cartel operations also reveals that market-rigging arrangements are not self-policing. Moreover, joint production or marketing arrangements may reduce costs and increase competitive pressures. Thus, whether particular conduct should be condemned automatically or only when it in fact causes significant harm depends on the likelihood of such harm as well as on other possible effects. A brief detour examining the economics of cartels as well as new insights into transaction costs are therefore warranted.

A. THE ECONOMICS OF CARTELS AND TRANSACTION COSTS

The rationale for industry cartels—agreements among rivals to restrict output and raise prices—is founded on Adam Smith's model of perfect competition[1] outlined in our earlier analysis of the theory of competition and monopoly. Recalling the description of market demand for widgets as represented by a negatively sloped curve (i.e., as more is consumed, consumers will pay less—and vice versa), we observed then that a single-firm monopolist could increase its total revenues by cutting supply from 10 to 5 widgets while raising price from $.10 to $.60 per unit. (See Table 1, p. 66 supra.) Competitive firms or price-takers will

1. A. Smith, *An Inquiry into the Nature and Causes of the Wealth of Nations* (1776).

quickly see that they also can increase their profits by taking similar action in cooperation with each other, avoiding independent action.

Assume, for example, that ten competing firms supplied a total of 10 widgets to the market weekly. According to the demand schedule (Table 1), the market price for widgets would be only $.10 and weekly revenues would be limited to $1.00. However, acting in concert the ten firms could triple their weekly revenue by cutting production in half and selling their widgets at $.60 per unit. In this instance, each would agree to produce only one widget every other week, yet the industry's total revenue would not equal $3.00. Before one gets too enthusiastic about this plan, however, it should be noted that it deprives consumers of two of the benefits of a competitive market: lower prices and increased output. Not surprisingly, the Congress sought to outlaw such conduct under the Sherman Act.

In light of these substantial rewards, the failure of industry members to cooperate with each other so that their industry marginal revenue matches marginal cost may merely indicate that the industry understands such a policy of cooperation to be illegal. But we also know that such cooperation was not always considered unlawful, that the antitrust laws do not cover significant segments of the economy, and that not all businessmen scrupulously follow the law. Yet evidence of market-rigging, while not wholly absent, is not pervasive. This may be due solely to the secrecy surrounding such arrangements. The more likely reasons are the problems which make it difficult to form and operate cartels, despite their promise of substantially increased revenues.

Three significant hurdles to cartels stand out: First, the industry may be unable to solve internal administrative problems such as the assigning of production quotas and the sharing of aggregate profit data. Second, the established firms may fear that if they are successful in raising their immediate profits to a maximum, this would only encourage new producers to enter the industry. Third, the participating firms often do not, in fact, know the output level which will maximize their profits over the short run. As one astute observer summarized: "the 'competition' of businessmen— as the term is commonly understood—is rooted in the prohibitions of the law, avarice, distrust of actual rivals, fear of potential rivals, and simple miscalculation." D. Dewey, *Monopoly in Economics and Law* 8 (1959).

Even during one of the most celebrated price-fixing conspiracies—that of electrical equipment manufacturers during the 1950's—there was widespread cheating among the conspirators which often touched off bitter price wars. In a moment of candor, one General Electric Company executive revealed the basis for his group's temporary refusal to adhere to the arrangement: "No one was living up to the arrangements and we . . . were being made suckers." Nor are these difficulties automatically surmounted when market-rigging agreements are supported by law. The IATA (International Air Transport Association) lawfully fixed passenger fares on almost all international airline routes. But the definition of a "sandwich" supplied passengers enroute required a plenary session in 1958, and lengthy debate preceded the Association's subsequent decision to raise the surcharge for inflight movies.

Two problems are central to the tendency of market-rigging agreements to falter. First, the different firms participating in the arrangement most likely have divergent costs and market shares. As a consequence they will have very different ideas concerning the appropriate price level and the equitable distribution of market shares. The growing firm will expect an increased share of the market in the future, the declining firm will contend that the agreement should maintain its quota. These and similar differences usually make it difficult in the first place to reach any understanding which each participant will find acceptable and will observe. Smoke filled rooms and hard drinking may make compromise possible, but they cannot eliminate differences in price and output preferences. The IATA splintered into two camps almost from its inception. One group having lower costs constantly pushed for low transatlantic fares to encourage higher volume; airlines having higher costs, on the other hand, argued for a higher rate structure.

Second, once an agreement is reached to fix a price substantially above marginal cost, each participant will then have a strong incentive to cheat. As long as others can be relied upon to honor their commitments, and as long as chiseling can be done covertly, honesty in observing the price-fixing agreement appears a foolish policy. That is, each member finds he could substantially increase his profits by undercutting the fixed price, gaining additional sales at a price equal to (or, perhaps, even above) his marginal cost. This is well illustrated by the following figure:

FIGURE 9: THE TEMPTATION TO CHISEL

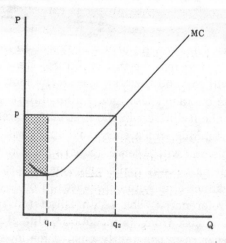

Here it is assumed that there are four firms in the industry with identical cost curves (*MC*), able to supply the entire market (q_2), but that each is constrained by the cartel to one quarter of the output (q_1). Advantageous as the arrangement is to each participant, as reflected by the amount that the price (p) exceeds cost at the output (the shaded rectangle), this situation also produces a powerful temptation for each firm to chisel since each could then increase its total revenues by increasing output to q_2. As long as the price at least equals marginal cost. increased revenues generally will bring increased profits. The pressure to prevent this kind of chiseling encourages the cartel to lower the price nearer to the marginal cost. Whenever the cartel price is set substantially above a member's marginal cost the cartel is likely to disintegrate unless it can effectively detect cheating and police its members.

Incidentally, these two problems often interact with each other. Those cartel participants least satisfied with the original agreement may prove to be especially likely to chisel and thereby cause its disintegration. Maintenance of the cartel also depends on erecting barriers to new entry—or co-opting new entrants by admitting them into the cartel. The latter policy also will destroy the cartel since it will soon eliminate all reason for its existence; that is, the members of the cartel will have to accept a smaller share of the market or output will increase and price will be reduced.

Participation in a cartel, despite the difficulties mentioned, is worthwhile under many market conditions; the profits can be extraordinary. Where conditions conducive to competition are present, the cartel is probably doomed because policing dozens of firms where entry is easy will prove impracticable. Likewise a cartel is unnecessary where one firm is a monopolist and controls the entire output of a single product such as local telephone service. But between these extremes, that is, under the conditions facing many firms, the urge to create a cartel is enduring and universal so long as marginal revenue (price) exceeds marginal cost.

On the other hand, unless assured of continued government support, every cartel contains the seeds of its own destruction. Theory and empirical evidence both suggest a relatively short lifespan for most cartels. In addition, industry cartels are asserted to have beneficial effects in some cases. For example, a cartel may protect an industry from the extremes of ruinous competition, thereby maintaining needed capacity, especially where fixed costs constitute a large percentage of the total costs (as with railroads). It may also permit the avoidance of concentration, thus preserving both individual firms and employment. And insulated from some of the most urgent competitive pressures, firms become free to finance desirable innovation and conduct other research activities as well as to protect the quality of their products from debasement.

Each of these alleged benefits is disputed. Ultimately the issue becomes that of whether the marketplace can be relied upon fully to evaluate the value or worth of a particular activity. Is it desirable, for example, to foster research that cannot support itself by useful products in the market? If consumers are unwilling, by their purchase decisions, to support quality, should industry groups be permitted to impose minimum quality standards? Frequent government intervention to assure public health and safety or to protect the public from substantial economic harm reflects a judgment that the marketplace does not adequately balance all interests. Nevertheless, it does not support private cartel arrangements as a substitute for market performance. These and similar issues, then, underlie most significant applications of Section 1 of the Sherman Act to cartels.

On the other hand, not all joint activity is designed to restrict output and raise prices. Firms frequently merge or integrate partially by contract to create partnerships and new firms or to achieve specific functions. These arrangements among noncompetitors, and even contractual arrangements among competitors, may be designed to achieve a more efficient or effective organization. Whatever the outcome in fact, the driving purpose of the collaboration is that the new firm or organizational form will contribute to competition—the very opposite of a cartel.

[handwritten margin note: COASE PTED OUT THAT DISTINCTION BTWN K FOR A SINGLE T/A, THE ORGANIZATION OF A FIRM, OR THE STRUCTURE OF A MKT IN WHICH THE 1ST TWO OPERATE IS NOT SHARPLY MARKED]

Professor Ronald Coase first outlined these views almost fifty years ago in pointing out that the distinction among contracts for a single transaction, the organization of a firm, or the structure of a market in which the first two operate, is not sharply marked. Coase, *The Nature of the Firm*, 4 Economics (n.s.) 386 (1937). Rather, they are just points on a continuum of methods of organization.

Building on this understanding, Professor Oliver Williamson developed the economics of transaction costs to explain further alternative organizational forms. O. Williamson, *Markets and Hierarchies* (1975). He has shown, for example, that firms perform more than production functions; their operation as a governance mechanism is to economize on transaction costs. Thus, a firm will change its form, grow larger or smaller, make arrangements with other firms for production or distribution, etc., to reduce costs or otherwise improve the organization of economic transaction.[2] Production cost savings matter—they are not limited to the physical expenses of running a plant; savings in organization translate into real cost savings.

[handwritten margin note: JOINT ARRANGEMENTS MAY LEAD TO EFFICIENCY BENEFITS]

Transaction cost economics has significant implications for antitrust. It illustrates that joint product or sale arrangements or other forms of cooperation may serve efficiency instead of cartel functions. In point of fact, competitive market

2. Transaction cost analysis explains that the economic institutions of capitalism are designed to economize on transaction costs. O. Williamson, *The Economic Institutions of Capitalism* (1985).

pressures are likely to lead firms to cooperate, which in turn may increase output, lower prices, and provide benefits to consumers and the economy. There is, in other words, no "right degree" of firm or interfirm organization in a market. The difficulty for antitrust is in discerning the objectives and likely effect of joint arrangements, and of deciding whether they are sufficiently beneficial to be allowed (in light of the risks that they may in fact be harmful).

As is discussed in this section, the Supreme Court has begun to recognize these competing ideas; its decisions now reflect an understanding that markets and firms are on the same continuum. See Copperweld Corp. v. Independence Tube Corp., 467 U.S. 752 (1984) (overruling of intraenterprise conspiracy doctrine). Thus, it has held that firms and even entire industries may cooperate when interfirm organization is likely to result in more efficient production. See NCAA v. University of Oklahoma, 468 U.S. 85 (1984); Broadcast Music, Inc. v. Columbia Broadcasting System, Inc., 441 U.S. 1 (1979). But see Arizona v. Maricopa County Medical Soc'y, 457 U.S. 332 (1982). At times these new rulings seem a sharp departure from precedent, although few cases are in fact overruled. One consequence is that the Court often has difficulty in deciding whether an arrangement is likely to enhance allocative efficiency on the one hand, or monopolize a market on the other. At this point there are still few reliable guides.

See, e.g., Aspen Skiing Co. v. Aspen Highlands
Skiing Corp., 105 S.Ct. 2847 (1985) (discussed pp.
148–49 supra); Hospitals Corp. of America, 3 CCH
Trade Reg. Rep. ¶ 22,301 (FTC, Oct. 25, 1985) (rejecting efficiency defense where the acquisition of 5
hospitals created a substantial market share).

B. PRICE–FIXING

It is now well established that explicit agreements by competing or independent firms to fix
prices are a primary concern of Section 1 of the
Sherman Act. This was acknowledged in the earliest cases. Where evidence of agreement or con-
spiratorial conduct was not contested, judicial analysis concentrated on whether evidence of economic
injury or extenuating circumstances justifying the
arrangement should be permitted. Did the Sherman Act condemn every price-fixing agreement
automatically? Must the plaintiff establish that
the agreement was harmful to competition or competitors? Or, is the arrangement illegal unless the
defendants can justify it by pointing to societal
benefits? As succeeding sections will recount, the
history of judicial treatment of price-fixing involves a typical ebb and flow process—of strict
rules and encroaching exceptions. It is recounted
in considerable detail here because the study of the
judicial weaving is instructive for later application
of the Sherman and Clayton Acts to other practices.

1. EARLY DEVELOPMENTS

The first Section 1 case to reach the Supreme Court, United States v. Trans-Missouri Freight Ass'n, 166 U.S. 290 (1897), involved an effort by 18 railroads controlling traffic west of the Mississippi to eliminate fratricidal rate wars. The railroads created an association to establish freight rates for all participants. When challenged by the government, they conceded that their contracts limited each railroad's freedom of commercial action. Nevertheless, the railroads argued that they were exempt from the Sherman Act on the basis of being regulated carriers under the Interstate Commerce Act, and that in any case the rates they fixed were legal because these rates were reasonable and therefore valid under common law. The lower court sustained these arguments. A closely divided Supreme Court reversed the decision. It held that railroads were not exempt from the Sherman Act, and that it was unnecessary to consider whether the restraint was valid at common law. The Court stated that Section 1 condemned "every" restraint of trade; it recognized no exceptions. Thus, reading the Sherman Act literally, the Court appeared to condemn all agreements in restraint of trade, not just unreasonable ones. On the other hand, as Judge Bork has carefully developed, Justice Peckham's opinion for the majority also suggested that the agreement was illegal because it suppressed competition—and that this was the reason for prohibiting the arrangement regardless of whether the rates were reasonable. R. Bork, *The Antitrust Paradox* 23 (1978).

Two cases decided within the next year further developed both sides of this analysis. While still reading the Sherman Act literally and ruling, once again, that price-fixing agreements were within the prohibition of "every" trade restraint (without regard to reasonableness), the Court's approach also suggested that the antitrust law would not be applied in so sweeping a fashion. Specifically, in Hopkins v. United States, 171 U.S. 578, 592 (1898), the Court read *Trans-Missouri* as applying only to "direct" agreements in restraint of trade; that is, only those agreements whose main purpose was to fix prices were condemned. Covenants not to compete in connection with the sale of business goodwill and similar ancillary agreements, for example, were not threatened by the Sherman Act. And in United States v. Joint-Traffic Ass'n, 171 U.S. 505 (1898), the Court distinguished price agreements from ordinary sale, lease, partnership and incorporation contracts on the ground that the elimination of actual or potential rivalry was permissible where it served to support an integration of the parties' productive economic activities or facilities. Economic efficiency was, in other words, recognized early on as a justification for arrangements that might otherwise restrain trade in violation of the law. Thus, the scope of *Trans-Missouri's* condemnation of "every" trade restraint was placed in doubt.

This first phase in the development of the Sherman law was completed with an extraordinarily
suggestive opinion by William Howard Taft, then a
circuit judge. He relied on an expansive reading of
the common law to relate the rules of antitrust to
the goals of the Act. In United States v. Addyston
Pipe & Steel Co., 85 Fed. 271 (6th Cir.1898), six
leading producers of cast iron pipe conceded that
they had agreed among themselves to divide the
southern and western markets into regional monopolies and had instituted a system of fixed prices
for each territory. The evidence showed that the
prices agreed upon were just low enough to discourage entry by eastern manufacturers, and that
without the agreements prices might have been
lower if the local firms had competed among themselves. The defense concentrated on two separate
contentions. First, the defendants argued that the
purpose of the arrangement was not monopoly but
the avoidance of ruinous price competition in the
industry. They pointed to the previous high fatali-
ty rate among cast iron pipe firms. Second, they
sought to prove that the prices at which such pipe
was sold in each region were reasonable. Since
consumers were not injured, the defendants argued
the public had not been harmed and the Sherman
Act provided no remedy for nonexistent harms.

Neither defense convinced the circuit court. Instead, it held that the effect of the agreements was
to deprive the public of the benefits of competition.
Seeking to build an airtight per se prohibition of

price-fixing agreements, Judge Taft read the prevailing common law as voiding all price-fixing agreements unless they were ancillary to some legitimate cause. The law, as Taft saw it, made naked restraints in which the "sole object" is the elimination of competition per se illegal. Consequently, he ruled that even under *Joint-Traffic's* reading of the Sherman Act, the defense of reasonableness was irrelevant. On the other hand, some restrictions on competition are desirable and here Taft drew from his reading of the common law the concept of "ancillary" restraints. The idea was that where the purpose of the agreement served a legitimate purpose (such as the sale of a business or property or the creation of a partnership), the subordinate price restraint enhanced the basic arrangement and thereby should be preserved. In such a case the benefits were likely to outweigh the losses and should not be automatically outlawed. When measured by this standard, the pipe producers' agreements were clearly not ancillary—and thus were illegal.

Despite the force of this analysis, its impact during the formative years of the Sherman law was limited. Almost as an afterthought, Taft had also noted in *Addyston Pipe* that "if it were important, we should unhesitatingly find that the prices charged in the instances which were in evidence were unreasonable." Latching on to this statement, the Supreme Court muted the significance of Taft's ruling by affirming (but modifying the decree of) the circuit court, and by emphasizing the finding that the prices fixed were in fact unreasonable. (175 U.S. 211 (1889).) The implication seemed to be that reasonableness might be sustained as a defense.

2. DEVELOPMENT OF THE RULE OF REASON

A new Supreme Court majority[3] seemingly reversed the trend toward a per se prohibition of price-fixing in *Standard Oil of N.J. v. United States*, 221 U.S. 1 (1911) (also examined pp. 124–27 supra). In a lengthy and confusing opinion focused upon the defendant's efforts to monopolize the sale of petroleum products, Chief Justice White reread Section 1 of the Sherman Act as condemning only every *undue or unreasonable* restraint of trade. He asserted that to prohibit every trade restraint would be impractical and contrary to the Congressional desire. Applying a "standard of reason" to determine whether an agreement is prohibited as a restraint of trade depends, he concluded, on the purpose of the arrangement, the character (i.e., power) of the parties, and the necessary effect of their actions.

Standard Oil (N.J.) was not a direct holding that price-fixing was permissible if reasonable, however. The defendant's monopolizing activities were the

3. Chief Justice White, who had dissented in *Trans-Missouri* and *Joint-Traffic*, wrote the Court's opinion in *Standard Oil (N.J.)*.

Court's concern. Moreover, it noted that some conduct was conclusively presumed to be undesirable and harmful, but the scope and content of this unelaborated conclusion was unclear. Thus in *Standard Oil (N.J.)* the Court appeared to create a new rule of uncertain content which emphasized behavior and recognized that agreements between independent firms have a wide range of possible effects; yet it also acknowledged that some conduct may be inherently unreasonable.

The next antitrust case presented to the Supreme Court involving a charge of price-fixing, *Chicago Bd. of Trade v. United States*, 246 U.S. 231 (1918), is important for two reasons: (1) because it is still the leading case outlining the reasonableness standard, and (2) as an illustration of how that standard has been applied generally so as to find no antitrust liability. While the rule of reason standard no longer governs price-fixing agreements, if it ever did, this measure of business conduct is widely applied throughout antitrust. Its development, in terms of theory and application needs to be carefully traced and thoroughly understood if one is to gain a sure foothold in antitrust.

In *Chicago Bd. of Trade* the government had charged that a grain exchange rule requiring members to adhere to their closing bid on the "call"—which had the effect of confining price competition to the time the exchange was open—was illegal because it fixed prices during part of the business day. The call rule required members of the exchange to establish their off-hour trading price for "to arrive" grain at a special call session. The government claimed that the purpose and effect of the rule was to fix the price for trading in "to arrive" grain after the exchange's daily and week-end closing times; members could not change their price during this time to reflect fluctuating conditions—as they would in an unregulated market. Yet the exchange's call rule did not seek to set the level of that to arrive price; participants in the call session were free to compete on the price for the "to arrive" grain.

Writing for the Court, Justice Brandeis rejected this claim of per se illegality in now famous dictum stating more specifically the factors to be considered under *Standard Oil's* "rule of reason":

> [T]he legality of an agreement or regulation cannot be determined by so simple a test, as whether it restrains competition. Every agreement concerning trade, every regulation of trade, restrains. To bind, to restrain, is of their very essence. The true test of legality is whether the restraint imposed is such as merely regulates and perhaps thereby promotes competition or whether it is such as may suppress or even destroy competition. To determine that question the court must ordinarily consider the facts peculiar to the business to which the restraint is applied; its condition before and after the restraint was imposed; the nature of the restraint and its effect, actual or probable. The history of

/ PURPOSE OF RESTRAINT

the restraint, the evil believed to exist, the reason for adopting the particular remedy, the purpose or end sought to be attained, are all relevant facts. This is not because a good intention will save an otherwise objectionable regulation or the reverse; but because knowledge of intent may help the court to interpret facts and to predict consequences.

Following these directions, the Court ruled in *Chicago Bd. of Trade* that the exchange requirement restricting its members' hours of operation and prices while the exchange was closed were reasonable. In doing so, the Court continued its practice of not examining actual prices or their reasonableness. Instead it found that the rules fostered the exchange market; and regulating competition, in contrast to preventing it, was not always to be discouraged. The critical factors relied upon to evaluate the call rule were its purpose and effect, which, according to the Court, were: to regulate the exchange's hours of business, to break up the monopoly previously held by a limited number of warehouses willing to make evening purchases—which was thought to be particularly unfair to unsuspecting country dealers and farmers—and to perfect the operation of the commodity exchange by increasing the number of transactions made there. While a careful analysis of each of these arguments suggests an equally persuasive contrary result,[4] the case does suggest the where

CRITICAL FACTORS RELIED ON / CBOT → / PURPOSE & EFFECT

4. For example, if country dealers or farmers were in fact being unfairly taken advantage of by a few monopolistic ware-

and how of the application of the reasonableness standard. The "call rule's" primary aim was found to be the creation of a public market where commodity prices could be determined competitively. That is to say, according to the Court, the rule sought to further rather than to suppress competition, and in this light it was acceptable under the reasonableness test.

This flexible view of the Sherman Act—even as applied to price-fixing agreements—dominated antitrust for a decade and, as noted below, continues to resurface regularly. Indeed, the rule of reason's subsequent application in monopolization (see *United States Steel*, p. 128 supra) and trade association (Maple Flooring Ass'n v. United States, p. 236 infra) cases shortly thereafter suggested to some that price-fixing might also survive Sherman Act scrutiny.

Before returning to the law of price-fixing, it is worth noting that the judicial treatment of the reasonableness defense to a price-fixing charge is significant because it is typical of the evolution of antitrust law, and similar developments have occurred in almost every other area where antitrust concepts have been applied. Defendants will first

housemen, a response more consistent with the Sherman Act would be to increase competition by encouraging others to enter the off-hour market with offers of competitive prices; if the concern is over the seller's lack of current price information, the exchange could circulate such information to these dealers and farmers. Note, these alternatives are less restrictive than the exchange's "call rule" which had the effect of denying such sellers an opportunity to sell their "to arrive" grain to member brokers at prices responsive to changing conditions.

argue that their primary conduct was lawful—here, that price-fixing violates neither the common law nor the Sherman Act. After that contention is categorically dismissed, as in *Addyston Pipe*, the defense erects a second line of rebuttal. It asserts that the market-rigging being attacked does not violate the Sherman Act's prohibition of "undue" restraints because the arrangement is reasonable—here, that the fixed price was reasonable. Not only is the agreement said to be harmless to consumers and competitors, but it is also said to help market participants avoid the concededly disruptive and often harmful effects of intense price rivalry.

In evaluating this claim in regard to price-fixing charges, several responses must be considered. No price is intrinsically reasonable, except by reference to its determination in a competitive market. The function of price is to allocate resources and production, and price-fixing distorts this market operation. Courts do not have the facilities for measuring marginal cost upon which a theoretically reasonable price would be based; in fact, one of the constant criticisms of the regulatory commissions is their inability to measure marginal cost accurately. Price reasonableness is necessarily an ever changing concept responsive to market and cost conditions. What is reasonable one day may not be the next. In order to prevent abuse of the reasonableness defense, then, courts would have to exercise daily supervision over business pricing.

Not only does this seem clearly undesirable from the businessman's point of view, but it is also beyond judicial competence. Finally, price-fixing agreements concentrate market power and impair the competitive process. Unless an overriding need is fulfilled by the arrangement, its effect is to destroy independent values worth preserving.

3. THE RISE OF THE PER SE APPROACH

Perhaps implicitly recognizing some of these problems, at least with regard to price-fixing, the Supreme Court dispelled at its next opportunity any notion that price-fixing could be tested by a reasonableness standard. In United States v. Trenton Potteries Co., 273 U.S. 392 (1927), the makers of 82 percent of toilets and other bathroom fixtures belonged to an association that had fixed the prices of sanitary pottery and had limited sales to "legitimate" jobbers. Since the court of appeals had reversed a criminal conviction on the ground that the jury had not been allowed to consider the reasonableness of the prices fixed by the defendants, the issue of whether reasonableness constituted a defense was squarely before the Court. Justice Stone's response seemed unequivocal:

The aim and result of every price-fixing agreement, if effective, is in the elimination of one form of competition. The power to fix prices, whether reasonably exercised or not, involves power to control the market and to fix arbitrary

and unreasonable prices. The reasonable price
fixed today may through economic and business
changes become the unreasonable price of to-
morrow. Once established, it may be maintained unchanged because of the absence of competition secured by the agreement for a price
reasonable when fixed. Agreements which create such potential power may well be held to be
in themselves unreasonable or unlawful restraints, without the necessity of minute inquiry
whether a particular price is reasonable or unreasonable as fixed and without placing on the
government in enforcing the Sherman Law the
burden of ascertaining from day to day whether
it has become unreasonable through the mere
variation of economic conditions. Moreover, in
the absence of express legislation requiring it, we
should hesitate to adopt a construction making
the difference between legal and illegal conduct
in the field of business relations depend upon so
uncertain a test as whether prices are reasonable—a determination which can be satisfactorily
made only after a complete survey of our economic organization and a choice between rival
philosophies.

Read literally, this analysis holds that proof of
the mere existence of a price-fixing agreement
establishes defendant's illegal purpose and that the
prosecution need demonstrate nothing further. It
need not show that the prices fixed are unreasonable, that the defendants had the power to impose

their wishes on the market, or that the agreement injured anyone (by causing them to pay supracompetitive prices). That is, the action of agreeing to fix prices is in itself (i.e., per se) illegal. The circumstances surrounding the action and the consequences flowing from it are irrelevant. On the other hand, defendants' control of 82 percent of the market was itself substantial evidence of market power (although the trial evidence in fact suggested that pricing discipline was weak and that exhortations not to sell at off-list prices were often unsuccessful); nor did the Court apparently doubt that the arrangement had an undesirable impact.

These implicit limitations on the holding in *Trenton Potteries* were seized upon by the Court only six years later when a price-fixing case was presented in the midst of the Great Depression. That economic catastrophe hit the coal industry particularly hard: between 1929 and 1933 prices of bituminous fell 25 percent while output declined by 38 percent. To cope with these conditions, 137 coal companies, who accounted for almost 75 percent of all production in the Appalachian region and 12 percent of national coal output, formed a new company which was to serve as the exclusive selling agent for member firms. The agency was instructed to get the "best prices obtainable" and if all output could not be sold, to allocate orders fairly among member firms. In effect it served as a sales cartel, but with far from complete control over the coal market. The government's challenge to the agency was successful before a three-judge district court which adhered closely to the principles set forth in *Trenton Potteries;* that is, the combination was designed to eliminate competition, and could not be interpreted as a "bona fide corporate organization resulting from normal growth and development."

Responding to the "deplorable" economic conditions of the coal industry and to the obvious need for reform and reorganization, the Supreme Court reversed the decision in Appalachian Coals, Inc. v. United States, 288 U.S. 344 (1933). It stated that the purpose of the Sherman Act was to prevent "undue" restraints on interstate commerce. Emphasizing the "essential standard of reasonableness," the Court called for "a close and objective scrutiny of particular conditions and purposes" in every case: "Realities must dominate the judgment. The mere fact that the parties to an agreement eliminate competition between themselves is not enough to condemn it." Starting from the premise that the proposed sales agency for marketing the members' coal production had no power either to fix or affect prices,[5] the Court accepted the defendants' argument that collaboration for legitimate purposes—such as distributing "distress" (i.e., odd-size) coal and preventing "pyramid" sales (i.e., multiple or fraudulent sales)—was law-

5. This aspect of the Court's analysis, which relied on the existence of competition from other powerful sellers and buyers of coal and on an allegedly inexhaustible supply, seems doubtful and probably would not be asserted by the Court today.

ful. It also accepted the defendant's professed intention of fostering "a better and more orderly" marketing system rather than a system restricting output. Finally, the Court held that the issue of legality ultimately rested on the likely effect of the agreement which had not yet been implemented; purpose or intention was not enough to condemn it.[6]

Despite the Court's efforts to paper over the differences, its decision in *Appalachian Coals* was an obvious departure from *Trenton Potteries* and the per se rule enunciated there. The question was which approach would prevail. Would *Appalachian Coals'* return to the rule of reason survive the Depression? That question was answered decisively—and negatively—in United States v. Socony Vacuum Oil Co., 310 U.S. 150 (1940) (*Madison Oil*) where the Court explicitly adopted a rigid per se rule condemning all price-fixing arrangements. *Madison Oil* is now the definitive case on the Sherman Act's application to price-fixing cartels.

In many respects the facts presented in *Madison Oil* were substantially similar to those before the Court in *Appalachian Coals*. The oil refining industry was depressed and independent producers faced panic market conditions. Decreased demand was aggravated by increased supplies of gasoline from new oil fields. Independent refiners had no

6. While the district court was to retain jurisdiction, it never reviewed the association's activities since Congress explicitly approved such marketing measures in several Depression statutes.

storage facilities and had been dumping gasoline in the Midwestern market at give-away prices.[7] In response a group of major refining companies agreed to buy surplus ("distress") gasoline from the independents, disposing of it in a more "orderly manner"—that is, so as not to depress prices. The mechanics of the arrangement required that each major firm be assigned one or more independents as a "dancing partner" whose surplus it would purchase. While the purchased gasoline eventually did reach the market, its effect on prices was thought to be less significant. By manipulating the relatively thin spot market, it was believed (by the Court) that the defendants had managed to keep gasoline prices above the level that competitive conditions in the industry would otherwise have brought about.

Although the major oil companies had not explicitly agreed on the price at which they would sell their oil, the Court had no difficulty finding that the purpose of the arrangement was to curtail competition and raise prices. Following the Depression precedent of *Appalachian Coals,* the defendants argued that their buying program served to stabilize the market; it was intended only to remedy "competitive evils." But the Court rejected this defense as having "no legal justifica-

7. Even in these post OPEC-cartel times, the trial record makes fascinating reading. The "supply of oil from this [East Texas] field was so great that at one time crude oil sank to 10 or 15 cents a barrel and gasoline was sold in the East Texas field for 2⅛¢ a gallon." Id. at 170–71.

tion"; the reasonableness of the fixed prices was
no defense. The thrust of the Sherman Act is
deeper:

> Any combination which tampers with price
> structures is engaged in an unlawful activity.
> Even though the members of the price-fixing
> group were in no position to control the market,
> to the extent that they raised, lowered, or stabi-
> lized prices they would be directly interfering
> with the free play of market forces. The Act
> places all such schemes beyond the pale and
> protects that vital part of our economy against
> any degree of interference. Congress has not
> left with us the determination of whether or not
> particular price-fixing schemes are wise or un-
> wise, healthy or destructive. . . .

> Under the Sherman Act a combination formed
> for the purpose and with the effect of raising,
> depressing, fixing, pegging, or stabilizing the
> price of a commodity in interstate or foreign
> commerce is illegal per se.

Even the limited aim of price stabilization—i.e., of
placing a floor under the market—was condemned
as illegal:

> market manipulation in its various manifesta-
> tions is implicitly an artificial stimulus applied
> to (or at times a brake on) market prices, a force
> which distorts those prices, a factor which pre-
> vents the determination of those prices by free
> competition alone.

FN 39 ~ THE PWR TO CONTROL

PRICES IS
NOT
NECESSARY
BUT TO
MORE
ILLEGAL
P.F.

Finally, in rejecting the argument that the defendants' market power was too limited to control prices, the Court, in its celebrated footnote 59, went so far as to indicate (in dicta) that effective power to implement the purpose was not a necessary element in proving illegal price-fixing; the offense is the illegal purpose as shown by the agreement. While the Court's language can be read as condemning any price-fixing agreement whether or not the parties could act so as to have any impact on prices, a more sensible reading does not deny a de minimus limitation. The concern expressed by critics of this footnote is more theoretical than practical. If the parties' actions can have no impact on prices, no reason would exist for them to agree to fix them. The aim of the Court's ruling is to condemn market-rigging arrangements having less than total domination or control over a market; the latter may also cause at least temporary injury and are not tolerated under the Sherman Act.

The standard of *Madison Oil* has withstood the test of time, and the Court has not retreated from its strict stance. In reviewing a similar stabilization plan under Section 5 of the FTC Act, in Virginia Excelsior Mills v. FTC, 256 F.2d 538, 541 (4th Cir.1958), the court of appeals observed: "What contrary suggestion may be found in Appalachian Coals, Inc. v. United States, . . . has not survived the strong and consistent course of subsequent decision." Note also that the rule of *Madis-*

on Oil condemns—at least in dicta—any price tampering.

Later cases applied this rule of per se illegality to maximum price-fixing, even though the potential public injury and economic rationale is distinct.[8] Kiefer-Stewart Co. v. Joseph E. Seagram & Sons, Inc., 340 U.S. 211 (1951); see Albrecht v. Herald Co., 390 U.S. 145 (1968) (vertical price fixing). The Supreme Court reaffirmed this approach in Arizona v. Maricopa County Medical Soc'y, 457 U.S. 332 (1982) when it struck down an agreement among physicians setting the maximum fees they would charge for their services.[9] There 70 percent of the medical practitioners in Maricopa County (which includes Phoenix) established a plan whereby they agreed not to charge patients more than a

8. The benefits from maximum price-fixing are: (a) consumers are protected from temporary exploitation; (b) public anti-inflation policy is served; (c) industry interests are served by increasing demand and reassuring buyers against price disruptions; and (d) they allow low-price sellers to identify themselves and are less costly ways for making low price agreements with buyers. Among the possible harms from forced price ceilings are (a) the parties may select an entry-discouraging price; (b) the agreement may be an implicit arrangement to forego additional service or quality improvements (c) the parties may be selecting some mechanism other than price for allocating short supplies; and (d) the price selected may in fact become the minimum and in any case be an occasion for discussing prices generally. See generally Easterbrook, *Maximum Price Fixing,* 48 U.Chi.L.Rev. 886 (1981). Even accepting this benefit-harm analysis, the legal issue is what explains any given maximum price agreement and whether courts can distinguish between harmful cartels and beneficial maximum price agreements.

9. See also Gerhart, *The Supreme Court and Antitrust Analysis: The (Near) Triumph of the Chicago School,* 1982 Sup.Ct. Rev. 319.

specified fee for identified services; several insurance companies in turn agreed to pay the full cost of these services provided by doctors participating in the plan; and the participating doctors were identified in a list provided consumers. The doctors argued that this agreement in fact reduced prices to consumers by lowering information search costs, that the participating insurance companies were acting in the consumers' interests, and that the medical profession met higher standards and should not be subject to the usual antitrust (per se) rule. These considerations were rejected by the Court. It believed that similar ends could be achieved without maximum price fixing and it feared the anticompetitive potential of price fixing; these concerns justified a rigorous rule without exceptions. However, the decision seems questionable. It seems unlikely that the insurers would have participated in a cartel since it was not in their interest to increase their costs or protect the physicians. The likely effect of the program seemed to be that it would lower consumer costs. And the application of a per se approach prevented consideration of the effect of the plan on prices or output.

[handwritten margin note: BuT see CLASS NOT... unless... PHYSICIANS were in control of assoc, in MARICOPA but not in HAHN]

Nor is it permissible in most instances for independent firms to enter into arrangements where the effect of the agreement on price is indirect. Thus, agreements to establish standard charges for check cashing or credit servicing, to change prices at the same time, or not to advertise prices are per se illegal. For example, in Catalano, Inc. v. Target Sales, Inc., 446 U.S. 643 (1980) (per curiam), the Court held that an agreement among beer distributors to eliminate free short-term credit on sales to retailers was "as plainly uncompetitive as a direct agreement to raise prices"—and hence was unlawful per se. Since extending interest-free credit is the equivalent of giving the retailers a discount equal to the value of the use of the purchase price for that time period, the credit terms were viewed as an inseparable part of the overall retail price. Similarly, in Plymouth Dealers' Ass'n of Northern California v. United States, 279 F.2d 128 (9th Cir. 1960), it was held illegal for competing new car dealers to agree upon a "list price" even though customers invariably bargained over the price and the defendants almost never sold cars at that price—and the agreement was in response to customer animosity over dealer pricing practices. The arrangement established an agreed upon starting price—that is, the agreement affected prices even though it did not fix them—which violated the airtight rule of *Madison Oil*. Finally, an agreement among buyers of a product, rather than among sellers, to reduce the durum wheat content of high quality macaroni violates the per se rule. Durum wheat was in short supply and the purpose of the agreement was to keep the price of wheat low. National Macaroni Mfrs. Ass'n v. FTC, 345 F.2d 421 (7th Cir.1965).

4. CURRENT DEVELOPMENTS

The formulation of the per se rule against price-fixing and the rigidity of its application have been subject to occasional question and analysis. By focusing almost exclusively on evidence of a conspiracy to fix prices, the law has made it relatively easy to prosecute unsuccessful cartels (where disgruntled participants are willing to testify against those who cheated or decided to leave the cartel) while providing no effective measure against cartels that have overcome the usual problems of finding an acceptable price, allocating sales quotas to the participants, or discouraging new entrants attracted by the cartel price. On the other hand, the per se rule also drives such cartels underground and makes it difficult for them to operate without the elaborate machinery necessary to prevent evasion by low cost participants with unused capacity. Thus the elimination of formal cartels from American industry has been called the single most important achievement of the antitrust laws. R. Posner, *Antitrust Law* 39 (1976). Of greater concern is the tendency to apply the rule of automatic illegality where price-fixing may be only ancillary to an otherwise desirable arrangement (e.g., vertical distribution). Although the Supreme Court has reiterated its long-standing rule prohibiting resale price agreements (see Continental T.V., Inc. v. GTE Sylvania Inc., 433 U.S. 36, 51 n. 18 (1977) discussed pp. 302–05 infra), it has provided clarification of both the per se and rule of reason

and their relationship to price agreements—in recent years.

As Professor Areeda has carefully explained, despite the clear division between per se and rule of
reason requirements, the Supreme Court's antitrust opinions cannot be neatly divided into two
categories. See 7 P. Areeda, *Antitrust Law* ¶ 1511
(1986). The per se rule is not so tightly drawn as
to permit no exceptions; for example, the price
fixing characterization can sometimes be avoided if
the arrangement increases efficiency even though
the conduct might ordinarily be viewed as price
fixing. Similarly, application of the rule of reason
may result in an arrangement being found illegal
on a limited record; it "does not always require
refined fact-finding or balancing." Five recent decisions illustrate this new-found flexibility in antitrust rules and, correspondingly, the difficulty of
predicting case outcomes.

(1) In National Soc'y of Professional Engineers v.
United States, 435 U.S. 679 (1978), the Court held
that a professional society's canon of ethics prohibiting competitive bidding among its members violated Section 1. In doing so, it rejected defendant's
claim that the restriction was justified "because
bidding on engineering services is inherently im-
precise, would lead to deceptively low bids, and
would thereby tempt individual engineers to do
inferior work with consequent risk to public safety
and health." But the Court did not apply the per
se rule even though the practice appeared to have

a direct price effect, partly because a learned profession was involved. (In Goldfarb v. Virginia State Bar, 421 U.S. 773, 788 n. 17 (1975), the Court had indicated that although covered by the antitrust laws the learned professions were subject to less rigorous rules.) Instead the Court engaged in a rule of reason analysis, which it said, required a balancing of the restraint's anticompetitive effects against its procompetitive aspects. Thus, in this instance, the Court rejected the professional group's justification as legally insufficient because that inquiry "is confined to a consideration of [the] impact [of the restraint] on competitive conditions," and the engineers' had not claimed that their ban on competitive bidding enhanced competition.

Read literally, as some lower courts have done,[10] the Court seemed to be taking away with one hand what it was granting with the other. That is, the Court's opinion could be read as narrowing the per se rule's application only to the most direct price-fixing agreements while more readily finding agreements not covered by the per se rule illegal under the rule of reason standard. Neither interpretation seems complete. As illustrated by the Court's per curiam decision in 1980 in *Catalano,* p. 185 supra, agreements such as those restricting credit terms, which are inseparable from prices, are still governed by the per se rule. Similarly,

10. See, e.g., Smith v. Pro Football, Inc., 593 F.2d 1173, 1186–87 (D.C.Cir.1978).

the Court in *Professional Engineers* specifically cited with approval the Third Circuit's decision in Tripoli Co. v. Wella Corp., 425 F.2d 932 (3d Cir.1970), cert. denied, 400 U.S. 831 (1970), that upheld marketing restraints related to the safety of a product, even though the restraints did not necessarily enhance competition, because they were ancillary to the seller's purpose of protecting public safety or itself from product liability.[11]

(2) This analysis, that redeeming factors can be weighed under the rule of reason, is further supported by the Court's action in Broadcast Music, Inc. v. Columbia Broadcasting System, Inc., 441 U.S. 1 (1979) (BMI). The facts of the case are not easily summarized; they depend on an understanding of the copyright as well as the antitrust laws. Since 1897 musical compositions have been protected by copyright laws which give owners the right to license the public performance of their works for

---

11. Dicta in *Catalano,* however, summarized *Professional Engineers* as applying a per se rule as follows: "an agreement among competing firms of professional engineers to refuse to discuss prices among potential customers until after negotiations have resulted in the initial selection of an engineer . . . was held unlawful without requiring further inquiry." While there is language in *Professional Engineers* possibly justifying this categorization, the Court's discussion there of the association's asserted justifications is meaningful only in the context of a rule of reason analysis. There are, in addition, other questionable statements in *Catalano*—e.g., its citation of Sugar Institute, Inc. v. United States, 297 U.S. 553 (1936), as a per se decision. The Court's characterization of *Professional Engineers* seems erroneous and perhaps should be attributed more to the fact that *Catalano* was a summary reversal drafted without benefit of briefs or oral argument on the merits than to a deliberate recasting of the rule of reason.

profit. However, in order to collect royalties the owners must enforce their rights and this can be difficult—it is easy for performers to use a copyrighted work and the performances can be frequent, fleeting and widespread. Individual composers are in fact seldom in a position to negotiate with performers or to sue against unauthorized use. As a consequence, since 1914 owners of musical compositions have been organized, first into the American Society of Composers, Authors, and Publishers (ASCAP), and since 1939 also in Broadcast Music, Inc. (BMI). These groups were subject to an earlier government antitrust action which was ultimately settled; under the subsequent court order, both ASCAP and BMI were authorized to grant blanket licenses for all works provided that they held only a nonexclusive license that would allow users the option of contracting directly with individual composers. The effect was that the two organizations acted as a license clearing house for their members. Those dealing with ASCAP or BMI were given a blanket license authorizing the user to perform the entire repertory without regard to the number of times the works were played. In return, the users paid a royalty measured either by a specified fee or by a percentage of the user's advertising revenues.

Deciding that the cost of its blanket contracts was rising unreasonably, CBS sought a license on a per use basis from both ASCAP and BMI. When they refused, it sued for violation of the Sherman

Act including price-fixing, and the sole issue before the Court was whether the blanket license arrangement was within the per se category. Again the Court opted for the rule of reason approach even though agreements among competitors regarding the terms on which they will deal with their customers are generally within the per se rule. The Court acknowledged that under the blanket license arrangement prices of differing compositions are melded into a single fee, but it contended that this method of pricing is not plainly anticompetitive or without substantial justification. In explaining why the rule of reason was to be applied here, the Court emphasized the Sherman Act's flexibility in responding to complex marketing situations:

> The Sherman Act has always been discriminatingly applied in light of economic realities. There are situations in which competitors have been permitted to form joint selling agencies or other pooled activities, subject to strict limitations under the antitrust laws to guarantee against abuse of the collective power thus created. . . . This case appears to us to involve such a situation. The extraordinary number of users, spread across the land, the ease with which a performance may be broadcast, the sheer volume of copyrighted compositions, the enormous quantity of separate performances each year, the impracticability of negotiating individual licenses for each composition, and the

ephemeral nature of each performance all combine to create unique market conditions for performance rights to recorded music.

Critical to the Court's choice between the per se and rule of reason standard was its conclusion that the marketing arrangements appeared to be reasonably necessary if the rights granted composers under the copyright laws were to be developed. The Court was also strongly affected by the defendants' use of this arrangement to achieve market integration and to gain related efficiencies negotiating for and monitoring the use of the compositions. The alternative of individual negotiation and enforcement was considered less desirable; it would be more costly and would delay the marketing of compositions and, in any case, was separately available to the plaintiff. The Court saw no reason to deny the composers this opportunity to maximize their return. One test under the rule of reason therefore seems to be whether the practice is primarily designed to increase economic efficiency—and, as a consequence, to make the market more competitive.

(3) In *NCAA v. University of Oklahoma*, 468 U.S. 85 (1984), the Court ruled that an agreement among NCAA colleges restricting the number of times each team's football games could be televised inhibited rather than enhanced competition, and thus violated Section 1 of the Sherman Act. Despite the horizontal price-fixing and output limiting aspects of the agreement, the per se rule was

considered inappropriate. In determining that the television agreement should be tested under a rule of reason, the Court relied on the fact that the "horizontal restraints on competition are essential if the product is to be available at all"; the NCAA is a joint venture that required some degree of collaboration if it was to succeed. The issue, therefore, was (1) whether the television plan—an exclusive, joint marketing arrangement—for college football's existence was necessary (it was not, contrast *BMI*); (2) whether college game attendance would suffer if the plan were unavailable (this was ruled an invalid defense since it was based on the unreasonableness of competition, compare *Professional Engineers*); (3) and whether the plan was needed to preserve competitive balance (again, this argument was rejected because it was not related to a neutral standard, any readily identifiable group of competitors, or the television plan). The Court therefore concluded the lower court's findings were correct and that the plan was anticompetitive.

The *NCAA* opinion reinforced the view first established in *BMI* that competitor collaboration can be procompetitive and thus should not be summarily rejected (as once was the case, see United States v. Topco Assoc., Inc., 405 U.S. 596, 608 (1972) (discussed pp. 206–11 infra)) by simply labeling the arrangement a horizontal restraint subject to per se prohibition. This view seems a distinct and important advance in antitrust analysis. The difficulty with *NCAA* is that the Court quickly deviated from this approach. For example, the Court said that proof of market power is not necessary for finding liability under the rule of reason ("the absence of market power does not justify a naked restriction on price or output"), a comment that reveals but does not answer several puzzles. Does it mean that a naked restraint (in contrast to the NCAA's television plan) is tested by a rule of reason inquiry and presumably an efficiency defense? Similarly, the Court's statement that the "essential inquiry . . . is whether or not the challenged restraint enhances competition" can hardly mean what it says, namely, that defendants must now prove that their conduct is procompetitive. Repeating the statement in *Professional Engineers* that only the effect on competition is relevant under a rule of reason inquiry, the Court again failed to give content to "competition" in this context.

(4) In Copperweld Corp. v. Independence Tube Corp., 467 U.S. 752 (1984), the Court expressly overruled the intra-enterprise conspiracy doctrine and held that a parent and its wholly owned subsidiary could not be "conspiring entities" under the Sherman Act. Recognizing that the prior doctrine elevated form over substance, the Court relied on the fact that the parent and sub were one economic actor and that a firm cannot enhance its market power by separately incorporating a division. Probably the major surprise of the decision is that

only five members of the Court joined the opinion; one did not participate and three dissented. More important, however, was the fact that a clear majority adopted a consumer welfare approach to antitrust that accepts collaboration where output will not be restricted or prices increased.

(5) Finally, in Monsanto Co. v. Spray-Rite Service Corp., 465 U.S. 752 (1984) (discussed p. 307 infra), the Court ruled that vertical price fixing cannot be inferred simply from the existence of dealer complaints to their manufacturer about prices or even from constant communication between dealers and manufacturers about price. The lower court's per se approach of inferring an agreement from a termination in response to price complaints was rejected. Instead, the Court ruled (and found) "evidence that tends to exclude the possibility that the manufacturer and nonterminated distributors were acting independently." The *Monsanto* Court thus continued its movement away from the labeling approach in antitrust. Rather, the focus is to be on economic and efficiency considerations.

These cases reflect the increasing importance of the rule of reason in antitrust analysis. In these and other opinions,[12] the Court is clearly limiting

12. This description of five cases is selective. Others should be included in a complete analysis. See also Jefferson Parish Hosp. Dist. No. 2 v. Hyde, 466 U.S. 2 (1984) (discussed pp. 326–27 infra); Northwest Wholesale Stationers, Inc. v. Pacific Stationery and Printing Co., 105 S.Ct. 2613 (1985) (discussed pp. 224–25 infra).

the scope of the per se rule "through expansion of the characterization process, through contraction of the sorts of conduct to which [the per se rule applies], and through refinements of the alternative approach, the rule of reason." Hutchinson, *Antitrust 1984: Five Decisions in Search of a Theory*, 1984 Sup.Ct.Rev. 69, 143. But a clean break with the old language and the per se/rule of reason characterization process of antitrust has yet to occur. Whether the old dichotomy between the rule of reason and per se rule still exists much less is helpful to analysis seems increasingly doubtful. It seems possible but perhaps not probable that the Court will consider abandoning the per se category altogether, thus focusing on the likely economic effect of the particular arrangement. The effect of such a move would require greater concentration on the ambiguous meanings of "competition" and "efficiency" when applying the rule of reason. But this is not the Court's approach in the mid-1980's. The Supreme Court's current division has given particular importance to the views of Justice John Paul Stevens, and they have proven especially difficult to reconcile.

C. A COMMENT ON THE PER SE AND RULE OF REASON APPROACHES

The adoption of a per se test of illegality for price-fixing agreements, and its subsequent application to other market-rigging arrangements focuses attention on the use of per se rules as an enforcement device. Until the recent swing away from per se rules, it was not uncommon for antitrust courts to adopt rules for automatically condemning certain practices after first studying them under the rule of reason. As the courts became familiar with a particular practice, its purposes and effects, they were in a better position to determine whether the practice fit within a range of legitimate business efforts and promoted competitive rivalry, or whether its primary thrust and likely effect was anticompetitive. Once convinced that the particular scheme was unlikely to have any redeeming features, the courts quickly moved toward a per se prohibition.

Justif's for the per se rule

This process is undoubtedly affected by the advantages and limitations of each approach. One justification for a per se approach is its advantage of clear prohibition. The temptation to fix prices is strong (since the rewards—at least in the short-run—can be very large); if its legality is in doubt or it might be justified, many will undoubtedly test the outer boundaries of permissible conduct in the expectation or hope of either going unapprehended or of being able to explain the result as reasonable. Per se rules not only warn businesses in advance that a practice is prohibited, but they also encourage them from unnecessarily retesting the issue. Law enforcement is, as a consequence, more efficient. And since the defendants would enjoy the benefits of the practice until it was detected and they were convicted, a clear line often seems a necessity.

These contentions are not without counter-arguments. By drawing bright-line prohibitions, courts are also advising businesses how close to the line of illegality they may safely tread—that is, before the conduct is illegal per se; conduct not within the reach of the per se rule is still measured under the rule of reason, however. More serious is the concern that in the process of labeling a particular arrangement automatically illegal, some useful (i.e., efficiency enhancing) activities will be condemned. As *BMI* illustrates, even price-fixing agreements may serve necessary and beneficial purposes. Do we really want to prohibit joint drilling ventures by oil companies in expensive explorations for new sources merely because the price of any discovered oil will be fixed by two or more firms; or, what of the products of joint research laboratories which individual firms could not sponsor? If the rule reaches such activities, the cost of a per se test may be too high. The pressure inevitably, then, is either to define per se illegality narrowly or to find exceptions or limitations to its application. But at some point, of course, whatever advantages are offered by a per se approach then may dissipate.

In light of the Sherman Act's criminal penalties and of private treble damage claims for antitrust violations, one can also question the need for per se rules as a deterrent; but such arguments are difficult to evaluate. Perhaps more worrisome is whether criminal penalties should apply to per se rules or, stated alternatively, should per se rules ever apply to criminal statutes.

One final point in the rationale for per se rules is that their ultimate justification rests on the savings they offer for trials and law enforcement. If the courts are convinced that price-fixing is never reasonable or justified, evidence of either reasonableness or justifiability wastes judicial time and burdens the court system unnecessarily. Moreover, courts are saved from the quagmire of evaluating conflicting economic claims by per se rules; evidence of reasonableness or effect is superfluous. On the other hand, fairness and justice normally command that one charged with causing harm have an opportunity to show that such harm has not (or will not) occur—in fact it is usually the state's obligation to show that some harm has occurred. Moreover, judicial difficulty in evaluating the evidence is little excuse. It merely makes the case more pressing for competent tribunals knowledgeable in economics as well as law. Whatever time and effort are required, within tolerable limits, is generally thought to be one of the necessary costs of decency and civilization.

The ultimate balance obviously depends on the soundness of the policy implemented by a per se rule. Horizontal price-fixing, where the primary purpose is to restrict output and to raise price, seems a sensible candidate. As more is learned about transaction economics, however, this support of the per se approach is fading. Vertical arrangements disturbing only intraband competition, on the other hand, seem clearly better suited to a rule of reason standard. (See Chapter 8.)

Considerable controversy has also surrounded the procedural impact of a per se rule. Does it merely satisfy plaintiff's obligation to prove competitive injury by presuming an illegal effect (once a purpose to fix prices is shown), or is the presumption conclusive thus denying the defendant the opportunity to show justification. A quick review suggests that where there is clear evidence of a price-fixing purpose, as in *Madison Oil*, the presumption is conclusive. But where the purpose is less evident, as in *Chicago Board of Trade*, the courts have also considered the parties' alleged purpose, power and effect. Such a test, however, merely identifies the limits of a per se rule on price-fixing, not its procedural impact. *The Attorney General's National Committee to Study the Antitrust Laws* attempted, in 1954, to reconcile the seemingly conflicting cases by distinguishing cases involving direct price-fixing activities from those where the agreement relates instead to the processes of price formation. With respect to direct price-fixing, the practice could not be justified, according to the Committee; however, the illegality of agreements only affecting price formation depended on the significance of the competition eliminated in comparison with any other purposes or effects of

the challenged practices. Others have suggested
that the per se rule creates only a rebuttable
presumption.

In any event, neither approach is consistent with
the case law. That is to say, practices which
merely affect price formation are sometimes held
to be illegal per se, permitting no explanation,
whereas other courts examining agreements seemingly intent only on fixing prices have also examined possible justifications. Judge Robert Bork
has persuasively demonstrated that the case law is
not reconcilable, that there are in fact two principal lines of decision. Bork, *The Rule of Reason
and the Per Se Concept: Price Fixing and Market
Division,* 74 Yale L.J. 775 (1965); 75 id. 373 (1966).
One he terms the "main tradition," the other he
labels the "Brandeis tradition." Whether the presumptive or conclusive illegality approach is taken
under the per se rule depends upon the views
which particular Supreme Court justices have of
the ultimate purposes and values which the antitrust laws are to implement. This analysis, however, makes no attempt to produce a clear statement
of current law.

What all this adds up to, then, is that the application of a label of per se illegality to particular
conduct may or may not deny a defendant an
opportunity to justify the practice and demonstrate
that its effect is likely to be beneficial. (Where
price-fixing is found, the usual result now is to
allow no justification; on the other hand, justifica-

tion is invariably submitted by the defendant in seeking to explain the agreement's legitimate purposes.) At the least, the burden will be on the defendant, and the courts will view such justification skeptically.

D. MARKET ALLOCATIONS AND PRODUCTION CONTROLS

Prices can be controlled not only by direct price-fixing agreements, but also indirectly by agreements among firms not to compete with one another. Withdrawing supplies from a market has the effect of moving the supply curve to the left, which raises the equilibrium price:

FIGURE 10: RESTRICTING OUTPUT

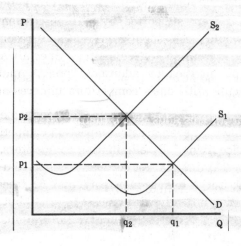

That is, if company Able withdraws from a market, available supply is reduced and the supply curve will move from S_1 to S_2. Without a change in demand, equilibrium will be achieved by an increase in price from p_1 to p_2.

Agreements to divide markets take many forms. Firms may agree to allocate markets geographically, for example, one serving the North and the other the South. Or they may agree to assign customers functionally by class (one serving wholesalers and the other retailers) or technically by type of product (e.g., home and professional movie or stereo equipment). Such agreements are invariably justified on the grounds they permit more efficient production and marketing. Production facilities can be concentrated and scale economies supported; distribution costs can be reduced and transportation limited. The flaw in the argument for "more rational" organization of production is that if it were supported by market efficiencies, firms would seek such gains without resort to market allocation agreements. Specialization would be justified by additional profits, making agreements with one's competitors unnecessary.

Market division agreements may in some respects have an even greater impact on competition than price-fixing. By eliminating competitors, the single remaining market occupant—albeit in a limited territory—has a monopoly and is freed of competition not only with respect to prices but also with respect to service, quality, innovation, etc.

Moreover, market allocation arrangements may not have to resolve the same internal divisions between different cost producers which frequently cause price agreements to crumble. On the other hand, the disputes likely to limit the scope and term of price-fixing agreements also face firms seeking to allocate markets. If the remaining firm sets the price above marginal cost, new entrants are invited; if the latter are immediately "co-opted" by inclusion in the market sharing, then the same spoils must be further subdivided, making the arrangements less attractive.

In general, courts have treated horizontal market division arrangements as they have price-fixing. The rule has its origins in *Addyston Pipe*, p. 167 supra, where the defendants agreed not to compete with each other in various areas and devised an elaborate system of allocating business among participants. While the court in *Addyston Pipe* seemingly would have condemned the market allocation agreement alone, the significance of its condemnation of the defendants' market division was diminished because the lion's share of the court's attention was directed toward the price-fixing aspects of the plan. Moreover, in National Ass'n of Window Glass Mfrs. v. United States, 263 U.S. 403 (1923), the Court upheld a production control agreement whereby all manufacturers of handblown window glass agreed to operate only one-half of the year because of a labor shortage. It ruled, by Justice Holmes, that the pact's legality depended on the particular facts, and here the agreement "to meet the short supply of men" was not a combination in unreasonable restraint of trade.

Thus it was not until Timken Roller Bearing Co. v. United States, 341 U.S. 593 (1951), that a division of markets among competitors was directly ruled unlawful. There the Court condemned an allocation of territories throughout worldwide markets between the dominant American producer of tapered roller bearings and British and French firms (the latter controlled by Timken and its British competitor). However, the reach of this holding, and whether a per se or rule of reason approach was being applied, remained in doubt. The power of the parties and the effect of the agreement on output and price was evident; thus the arrangement could not have survived under either the per se or rule of reason test. Moreover, the defendants were also convicted of having fixed prices, and in finding the arrangement illegal, the Court elliptically said: "Our prior decisions plainly establish that agreements providing for an aggregation of trade restraints such as those existing in this case are illegal under the Act." This comment left unanswered the question of whether market allocations alone, without price-fixing, were per se illegal.

The next case to reach the Supreme Court, United States v. Sealy, Inc., 388 U.S. 350 (1967), moved closer to a per se rule for horizontal market division but still did not fully resolve the question of how such arrangements were to be assessed. There several mattress manufacturers formed a joint company which developed the Sealy trademark and advertised mattresses sold under its label regionally and nationally. The "parent" Sealy company licensed each of the shareholder-manufacturers to make and sell mattresses under the Sealy label. Each was also assigned an exclusive territory and told the retail price at which it could sell the Sealy brand mattresses. After trial the lower court held the price-fixing illegal but rejected the government's charge that the market division was unreasonable. Thus, on appeal the issue before the Supreme Court was the legality of the territorial allocation. The Court reversed the trial court, holding the arrangement did not warrant a rule of reason inquiry (i.e., it was apparently per se unlawful). Again, however, the Court did not rely solely on the effect of the market division on competition; instead it followed the approach taken in *Timken* of looking at the "aggregation of trade restraints"—here the price fixing in addition to the market division—even though the price-fixing was separately condemned.

Whatever question remained of the legal rule applicable under the Sherman Act to horizontal territorial restraints was finally eliminated in United States v. Topco Associates, Inc., 405 U.S. 596 (1972), where the Court explicitly ruled that market allocations are per se illegal whether or not ancillary to price-fixing or other market-rigging arrangements. The facts in *Topco* were similar to those in *Sealy* except for the absence of any price fixing. (*Topco* was also similar to a hypothetical case posed in *Sealy* where the Court suggested that small grocers might be allowed to allocate territories in order to band together under a common name and common advertisements.) Specifically, in *Topco* a group of small- and medium-sized supermarket chains with 6 percent of the market created a joint subsidiary to market private label (house brand) products through their stores in competition with the larger supermarket chains such as A & P and Safeway. The latter each had their own branded goods and the Topco participants were generally too small to market private label goods on their own. The joint venture to market goods under a private label was not challenged. (See also p. 248 infra.) What condemned the arrangement, according to the Court, was its provision for dividing markets on the sale of Topco branded goods.

In reaching this result and applying a per se rule, the Court specifically rejected the lower court's analysis that the defendant supermarkets lacked market power, that the arrangement did not reduce competition among them or in the market, and that the restrictions were necessary for the joint venture to succeed. These it said were arguments for Congress, not the courts which are ill-equipped to measure whether constraints on competition in one area are overcome by improvements in competition elsewhere. Since the market division necessarily eliminated competition among sellers of Topco private label products, the agreement restrained competition and was per se illegal.

Although sometimes defended as a necessary response to overly restrictive marketing arrangements, *Sealy* and *Topco* are also strongly criticized for (a) ignoring the fact that since they were without market power the participants could not have limited output or affected competition and price, and (b) failing to evaluate the economic necessity of and benefit to competition from the arrangement. Since both analyses have substantial economic support—and are consistent with the Court's 1977 decision in *Sylvania* (discussed p. 302 infra)[13]—they deserve closer analysis.

The first argument on market power is simply that the division of territorial markets among firms selling a branded product in competition with other products cannot adversely affect competition or consumers unless one brand has substantial market power and interbrand competition is as a consequence adversely affected. That is, an agreement dividing territories among those holding only 6 percent of sales (as in *Topco*) generally cannot force the seller of the other 94 percent to follow its prices, quality or service. While un-

13. Judge Posner once speculated that *Sylvania* overrules *Topco*. Posner, *The Next Step in the Antitrust Treatment of Restricted Distribution: Per Se Legality,* 48 U.Chi.L.Rev. 6, 25 (1981); accord Rothery Storage & Van Co. v. Atlas Van Lines, Inc., 792 F.2d 210 (D.C.Cir.1986) (Bork, J.).

doubtedly correct, this argument could also be made against the *Madison Oil* per se price-fixing rule, at least as it was extended in footnote 59 to situations where there is no evidence that the cartel participants have market power. See p. 182 supra.

There is a distinction in the territorial division cases (probably not as prevalent in the price-fixing cases), however, and it moves us to the second argument, namely the *justification* for the territorial allocation. The concern of both the Sealy and Topco licensees was that without the protection of exclusive territories, the retail participants would not be willing to promote the product, provide customer service or otherwise engage in activities designed to penetrate the market. They would be afraid that sellers of Sealy mattresses or Topco labels in adjoining areas would seek a "free ride" on the advertising or service promises of a direct competitor and, not having incurred the advertising or other cost, would thereby be able to undercut the price. Thus, the exclusive territory here is arguably a necessary component for the success of the Sealy mattress or Topco private label ventures. If denied them, competition would suffer from the loss or reduced vigor of the Sealy or Topco enterprises. (Note the similarity of this argument in *BMI* and *NCAA* that competition collaboration was an "essential element" of the product or service being marketed.)

Another ground of criticism, stated most forcefully by Professor Wesley Liebler, *Book Review,* 66

Calif.L.Rev. 1317, 1333–40 (1978), is that the Court mischaracterized the arrangement in *Sealy* (and possibly in *Topco*) as horizontal interbrand restraints subject to a per se rule, when in point of fact they only constituted an agreement within a "firm," with the latter defined as an organization promoting one brand or product in competition with other like products. Sealy mattresses and Topco label products are in direct competition with other branded mattresses or food products. Where one firm integrates vertically or allocates territories among its distributors, the courts now permit such practices subject to a rule of reason test. See pp. 302–05 infra. Alternatively, if several firms engage in a joint venture, a similar rule of reason approach is taken. Thus as Professor Liebler notes, the semantic distinction between horizontal or vertical agreements or the title attached to the arrangement should be wholly irrelevant. What counts is whether the participants have the power to restrict output and thereby to restrain trade— i.e., can they act like a monopolist or a cartel. If the arrangement affects several products in competition with each other or has interbrand effects, then the horizontal rules of per se illegality have greater justification. Even here it can be argued that without power to alter output and prices, the agreement should not be condemned out of hand. However, in that circumstance the potential harm likely to flow from a horizontal market allocation may be so substantial and the likely benefits so small that a per se rule may be appropriate. Where only intrabrand competition is affected, by contrast, the arrangement will usually be unable to hinder competition and will probably produce marketing efficiencies or other benefits. Therefore a rule of reason approach seems more consistent with consumer welfare where the agreements affect only one product.

The current legal status of market allocations is uncertain. That the law has changed since *Sealy* and *Topco* is clear. Perhaps illustrative of that movement is the FTC's split decision approving a consent settlement that allowed the *GM-Toyota* joint venture. General Motors Corp., 48 Fed.Reg. 57,314 (1983) (statement of Chairman Miller and Commissioners Douglas and Calvani); id. at 57,252 & 57,254 (dissenting statements of Commissioners Pertschuk and Bailey). It permitted GM, the U.S. and world's largest seller of passenger cars, to form a joint venture with Toyota, the third largest seller of passenger cars world-wide, the largest foreign seller in the U.S., and the fourth largest seller in the U.S. Under the agreement, the venture would manufacture between 200,000 to 250,000 subcompacts at an idle GM plant in California; the price was to be set by the parent companies. The consent decree limited the agreement to 12 years and otherwise sought to keep the parents competitive. In accepting this arrangement, the Commission majority emphasized its procompetitive features, especially the opportunity for GM to learn about more efficient Japanese manufacturing and management methods.[14]

E. BOYCOTTS

The evolution of a per se rule, the limits of its application, and the return to a rule of reason approach (at least in fact if not in name), are probably most clearly illustrated in the judicial treatment of exclusionary agreements through which several competing firms agree to deal with or to isolate another firm. In contrast to cartel arrangements, where all competitors voluntarily join together to fix prices (and share monopoly rewards), etc., concerted refusals to deal usually involve only some of the firms competing with each other within a market. These collaborators band together to gain market power at the expense of other competitors—destroying or coercing their competitors. Such organized refusals to deal with a particular firm are usually given the pejorative label of boycotts.

1. PURPOSES AND ECONOMIC EFFECTS

Group refusals to deal with a competing firm, or decisions to boycott it, serve a variety of objectives. One obvious and perhaps not infrequent purpose is

14. For a very different FTC approach to joint ventures, as an illegal market division, see Yamaha Motor Co. v. FTC, 657 F.2d 971 (8th Cir.1981), cert. denied, 456 U.S. 915 (1982). See also pp. 248–57.

the elimination or disciplining of troublesome competitors. Boycotts may, for example, be used to police a price-fixing agreement. More generally, they can be used to punish maverick price cutters or others not adhering to industry custom. If concerted refusals to deal were only designed to increase the group's profits, there is little question that all boycotts would be condemned by a simple per se approach under Section 1 of the Sherman Act.

But not all refusals to deal can be classified so simply. They are sometimes designed to serve economic efficiency or to advance the group's general economic self-interest without being aimed at adversely affecting any other group's profits, or even to advance social and moral objectives unrelated to the group's business or economic interests. For example, all used car dealers in a city might band together to form a trade association for the purpose of improving trading practices and their members' public image. The dealers could agree, under the association's sponsorship, to abstain from the use of deceptive advertising, reliance on pressure sales tactics, or, for that matter, dealing with firms polluting the atmosphere, wasting energy, or discriminating against minorities and women. Failure to abide by the terms of the agreement could be sanctioned by expulsion from the association and denial of its "fair dealer" seal of approval. Since the group is open to all used car dealers (and the sanction of expulsion may in fact inflict no economic penalty), its primary aim is not to punish nonparticipants. The reforming of advertising and sales practices, instead, promotes the group's overall economic interest, not its immediate profits. Punishing polluters and racial bigots is unlikely to improve the group's profits or its general economic interest.

Because group exclusionary tactics have different purposes and because some are not inconsistent with public policy, it is not clear whether the Sherman Act should condemn them under a uniform standard. It would seem necessary, at least initially, to evaluate their economic impact beyond the advantage they create for the group engaged in the boycott.

The primary economic effects of a "successful" concerted refusal to deal designed to keep others out or to inhibit their directly competing efforts lie in three directions: (1) injury to the intended victim of the boycott; (2) injury to competition by forcing the victim to accept the boycott terms—and thereby reducing its competitive vigor—or by forcing the victim out of business; and (3) injury to innocent neutrals caught in the middle of a secondary boycott.

These effects are not necessarily dependent on the purpose of the boycott. Whatever the group's objective, the boycott, if successful, may force the intended victim out of business; not only is injury to the victim then complete but competition may also be impaired by the elimination of a significant firm—especially if entry into the field is limited. Alternatively, a successful boycott may extract the victim's acquiescence. Then, at least for some boycotts, the result will be to lessen the primary victim's competitive rivalry. And regardless of the group's goals, secondary boycotts impair the competitive vigor of the innocent neutral. If the neutral business accedes to the boycott demands (because of the superior economic power of the group) it must forego the business of the intended victim, the alternative being to accept the loss of the business of the members of the boycotting group. In either case the neutral's business is likely to be reduced and its rivalry restricted.

As this analysis suggests, the legality of group boycotts under the Sherman Act may depend upon an evaluation of the potential benefits from the concerted refusal to deal with the firms and whether these outweigh—or should be considered against—the economic and other harms likely to result.

2. THE LEGAL STANDARD

The case law intuitively reflects these stresses. As a result, the legal test applicable to boycotts is still far from clear, although it is still commonly said that such arrangements are judged solely by a per se rule. A more accurate appraisal is that where the boycotters possess market power or exclusive access and the boycott is directly aimed at limiting or excluding competitors, it is subject to per se treatment; otherwise concerted refusals to deal are tested under a rule of reason approach. Today most concerted refusals to deal with a firm reflect mixed motives. Where more than one objective can be inferred, the legal test will depend on which purpose predominates—except that even if a rule of reason is applied, the arrangement will be subjected to strict scrutiny. Thus, one commentator has concluded that the Supreme Court's condemnation of group boycotts or concerted refusals to deal is limited to "naked horizontal agreements by which competing buyers or sellers adopt a common policy toward one or more suppliers or customers." Havighurst, *Doctors and Hospitals: An Antitrust Perspective on Traditional Relationships,* 1984 Duke L.J. 1071, 1104–05. Competitor controlled entities serving legitimate purposes, on the other hand, are treated under a rule of reason standard where actual effects on competition are closely examined.

The early cases dealing with boycotts revealed no clear line of decision. In Eastern States Retail Lumber Dealers' Ass'n v. United States, 234 U.S. 600 (1914), the Court easily invalidated an implied agreement by retailers to boycott direct-selling suppliers. This appeared to be a simple arrangement whose sole aim was the exclusion of competing wholesalers from the retail market. The retailers' argument that the direct selling wholesalers were infringing on their "exclusive right to trade" was rightly dismissed; these retailers had no license to control the retail market. At this early stage, the Court did not focus on whether all boycotts were bad or only those without reasonable justification. Nor was consideration given to whether the defendant retailers had market power or were simply defending themselves against free-riding interlopers.

Instead, the gravamen of the violation appeared to be the defendants' act of agreeing to coerce the wholesalers to leave the retail market, an analysis apparently borrowed from the labor boycott conspiracy cases then in the forefront of business regulation.

On the other hand, organized distribution of information about a firm or its orders, as a means of curbing abusive business conduct, was upheld in other cases. E.g., Cement Mfrs. Protective Ass'n v. United States, 268 U.S. 588 (1925). It seemed here that a boycott, if reasonably focused to gain legitimate ends such as preventing cement buyers from placing fraudulent orders, would be upheld. But in other cases the Court rejected agreements seeking to promote standard contracts with arbitration clauses or security provisions. United States v. First Nat. Pictures, Inc., 282 U.S. 44 (1930). In Paramount Famous Lasky Corp. v. United States, 282 U.S. 30 (1930), for example, the Court rejected as irrelevant the industry's claim that the clause in this agreement (no dealing with noncomplying firm exhibitors) and its enforcement were necessary to protect the industry against undesirable practices: "It may be that arbitration is well adapted to the needs of the motion picture industry; but when under the guise of arbitration parties enter into unusual arrangements which unreasonably suppress normal competition their action becomes illegal." Any indication that a rule of reason was being applied was countered by a subsequent sentence (quoting from an earlier decision): "The law is its own measure of right and wrong, of what it permits, or forbids, and the judgment of the courts cannot be set up against it in a supposed accommodation of its policy with the good intention of parties, and it may be, of some good results." These cases are reconcilable if one follows the purposes and effects of the arrangement. That is: those agreements designed to stifle competition were condemned as illegal without consideration of their benefits or justifications; those not aimed at suppressing lawful competition or merely ancillary to a legitimate purpose were evaluated as in *Cement Mfrs. Protective Ass'n* by balancing the benefits against the harm.

This framework does not answer all questions. For example, in Fashion Originators' Guild of America, Inc. v. FTC, 312 U.S. 457 (1941) (*FOGA*), the Court was faced with a boycott whose aim was to eliminate troublesome competitors, enhance the group's general economic interests, and promote compliance with common law (and state) standards of business conduct. Manufacturers of women's garments who claimed to be creators of original dress designs sought to stop "style piracy"—the practice by other manufacturers of copying their designs and selling these copies at much lower prices. To stop this practice the members of the Guild agreed that they would refuse to sell to retailers who also sold garments copied from a Guild member's designs. Thus, on the one hand, the members' aim was to stop an allegedly illegal or tortious act (the copying of original designs); however, the Guild was taking the law into its own hands and, in the process, excluding rivals from the market. The Supreme Court declared that the Guild agreement was an "unfair method of competition" proscribed by the FTC Act, and that it also constituted an offense under the Sherman Act. Concerted action by a powerful combination could not be justified, according to the Court, and the Trade Commission therefore was correct in not hearing evidence of the evils of style piracy or of the illegality of the copying practice under state law.

FOGA has been read as applying a per se test to group boycotts. However, a close reading of the Court's opinion suggests that a narrow rule of reason (or limited per se) approach was adopted. The Court considered the group's power (its market share) and the purpose for its organization (not public protection but self-interest as revealed by its restraints on advertising, regulation of sale days, limits on allowable discounts, etc.). It also noted the availability of a less restrictive alternative, namely relying on civil tort actions. What appeared to disturb the Court, and therefore may be the ultimate basis for its decision, was the elaborate private government which the defendants had established to police the agreement. This power could readily be used as a vehicle to implement a boycott excluding lawful competitors. The social purpose of limiting style piracy appeared to be heavily outweighed by the dangers of an extralegal guild government.

Next, in Klor's Inc. v. Broadway-Hale Stores, Inc., 359 U.S. 207 (1959), the Court appeared to edge closer to a per se approach. Plaintiff, a San Francisco appliance store, alleged that the defendant department store chain had used its buying power to coerce ten national appliance manufacturers and their distributors from selling appliances to the plaintiff. Not denying the allegations, the defendants moved for summary judgment arguing that there had been no public wrong—that the Sherman Act protects competition not competitors; the defendants' affidavits showed that the boycott had no apparent effect on competition in the consumer retail appliance market. Finding sufficient public injury for Sherman Act liability the Court rejected the defendants' contentions and stated: "Group boycotts, or concerted refusals by traders to deal with other traders, have long been held to be in the forbidden [per se] category."

Despite this explicit confirmation that boycotts are illegal per se, a close reading of the basic case again suggests a more limited analysis. Since the defendants in *Klor's* offered no justification for their conduct, one can read the case as involving only a summary rule of reason approach: the harms are substantial; no benefits are asserted; there is a less restrictive alternative (of individual refusals to deal as approved in *Colgate,* see p. 308 infra).[15] In this vein, a subsequent case involving exclusionary conduct acknowledged that boycott-type action would be illegal per se "absent any justification derived from the policy of another statute or *otherwise.*" Silver v. New York Stock Exchange, 373 U.S. 341, 348–49 (1963) (dicta). A strict per se approach would not permit such "other" justification. These exceptions have led some commentators to refer to the "soft per se rule" applicable to boycotts as distinguished from the more rigid rule applicable to price-fixing.

On the other hand, the Court in *Silver* held that the exchange had violated the Sherman Act because it excluded a broker from access to its facilities despite the absence of any evidence that the plaintiff-broker's exclusion was designed to or would injure competition. The Court did not consider, for example, whether the exclusion was in retaliation for undercutting prescribed commission rates. It was enough that access had been denied

---

15. In addition, the ruling in *Klor's* was aimed at boycotts promoting group profits. A footnote to the opinion (359 U.S. at 213 n. 7) specifically indicated that the Sherman Act "is aimed primarily at combinations having commercial objectives and is applied only to a very limited extent to organizations, like labor unions, which normally have other objectives."

without a hearing. The case thus can fairly be read as imposing a rigorous per se rule. It is similar to *FOGA* in another regard, namely its hostility to private government action and the use of such uncontrolled power to discipline competitors (although here governance by the exchange was specifically authorized in the 1934 Securities Exchange Act). The anomalous result, in any case, is that a legal cartel (the New York Stock Exchange) was held to have a legal duty under the antitrust laws to accord its members due process hearing rights. Another case which also supports this alternative, more rigid reading of the Sherman Act rule on boycotts is United States v. General Motors Corp., 384 U.S. 127 (1966). There the Court held that action by a group of automobile dealers encouraging GM to stop further sales to a discount outlet was a "classic conspiracy" amounting to a group boycott and therefore per se unlawful.

Although this view of the Sherman Act, that boycotts are suspect and generally subject to a per se rule, draws support from those otherwise holding contrary views on antitrust,[16] substantial criticism has been made of the condemnation of concerted refusals to deal in the boycott cases. The main criticism has been directed at *FOGA* and *Klor's* since on closer analysis neither boycotting group of defendants seems likely to have restricted output or adversely affected competition. In

---

16. Compare R. Posner, *Antitrust Law* 208–10 (1976), with L. Sullivan, *Antitrust* §§ 83–92 (1977).

FOGA there were 176 participating original design manufacturers in the guild. They continued to compete with each other and, in addition, faced strong competition. Moreover there were legitimate reasons for their conduct. Judge Bork, for example, has argued that the guild members were probably trying to prevent copiers of their original designs from getting a free ride on the product information made available by retailers to their consumers. That is, by forcing retailers to deal exclusively with only the original products, they were preventing the copiers from getting the advantage of the promotional efforts of these retailers. Another, and similar explanation, offered by Professor Liebler, which builds on Bork's theory and the argument made by FOGA in the Supreme Court, is that the designers of original dresses were merely seeking to protect an investment in their dress designs by making it more costly for others to copy their ideas and sell pirated goods. Liebler, "Integration and Competition," in *Vertical Integration in the Oil Industry* 14–15 (E. Mitchell ed. 1976). Under this property rights analysis, the legality of the arrangement should be measured by the ancillary purpose test. The question then is: does the benefit generated by this protection of the designers' interest in their dress designs justify the protection they sought and the means they used?[17] See 168 supra.

17. Similar analysis also provides justification for the boycott in *Klor's*. That is, Broadway (the defendant) might have been providing consumers with demonstrations and product

Two Supreme Court decisions further support this type of analysis. First, in NCAA v. University of Oklahoma, 468 U.S. 85 (1984) the Court applied a rule of reason standard, including a close evaluation of proffered justifications, before condemning the colleges' concerted refusal to televise games on other networks. (See the discussion pp. 192–94 supra.) Second, in Northwest Wholesale Stationers, Inc. v. Pacific Stationery & Printing Co., 105 S.Ct. 2613 (1985), the Court distinguished *FOGA* (which applied a per se rule) as limited to boycotts "likely to restrict competition without any offsetting efficiency gains." Where, however, the joint activity is not aimed at disadvantaging competitions it is unlikely to have predominantly anticompetitive consequences. Thus, in *Northwest Wholesale Stationers* a supplier of office supplies was expelled from a purchasing cooperative after it expanded its operations from retailing to include wholesale activities. The reason for the expulsion was disputed, and the district court granted summary judgment for the defendant under the rule of reason because there was no evidence of anticompetitive effect. The Supreme Court upheld this ruling unanimously, significantly narrowing the boycott rule: "Unless the cooperative possesses

information on appliances; after examining the product at Broadway, customers might then have gone next door to Klor's, a discounter, and purchased the products at a lower price. The response by Broadway to have Klor's cut off unless it also provided the service, seems a less threatening response to free riders which deserves rule of reason rather than per se treatment. Liebler, "Integration and Competition," supra at 13.

market power or exclusive access to an element
essential to effective competition, the conclusion
that expulsion is virtually always likely to have
anticompetitive effect [that a per se rule is applicable] is not warranted."

This moderate view of the applicable legal standard is further buttressed by other cases—some
upholding and others condemning group boycotts—
applying a rule of reason test. Examples include
cases involving actions regarding decisions on ethics by professional societies. Here the leading case
is still probably American Medical Ass'n v. United
States, 130 F.2d 233 (D.C.Cir.1942), aff'd, 317 U.S.
519 (1943).[18] The Medical Society in the District of
Columbia had warned hospitals that they might
lose its approval if their facilities were open to two
former members expelled because they had participated in group prepaid medical practice. The Society had ruled that salaried medical practice under
contract was unethical because it put an intermediary between the doctor and the patient. The Court
analyzed the practice differently. It condemned
this secondary boycott because the "unethical" conduct seemingly affected doctor income much more
than patient care; in fact the latter reason seemed
spurious. See also FTC v. Indiana Federation of
Dentists, 106 S.Ct. 2009 (1986).

18. See also Goldfarb v. Virginia State Bar, 421 U.S. 773
(1975) applying the Sherman Act to fee schedules recommended
for lawyers by bar associations; National Soc'y of Professional
Engineers v. United States, 435 U.S. 679 (1978), discussed p. 187
supra.

Where the rational nexus between the professional rule and public protection is much closer, courts are more willing to uphold self-regulation even if enforced by a group boycott. Thus in another prepaid medical plan action, the Supreme Court indicated, in dictum, that professional societies have substantial leeway in applying ethical constraints on their members. United States v. Oregon State Medical Soc., 343 U.S. 326, 336 (1952). Nor is this approach limited to professional groups. Perhaps its most frequent application is in professional sports. For example, in Molinas v. National Basketball Ass'n, 190 F.Supp. 241 (S.D. N.Y.1961), a professional basketball player who had been indefinitely suspended from the NBA for betting on his own team charged that the league and its members had engaged in an unlawful boycott. The court dismissed the complaint, however, because "a disciplinary rule invoked against gambling seems about as reasonable a rule as could be imagined." Likewise the Professional Golfers' Association rules restricting eligibility in PGA-sponsored tournaments was upheld as justified by the need "to insure that professional golf tournaments are not bogged down with great numbers of players of inferior ability." Deesen v. Professional Golfers' Ass'n, 358 F.2d 165, 170 (9th Cir.1966). Caution must still be exercised. The use, for example, of a trade association to test products and give a "seal of approval" may constitute an illegal boycott if nonobjective tests are used for the purpose of driving out competitors. See, e.g., Radiant Burners,

Inc. v. Peoples Gas Light & Coke Co., 364 U.S. 656 (1961). And where self-regulatory boycotts are permitted, such powers can be validly exercised only by observing the minimal needs of fair process including notice and an opportunity to be heard. See Silver v. New York Stock Exchange, 373 U.S. 341 (1963).

In sum, where the self-interest of the boycotting group and the proffered justifications merge, it is extremely difficult to satisfy the rule of reason standard applied under the Sherman (or FTC) Act. To survive, the reason for the boycott must be closely related to a lawful purpose; and where the rule is essential for the enterprise (as anti-gambling rules are for professional sports), it will be viewed sympathetically. Rules whose primary aims are to increase the group's power vis-a-vis nonmembers—such as reserve clauses restricting a professional athlete's opportunity to sell his talents to another team—are increasingly suspect. In the few cases where courts have considered noncommercial boycotts—concerted refusals to deal with social, moral or other objectives unrelated to the group's profits or economic self-interest—they have been reluctant to interfere under the Sherman Act. See, e.g., Missouri v. National Organization for Women, 620 F.2d 1301 (8th Cir.) (Sherman Act inapplicable to protest boycotts), cert. denied, 449 U.S. 842 (1980); Allied Int'l, Inc. v. Int'l Longshoremen's Ass'n, 640 F.2d 1368 (1st Cir.1981), cert. denied, 458 U.S. 1120 (1982).

CHAPTER VI

HORIZONTAL RESTRAINTS: PROBLEMS OF CHARACTERIZATION AND PROOF

Drawing the basic outlines of prohibited and permitted conduct is simply the first step in determining the application of Section 1 of the Sherman Act to horizontal restraints. Granted that businessmen are sophisticated and shrewd, and since their objective is profits, the temptation to increase profits by whatever means is strong. Nevertheless, the likelihood that knowledgeable businessmen will openly enter into agreements or conspiracies to fix prices, to allocate territories, or to boycott competitors is small; the probabilities of detection and of subsequent harsh sentences undoubtedly deter many. Others perceive and prefer the possibility of securing the same ends by less direct methods. Consequently, questions of enforcement arise essentially in the gray areas: have the parties so acted in concert as to indicate an implicit agreement on a course of conduct? Can their conduct reasonably be described as evidencing a price or territorial cartel or a group boycott? Or is their conduct "legitimate" business effort conforming with competitive markets and prices?

These problems of definition and characterization are typical "legal" issues. Those who have studied first year Contracts or Criminal Law have already wrestled with the concept of agreement. And much of law school education and legal practice focuses on matters of characterization—for example, when does conduct become so careless that it is unreasonable, and therefore negligent? The basic issues have already been considered when the legal rules applied to horizontal restraints were canvassed in Chapter 5 and that discussion will not be repeated here. On the other hand, the insights provided by economics tend to emerge even more sharply here since the questions focus on the vague and often illusory boundaries between legitimate competitive conduct and illegal collaborative or exclusionary action.

A. PROBLEMS OF CHARACTERIZATION

Whether particular business conduct is a cooperative exchange of information designed to perfect the operation of a freely competitive market or a significant step toward fixing prices or allocating sales territories—to pick typical but not exclusive examples—is critical. Exchanges of information are generally upheld and often even promoted by governmental agencies (for instance, the Department of Commerce's long-standing efforts to develop product and size standards). But price-fixing and market allocation, as we have seen, violate

Section 1 of the Sherman Act and may even be grounds for criminal prosecution. Despite this vast difference in impact and significance, in practice the distinction between the two is often narrow and actual cases are particularly difficult to classify.

[handwritten margin notes: NOTE, GESUY OK, SO, ISSUE 1: IS IT AN INFO EXCHANGE OR RESTR OF TRADE, ISSUE 2: IF IT IS AN INFO EXCHANGE IS IT OK (SEE NOTES), INFO EXCHANGES]

1. INFORMATION EXCHANGES

Exchanges of information between competing or related businesses often raise antitrust problems, especially when the data is disseminated through the assistance of a trade association. Occasionally the antitrust laws apply even to information exchanges between business and government. The regulation of these latter interchanges differs, however, because First Amendment considerations limit governmental restraints on business appeals to the government.

a. *Trade Associations*

Businessmen selling the same product or competing with one another may join together for a number of reasons, many of which are not questioned in antitrust and are often viewed as promoting competitive markets. Primary among these possibly "legitimate" bases for meetings between competitors is the dissemination of trade information among producers. Knowledge concerning current inventory levels or the availability of raw materials, for example, may help a firm to plan its production and to develop its market strategies, thereby reducing costs, increasing profits and possibly intensifying competition. As governmental supervision of business conduct continues to increase (covering not only deceptive practices and labor relations, but also extending to energy consumption and environmental effects), it becomes increasingly important for business with its experience and expertise to participate in the planning and implementation of such regulation. Consequently, a significant role for trade associations, especially where the comprising business units are numerous and relatively small (a customary structural description of a competitive market), is the representation of related business interests before governmental agencies. Trade associations may also promote the industry to potential customers—one example is institutional advertising by life insurance companies which implicitly attacks other industries such as savings and loan associations; because of free rider problems it could well prove more efficient for industry groups to advertise rather than for individual firms to do so. Other reasons for businesses to join a trade association include the advancement of technology through the sharing of product innovation, the encouragement of standardization, and the attainment of the advantages of a large economic organization such as establishing an industry credit bureau.

On the other hand, trade associations or similar information exchanges can also function as instruments through which firms fix prices, allocate sales territories and market shares, or boycott others. As Adam Smith noted long ago: "People of the same trade seldom meet together, even for merriment and diversion, but the conversation ends in a conspiracy against the public, or in some contrivance to raise prices." For example, even such simple trade association activities as reporting prices can facilitate the detection of off-list prices, thus aiding the enforcement of collusive pricing. Still, it is the agreement to fix prices rather than the opportunity that seemingly should be condemned—especially since trade groups perform desirable market functions.

Yet the dangers posed by information exchanges in certain circumstances should not be underestimated. Trade participants need not always state their desire to fix prices in order for trade meetings to have this effect. Industry management is frequently drawn from similar social strata; their bonds of friendship, group similarity, and identical interests are likely to discourage maverick (competitive) action, especially where common meetings are frequent and discussions therein concentrate on sensitive pricing and production issues. Thus, given such coincident interests, trade meetings and information exchanges may serve to facilitate oligopolistic price coordination, whereby competitive pressures and practices will be suppressed. (For the theory of oligopoly behavior, see ch. 3, pp. 78–85 supra.) That is, the information exchanges may make a rival's decisions more predictable and provide common guidelines as to "appropriate" price levels. One common difficulty of oligopoly pricing is that a participant's competitors may secretly cut some of their prices in order to capture additional orders. But as in the case of outright collusion, if all prices are publicized, oligopoly rivals can retaliate more readily, thus denying the benefits (additional orders) to the price shading firm. The result of information exchanges in an oligopoly situation may then be to encourage price stability and to fix prices.[1]

Membership in a trade association and the exchange of information concerning prices, output, inventories or any other aspect of the business come within the jurisdiction of Section 1 of the Sherman Act because an agreement or combination is present. Trade associations in themselves are statutory combinations. They may also involve agreements by members to exchange information and accordingly meet the traditional definition of a contract. Or, as suggested in the preceding paragraph on oligopoly coordination, a tacit agreement among trade association members may be inferred from their conduct.[2] Whatever

1. This is by no means a far-fetched theory. It tracks remarkably with the original plan of the trade association movement as "fathered" by corporate lawyer Arthur Jerome Eddy in his book, *The New Competition* (1912) (promoting "open price" plans).

2. The discussion which follows assumes that a statutory agreement exists; the focus here is on the informational activities and their legality. For a discussion of whether or not the participants have acted with sufficient concert to form a "contract, combination, . . . or conspiracy," see pp. 260–65 infra.

the jurisdictional basis, the question under Section 1 is whether this information exchange has a tendency to restrain trade unreasonably.

Where there may be no apparent (and effective) purpose to fix prices or otherwise limit competition among its members, the exchange of information facilitated by a trade association is usually tested under a rule of reason approach. Even though, as the Court acknowledged in Maple Flooring Mfrs. Ass'n v. United States, 268 U.S. 563, 582 (1925), it is not "open to question that the dissemination of pertinent information concerning any trade or business tends to stabilize that trade or business and to produce uniformity of price and trade practice," the mere exchange of information is not "an unreasonable restraint, or in any respect unlawful." This position has, it seems, survived the rule of *Madison Oil* (p. 179 supra) which found it illegal per se to agree on prices or otherwise tamper with the operation of a competitive market. Although this conclusion may seem anomalous at first glance, since the exchange of trade information itself alters the manner in which price and production levels are otherwise established, nevertheless, the mere exchange of information does not in itself require the recipients to follow a particular policy. And that basic distinction is generally relied upon in differentiating between price agreements and information exchanges under the antitrust laws. Of course, even under a rule of reason approach, programs for data dissemination can still be condemned as unreasonable trade restraints.

In fact, the early cases dealing with "open competition" plans (which admittedly sought to "keep prices at reasonably stable and normal levels") found such plans in violation of the Sherman Act. Thus, in American Column & Lumber Co. v. United States, 257 U.S. 377 (1921) (the *Hardwood* case), a trade association whose members produced one-third of the nation's hardwood lumber had adopted a plan requiring member firms to submit price lists, detailed daily sales and shipment reports (including invoice copies), monthly production and stock reports, etc. The plan as implemented was held to violate the Sherman Act. The association's central office summarized the reported data and forwarded weekly reports to the membership listing each transaction, the parties and price, and noting whether the price departed from the member's listed price. Moreover, in frequent meetings the members not only discussed market conditions but strongly urged each other to restrict output and maintain prices. By any standard, the Court concluded, this was "not the conduct of competitors but is . . . clearly that of men united in an agreement, express or implied, to act together and pursue a common purpose under a common guide." Still the case was not easily decided. There was, in fact, no agreement to limit production or charge a fixed price, as the Court openly acknowledged, and the contention that it is demonstrated by "the disposition of men to follow their most intelligent competitors" hardly supplies the missing link—

especially since the market conditions were not conducive to price leadership or other efforts to cut production. (For example, the plan involved only one-third of the industry and 365 sellers.) And in strong dissents, Justices Brandeis and Holmes argued that the Sherman Act should not be used to stifle discussion or require business rivals to compete blindly without the aid of relevant trade information.

After striking down a similar open price plan in the linseed oil industry (United States v. American Linseed Oil Co., 262 U.S. 371 (1923)), the Court approved the plans of two trade associations. In Maple Flooring Mfrs. Ass'n v. United States, 268 U.S. 563 (1925) the trade association disseminated information detailing members' average costs and summarizing all sales, prices and stocks—but without identifying current individual transactions; a single base point freight rate booklet (which would facilitate uniform pricing) was also distributed to them. But this information exchange did not unreasonably restrain trade, said the Court, especially since the evidence also showed that after the *Linseed Oil* case the association members stopped discussing prices and after the complaint was filed here the weekly summary no longer linked specific sellers with particular transactions. Other evidence established that the members' prices were not uniform and in fact were lower than those of nonassociation manufacturers. The Court was, it appears, influenced by the association's effort to stay within the letter of the antitrust laws.[3] At the same time, the incidental disclosure of price information among cement manufacturers as part of an elaborate statistical program was upheld in the face of price uniformity on the grounds that competing sellers of a fungible product were forced through product homogeneity to meet price changes and that the data was needed to counter the fraudulent practices of some buyers. Cement Mfrs. Protective Ass'n v. United States, 268 U.S. 588 (1925), also discussed p. 217 supra.

Then in Sugar Institute, Inc. v. United States, 297 U.S. 553 (1936) the Court considered an elaborate open price plan which (a) assured that price reductions would be promptly met by all members, (b) provided that price increases would be announced in advance but could later be withdrawn unless all sugar refiners followed suit, and (c) resulted in an agreement that no refiner would make secret price concessions from announced policies. The Court condemned only the last item—the spe-

3. A fair reading of the evidence would also support a contrary inference, namely that the association sought to facilitate an express price agreement or oligopoly pricing in the hardwood flooring industry. What other purpose is served by exchanging average cost data? Why else distribute a single base point freight rate book? But see Carlton, *A Reexamination of Delivered Pricing Systems*, 23 J.L. & Econ. 51 (1983); Haddock, *Basing Point Pricing: Competitive vs. Collusive Theories*, 72 Am.Econ.Rev. 289 (1982). Moreover, the market presented a ready opportunity for collusion. The association had only 22 members and their aggregate market share was 70 per cent.

cific agreement to abide by list prices until a new price was publicly announced. Otherwise the Court accepted the parties' justification for advance announcement of price moves (an industry custom which allowed customers a period of grace in which to purchase sugar at the former price) and repeated its observations set forth in *Maple Flooring* that price exchanges are not illegal simply because they may bring about stabilization of production and price; "competition does not become less free merely because of the distribution of knowledge of the essential factors entering into commercial transactions."

Sugar Institute can, of course, be explained as another Depression-inspired case authored by Chief Justice Hughes, whose views on antitrust (see, e.g., *Appalachian Coals*, discussed p. 178 supra) generally have not survived *Madison Oil's* per se condemnation of any agreements that tamper with the price structure, including efforts at establishing price floors or price stability. However, that characterization would not be fully accurate in this case.[4] One reason is that the basic rule of reason standard for information exchanges antedated *Sugar Institute* and was long accepted by the Supreme Court. Thus, without a more direct examination of trade associations, it seems clear the rule of *Maple Flooring* remains, notwithstanding the per se prohibition of price-fixing and price

4. See, e.g., United States v. Citizens & Southern Nat'l Bank, 422 U.S. 86, 113 (1975) ("the dissemination of price information is not itself a per se violation of the Sherman Act.")

stabilization agreements in *Madison Oil.* Further-more, this conclusion is buttressed by the economic and social values provided by trade exchanges, especially for smaller firms otherwise unable to present their views effectively before government and the public or uninformed about market facts and trends. As the Supreme Court observed: "The exchange of price data and other information among competitors does not invariably have anti-competitive effects; indeed such practices can in certain circumstances increase economic efficiency and render markets more, rather than less, com-petitive." United States v. United States Gypsum Co., 438 U.S. 422, 441 n. 16 (1978). But in order to be sustained, the exchanges should be limited to past prices not identifying particular transactions or parties and not binding the members to abide by announced prices—and the data should be publicly available. See Tag Mfrs. Institute v. FTC, 174 F.2d 452, 463 (1st Cir.1949).

Two decisions by the Supreme Court have nar-rowed this position as applied to verification of prices directly between suppliers, although their approaches differ. In United States v. Container Corp. of America, 393 U.S. 333 (1969), 18 firms shipped 90 percent of the cardboard cartons shipped in the Southeast. They established an informal price exchange whereby suppliers would provide each other, on request, price information on their most recent sales to a particular customer. Not surprisingly, therefore, a firm, once it had received this information, would often (but not always) quote the same price to that customer, and it was common for buyers to divide orders among suppliers. The market loosely met the structural tests of oligopoly (18 of the 51 firms in the market controlled 90 percent of the sales, and the six largest controlled almost 60 percent); and the industry had excess capacity despite rapid increases in demand. On the other hand, entry was easy and frequent and capacity had expanded rapidly. Conceding that these facts fit none of the precedents, the Court, in an elliptical opinion by Justice Douglas, condemned this information exchange on the ground that it tended to stabilize prices; that is, the price exchange between members narrowed the range of price reductions. The primary operative language is as follows:

> Price information exchanged in some markets may have no effect on a truly competitive price. But the corrugated container industry is dominated by relatively few sellers. The product is fungible and the competition for sales is price. The demand is inelastic, as buyers place orders only for immediate, short-run needs. The exchange of price data tends toward price uniformity. For a lower price does not mean a larger share of the available business but a sharing of the existing business at a lower return. Stabilizing prices as well as raising them is within the ban of § 1 of the Sherman Act. As we said in *United States v. Socony-Vacumn Oil Co.,* [Madis-

on Oil] . . . "in terms of market operations
stabilization is but one form of manipulation."
The inferences are irresistible that the exchange
of price information has had an anticompetitive
effect in the industry, chilling the vigor of price
competition. (Id. at 337.)

Despite the harshness of this language, the
Court's subsequent opinions made clear that
Container was not announcing a new per se rule
for price exchanges. See *Citizens & Southern Nat'l
Bank,* supra p. 238 n. 4. Nevertheless, it does
seem clear that a stricter test for interseller price
verification was to be applied in specific circumstances. Viewing the market as oligopolistic in
structure, the Court observed that price exchanges
identifying particular parties, transactions and
prices could be used to foster interdependent pricing (by preventing secret price concessions). That
is to say, the opinion could be read as applying a
rule of presumptive illegality to specific price exchanges among sellers in oligopolistic industries.

The difficulty with this view of *Container* is that
the market did not really fit the Court's analysis.
There were too many firms, entry was too easy,
and excess capacity pressed too hard on the market, for oligopoly pricing as it is normally understood to occur—and the dissent made this clear.
In addition, the Court's stated reasoning would
apply to generalized price exchanges, yet it left
undisturbed its precedents in *Cement Mfrs.* (exchange of price to specific customers) and *Maple*

Flooring (exchange of generalized price data). Finally, no consideration was given to the fact such price exchanges could enhance the buyer's opportunity to obtain a lower price (by playing one seller off against another). Besides, competitors in the corrugated container industry could frequently determine each other's prices from market observations and through reading trade papers.

This, then, set the stage for *United States v. United States Gypsum Co.,* 438 U.S. 422 (1978). Here manufacturers of gypsum board were charged with per se price-fixing by the government for checking current and future prices with competitors before making price concessions to buyers. (The government read the per se-type language of *Container* as overruling *Maple Flooring* and as establishing a new test for information exchanges.) The defendants argued, to the contrary, that they had only checked with the competitors on prices and sales terms in order to comply with the meeting competition requirements of the Robinson-Patman Act (discussed p. 419 infra). Their contention was that the Sherman Act could not condemn out of hand what the Robinson-Patman Act authorized, and that this was a "controlling circumstance" recognized in *Container* [5] as a defense to a Sher-

---

5. The language in *Container* being relied upon by defendants in *Gypsum* was as follows:

> While there was present here, as in *Cement Mfrs. Protective Ass'n v. United States* . . . , an exchange of prices to specific customers, there was absent the controlling circumstance, viz., . . . exchanged price information as a means of protecting their legal rights from fraudulent inducements to

man Act charge. Although unrelated aspects of the opinion were not supported by all Justices, those participating agreed that the mere exchange of price information without intent to fix prices is not criminal price-fixing per se and must be tested under the rule of reason. They also ruled that a seller could usually satisfy the requirements of the Robinson-Patman Act's meeting competition defense without direct price checking; and the dangers presented by interseller verification in an oligopolistic industry (here the eight largest companies had 94 percent of national sales) outweighed the marginal benefits that could occur from allowing this exchange. Thus the Court held that the meeting competition defense was not an exception to the rule in *Container* prohibiting direct price exchanges.

Two things should be noted about this development. First, one still cannot confidently state the legal test applicable to trade association activities. The Court used language of a per se test in *Container* but dealt with the case under a narrower-than-usual rule of reason standard. In *Gypsum,* by contrast, the Court spoke in the measured terms of the rule of reason, yet its treatment of the facts left little doubt that price exchanges were not favored in oligopolistically structured markets, suggesting that the Court may have adopted a sliding rule of reason approach ranging from a

deliver more cement than needed for a specific job. (393 U.S. at 335.)

wide open inquiry in competitively structured industries to a less hospitable rule of presumptive illegality for information exchanges in markets whose structures are highly concentrated. Second, it is not clear from the standpoint of economic analysis that price verification is likely to lead to higher prices, even in oligopoly markets. If a seller has excess capacity and other reasonable means are not available to check on alleged price concessions—probably a common situation, even in concentrated markets—price competition may in fact occur only if a seller can check on whether in fact the lower price was offered; otherwise the seller may lose more in profits than it gains in sales from a price cut. We still do not know, despite the assumption in *Gypsum,* whether price exchanges in oligopoly markets cost consumers more because of interdependent pricing than they gain from the price competition that results. This in turn raises a question of what the antitrust rule should be where the evidence of likely effect is absent or equivocal. See generally Easterbrook, *The Limits of Antitrust,* 63 Tex.L.Rev. 1 (1984).

b. Appeals to Government

The range of governmental regulation of business is wide and extensive. Subsidies, licenses, price and wage controls, and quality and safety measures are typical. Because government's decisions frequently have an extensive impact on business decisions and profits, it is not uncommon for trade associations and others to attempt to influence such governmental decisions in favor of their particular interests. The question then arises, does competitor collaboration, which seeks (and obtains) anticompetitive results through governmental decisions, violate Section 1 of the Sherman Act?

A threshold question is whether government action is in itself immune from prosecution. First, as seems obvious, the Sherman Act does not apply to actions of the federal government. Thus, cooperation between agencies of the federal government or combinations by federal officials and a private firm are not within the Act's reach. Cf. United States v. Rock Royal Co-op Ass'n, 307 U.S. 533, 560 (1939). Second, in Parker v. Brown, 317 U.S. 341 (1943) the Court upheld the activities of a California agency fixing raisin production and prices (even though this was done at the request of and with the concurrence of a majority of growers). The state regulation was not a burden on interstate commerce since it coincided with federal agricultural policy (for similar market restrictions); and, in any case, the Sherman Act's prohibition of contracts in restraint of trade by "any person" applied to private businesses, not government agencies. Still, such general immunity of government action from the Sherman Act does not necessarily protect collaborating businesses from antitrust attack.

The basic concern is where to draw the line between the rights of individuals and groups to petition government, on the one hand, and the manipulation of government for private ends, on the other. The criminal laws generally seek to stop bribery and other corrupt acts; public discussion and publicity tend to insure that official actions reflect the public interest. In deciding where to draw the line, it is useful to note that vexatious litigation may fully serve its purpose even though entry is not prevented. Merely delaying new competition can protect an occupant of a lucrative market, and successful predation in this form does not always require any particular advantage or a deep pocket or entail high antitrust visibility. See Salop & Scheffman, *Raising Rivals' Costs*, 73 Am. Econ.Rev. 267 (1983).

There are relatively few cases spelling out the limits of permissible business conduct, and they generally fall into two categories. One group suggests an area of immunity from antitrust liability. For example, in Eastern R.R. Presidents Conference v. Noerr Motor Freight, Inc., 365 U.S. 127 (1961), joint efforts by businessmen—here 24 railroads and an association of railroad presidents—to obtain legislative and executive action unfavorable to competing trucking firms did not violate the Sherman Act. The desirability of public participation in governmental processes, even though that participation is for selfish rather than "public" reasons, was held to outweigh antitrust considerations. Without noting the tautology, the Court there contended that the adoption of legislation reflected a determination that the result served the public interest, which a court should not overturn for private purposes. See also New Motor Vehicle Bd. v. Orrin W. Fox Co., 439 U.S. 96 (1978) (state regulatory scheme allowed existing dealers to protect and delay the establishment of new, competing dealers).

But in California Motor Transport Co. v. Trucking Unlimited, 404 U.S. 508 (1972), the Court sustained a complaint that a combination of the 19 largest trucking firms in California violated the Sherman Act when they opposed all applications, regardless of their merits, by smaller truckers before federal and state agencies as well as in all available courts. Also relying on allegations that the defendants had warned the small truckers that they could avoid the costs being inflicted on them only by not asking for new operating rights, the Court distinguished *Noerr* and ruled that conduct which amounted to a sham is not protected by the First Amendment. Implicit in this holding is the suggestion that misrepresentation or other unethical conduct is more readily reached under the Sherman Act when used to subvert adjudicative processes which are less able to protect themselves and where other constitutional values (i.e., due process) are implicated. Accord Otter Tail Power Co. v. United States, 410 U.S. 366, 379–80 (1973); id. 360 F.Supp. 451 (D.Minn.1973), summarily aff'd, 417 U.S. 901 (1974).

2. JOINT VENTURES AND OTHER APPLICATIONS OF THE RULE OF REASON

a. The Standard of Reasonableness

In considering the development of the Sherman Act, we previously noted the "rule of reason," which the Court first said, in *Standard Oil (N.J.)*, it would apply to measure the legality of business conduct and which it has applied increasingly in recent years. Except in special circumstances where a court has found a per se rule appropriate because the challenged conduct was without redeeming virtue or the risk and substantiality of anticompetitive harm outweighed possible benefits, the reasonableness of a particular practice determines its lawfulness. Under this standard, the court must evaluate the parties' *purposes;* determine whether they have the *power* to implement them; and assess what *effect* has (or could have) occurred. Although one once could have suggested—without undue cynicism—that the application of one test versus another automatically determined the outcome, this is no longer an accurate reading of the case law. See, e.g., *Professional Engineers* discussed p. 187 supra. They reflect instead different analytical approaches, and application of the rule of reason not infrequently leads to liability under the Sherman Act.

The areas in which the rule of reason can be applied are endless and attempts at categorization

seem fruitless. Even conduct seemingly within per
se proscriptions may, for other reasons, justify a
less rigid level of scrutiny. For example, the Supreme Court has ruled that agreements among
competitors to terminate short-term credit are the
equivalent of price-fixing and therefore subject to
the per se test of *Madison Oil*. Catalano, Inc. v.
Target Sales, Inc., 446 U.S. 643 (1980), discussed p.
185 supra. However, temporary situations may
justify cooperative action despite the supposed
sweep of the rules against price-fixing. The rule of
reason might well have been relied upon during
the 1974 and 1979 gasoline shortages to evaluate
joint efforts aimed at reducing gas lines. Service
station operators and oil companies could have
sought speedier service for customers by agreeing
to abandon all credit sales during the crisis, even
though such action probably would not have been
permissible once the immediate crisis passed and
the lines disappeared.

A fair reading of the cases suggests that in
addition to considering the purpose, power and
effect of the parties' collaboration, an antitrust
court should also consider whether reliance should
be placed upon less restrictive alternatives to
achieve similar ends. Thus, while individual service station operators could have abandoned credit
sales, they might have been unwilling (individually) to risk antagonizing their credit customers who
could have switched their allegiance when gas supplies became plentiful again and they had a choice.

With this background, the joint venture and related cases presented in the next section are particularly instructive.

b. Joint Ventures and Other Collaborative Efforts Tested by the Rule of Reason

The legality of a joint venture or similar collaborative effort by two or more firms involves related yet distinct questions. One is whether the act of joining together itself violates the antitrust laws. Consideration of this question is postponed, however, until Chapter 9 is reached, where the anti-merger law (Section 7 of the Clayton Act) is examined; in that context the primary focus of the law is on whether the new "partnership" will eliminate actual or potential competition among the venturers, thereby substantially lessening competition.[6] The other question concerns the venture's purposes and practices. Looking at the impact of the venture upon others, the issue centers on whether the group's objectives are legitimate. Of equal importance is the internal impact of the venture; that is, does it unduly restrict the participants in the venture or are the restrictions necessary and therefore valid.

Analytically these questions are indistinguishable from others previously discussed where firms

6. Section 1 of the Sherman Act generally has not been applied to combinations of individuals or firms into new business units; the new entity is generally not viewed as a statutory "combination." Compare United States v. Penn-Olin Chem. Co., 378 U.S. 158, 161 (1964), with id. at 177–81 (Douglas, J., dissenting).

collaborate rather than compete. However, the cases are frequently considered separately because joint ventures seemingly offer appealing benefits, on the one hand, and involve extremely close cooperation among the participants, on the other. Many, perhaps most, are measured under a rule of reason unless price-fixing or territorial divisions are encountered. The economic issues in these cases are not distinctive. Unless the venture offers gains in economic efficiency, there seems little reason to permit it—in fact, there may be reason to suspect that the venture seeks monopoly ends. Where efficiencies can be identified, they should be weighed against their costs. More specifically, what are the advantages of allowing automobile manufacturers to sponsor joint research into solving energy and environmental problems caused by the automobile? Will this cause the participants to abandon their individual efforts; would their individual efforts produce a greater number of breakthroughs for the same research investment; or is there no market incentive now to engage in such research? Cf. United States v. Automobile Mfrs Ass'n, 307 F.Supp. 617 (C.D.Cal.1969), aff'd per curiam sub nom., City of New York v. United States, 397 U.S. 248 (1970) (consent decree barring cooperative efforts to delay and obstruct development of automobile pollution control devices), modified and replaced sub nom., United States v. Motor Vehicle Mfrs Ass'n, 1982–83, CCH Trade Cas. ¶ 65,088 (C.D.Cal.1982). On another level, what gains and losses would result from allowing regional supermarket chains to market and promote private label goods in competition with the national chains? Whatever the purpose and format of the collaboration, the basic issues appear unchanged.

While it has been said, as in United States v. Line Material Co., 333 U.S. 287, 310 (1948), that joint research presents no problems of illegality in regard to "the mere size of . . . [the] group or the thoroughness of its research," that statement appears in the light of subsequent cases to be inadequately considered dictum. There are two lines of cases, dating back to the early 1950's, which outline the basic and competing approaches.

First in Timken Roller Bearing Co. v. United States, 341 U.S. 593 (1951), the Court refused to accept the defendant's "joint venture" analysis of its agreement with a British businessman to buy the stock of a British manufacturer of roller bearings. Looking at all the provisions of the arrangement, which included worldwide price agreements and market allocation covenants, the Court concluded that "prior decisions plainly establish that agreements providing for an aggregation of trade restraints such as those existing in this case are illegal under the [Sherman] Act." This analysis was also applied in United States v. Sealy, Inc., 388 U.S. 350 (1967), where a group of small manufacturers of mattresses created the "Sealy" trademark and sought to exploit it through joint advertising. While the Court appeared to accept the combination as a legitimate collaborative effort, it also ruled that the horizontal territorial divisions, whereby each participant agreed to confine its sales to an assigned area (in conjunction with a retail price-fixing clause), were illegal under the rule in *Timken*. Thus the Court declined to weigh the benefits of the arrangement against its harms to competition.

An even more rigid approach was taken in United States v. Topco Associates, 405 U.S. 596 (1972). There a group of regional supermarket chains had formed a joint buying association in order to promote and market private label goods in competition with similar goods offered by the national food chains. While the combination itself was again assumed to be lawful, the Court held that the territorial restrictions agreed upon, which assured each participant that other members of the venture would not use the private brand to compete with it, were illegal per se.

Both cases have been analyzed and criticized sharply, see the discussion pp. 205–11 supra, and that examination will not be repeated here. However, it should be noted that in each instance a group of smaller firms had combined to obtain some of the efficiencies enjoyed by larger competitors, but without permanently merging into a larger firm. The economic question which the Court declined to consider [7] was whether the restrictive

7. Particularly disturbing is the Court's scorn for a rule of reason approach which, it said, would "leave courts free to ramble through the wilds of economic theory in order to maintain a flexible approach." United States v. Topco Associates,

provisions (protecting the territorial allocation to each joint venture) were necessary and whether the harms of those provisions outweighed their gains. Nor did the Court consider, in its characterization of these arrangements as horizontal market divisions, whether the output of mattress or private label products could be restricted by these firms.

There is another approach, however, illustrated by the decision in United States v. Morgan, 118 F.Supp. 621 (S.D.N.Y.1953). Here the court examined the practice of investment bankers in the securities industry to form underwriting syndicates when they engage in selling new issues. During the initial offering, the syndicate agrees with the issuer on the price at which the security will be offered to the public in support of their effort to attract capital by marketing the stock in "an orderly way." The district court held that this joint support of the new issue market was not an unreasonable restraint of trade. The court relied upon the short-term nature of the combine and its necessity. After the issue was "floated," the combine was ended and new syndicates comprised of differing firms were constantly formed. Even more significant was the syndicate's role in raising entrepreneurial capital at a low cost. The

405 U.S. at 609 n. 10. But see Continental T.V., Inc. v. GTE Sylvania, Inc., 433 U.S. 36 (1977), discussed p. 302; Aspen Skiing Co. v. Aspen Highlands Skiing Corp., 105 S.Ct. 2847, 2857–58 (1985) (dicta focusing on absence of efficiency justification for defendant's conduct).

government was unable to point to any equally efficient alternative for raising capital; without the price-fixing provisions, it was highly unlikely that an investment banker would take the risk of underwriting a major issue. Whether the objective of a joint venture and its primary provisions will be upheld under the Sherman Act depends, then, on an overall assessment of its purposes as well as a close analysis of the likely benefits, potential harms and possible (less restrictive) alternatives. See also United States v. Pan American World Airways, Inc., 193 F.Supp. 18 (S.D.N.Y.1961), rev'd on other grounds 317 U.S. 296 (1963).

While the line of cases that would view joint research marketing or sales agency arrangements with suspicion or outright hostility have not been overruled, decisions of the Supreme Court since the mid-1970's have adopted an economically oriented approach. See *BMI,* p. 189 supra. The Supreme Court is far less willing to approve the application of per se type rules while, at the same time, it is hesitant to overturn the per se approach and rely solely on a rule of reason. See, e.g., Jefferson Parish Hosp. Dist. No. 2 v. Hyde, 466 U.S. 2 (1984) (tying arrangement) discussed pp. 326–27 infra. In the meantime, the applicable legal standards seem confused and their application is fraught with uncertainty. The standards applied as well as antitrust approval will often depend on the parties' market power, the justification for the arrangement, and similar factors.

As a venture becomes increasingly successful and attains a degree of market power, the group may be required to accept competing firms as members or adequately explain why they refused to do so. In Associated Press v. United States, 326 U.S. 1 (1945), the publishers of 1,200 newspapers who had formed a newsgathering organization were ordered to eliminate their restrictive membership rules which allowed members exclusive rights to AP stories in their locale and gave each member the power to exclude competitors from membership. This arrangement was viewed as an agreement to exclude competitors. The parties had not demonstrated that their restrictions were necessary to achieve economies of scale in their newsgathering activities. On the other hand, neither the parties nor the Court considered the influence of this restriction in providing members with an incentive to gather local news for the AP. Nor was there evidence that AP's market power was so substantial that the bylaws' denial of access to nonmembers of AP-developed news could suppress competition—and without market power the exclusive dealing provision would generally be upheld. Consequently, it is difficult to assess the final result.

Also concerned with the exclusionary effect of competitor collaboration is Silver v. New York Stock Exchange, 373 U.S. 341 (1963). There the Court relied on the Sherman Act to impose a due process-type "duty to explain and afford an opportunity to answer [charges]" before the Exchange could sever private telephone wire connections with a nonmember broker.

B. EVIDENCE OF AN AGREEMENT

Proof of an agreement among competing firms to fix prices or to engage in other similarly prohibited conduct is probably the single most important question in an antitrust trial. Businesses invariably rely on written records, so the parties can seldom dispute the identity of their prices or the location and time of their sales; since such records must be kept for other purposes (e.g., taxes, inventory control) it is not difficult to reconstruct prior sales transactions. But the defendants invariably challenge charges that their identical prices or their similar business actions were the result of an agreement or combination. And evidence showing the existence of a conspiracy to restrain trade is seldom preserved or readily available.

1. THE REQUIREMENT OF AN AGREEMENT

Before examining some of the peculiarities exhibited by antitrust cases involving issues of proof that the defendants conspired to restrain or monopolize trade, it should be noted carefully why proof of an agreement is even required. (As Chapter 3 demonstrated, the economic definition of monopoly focuses solely on price and output effects; and monopoly is condemned in economics because it results in higher prices and reduced output to the detriment of the consumer.) Several reasons can be readily suggested—namely, that the statute requires proof of an agreement, that the Sherman Act would otherwise impose criminal penalties on innocent or unavoidable conduct, and that this approach simplifies enforcement. None of these arguments is without substantial counterpoints, however.

It is true that Section 1 seemingly addresses only concerted activity (i.e., a "contract, combination . . . , or conspiracy"), implicitly absolving individual action—a view supported by the legislative purpose and history. But the statutory term "combination" appears sufficiently flexible to include interdependent yet still not concerted action. Nor does legislative history normally either override clear statutory language or provide an appropriate basis for ignoring policy considerations. More persuasive, perhaps, is the argument that by requiring evidence of agreement, harmful activity is thereby distinguished from harmless or unavoidable action. For example, identical pricing may only reflect similar product costs, intense rivalry or other beneficial and nonconspiratorial factors. Nor could businessmen be expected to compete vigorously when their reward for such activity would be a possible criminal sentence. This argument is not without its limitations, however. For requiring evidence of an agreement may place all oligopoly conduct beyond the reach of the Sherman Act. Finally, easing the enforcement task seems to have been one of the Supreme Court's goals in *Madison Oil* when (in dicta in footnote 59, see p. 182 supra) it stated that neither the adverse effect of the agreement nor the showing of substantial market power were necessary elements in proving an offense by defendants under Section 1.

The result is that Section 1 cases readily fit within conventional criminal conspiracy litigation. This simplified approach to the Sherman Act is something of a mixed blessing, however. Proof of a conspiracy is often difficult even though the rules of evidence seemingly favor the prosecution; juries are sensitive to the dangers of criminal conspiracy charges.[8] Emphasis on the "agreement" shifts attention from the impact of the defendants' actions, with the result that neither prosecutors nor courts consider the economic effects of challenged activities. Hence trivial conduct may be treated with the same solemnity (and resource commitment) accorded serious offenses.[9]

8. In this connection, one can recall the refusal of juries in the 1970's to convict any of the defendants in the major conspiracy cases brought against protestors of the Vietnam War, and in some of the Watergate trials, despite extremely strong evidence.

9. Judge Posner has suggested that the legal approach in fact encourages this result:

It is the large, unwieldly cartel that is most likely to collapse amidst mutual recriminations, thereby generating rich evidence of actual agreement. The cartel that requires minimum explicit coordination, perhaps because there are only a few sellers to coordinate, is apt to have a greater adverse effect on price and output and at the same time be in less danger of being detected and prosecuted.

Antitrust 95 (1974).

2. THE EVIDENTIARY REQUIREMENTS

The trial of a typical price-fixing case initially focuses on the defendants' actual agreement. Sometimes, as in *Madison Oil* and most trade association cases, there is no question that the parties expressly agreed with each other or at least failed to dispute what was said. Then the question becomes one of whether the agreed-upon or resulting actions constitute price-fixing within the coverage of Section 1.[10] At other times it is less obvious that an agreement or conspiracy existed. Invariably such trials involve a search for direct evidence, from documents or testimony, of what actually occurred as well as for indirect or circumstantial evidence exploring the parties' apparent purpose. It is the jury's (or trial court's) task to decide whether the defendants conspired and what it was they agreed upon.

Two leading Supreme Court cases, pointing in somewhat opposite directions, establish the outlines of the minimal evidence necessary for finding an agreement. In Interstate Circuit, Inc. v. United States, 306 U.S. 208 (1939) the evidence showed

10. Related questions include whether rules of apparent authority developed in agency law apply in an antitrust context to hold an unincorporated association liable for the misdeeds of its officers as well as whether the corporation is bound by the acts of its officers. In general, the rules have been restrictive and liability readily found. See American Soc'y of Mechanical Engineers v. Hydrolevel Corp., 456 U.S. 556 (1982); United States v. Koppers, Inc., 652 F.2d 290 (2d Cir.1981), cert. denied, 454 U.S. 1083 (1981).

that eight motion picture film distributors with 75 percent of the feature film market had made identical modifications in their contracts with two affiliated Texas exhibitors (theater owners) of first-run films. The complaint alleged that the distributors had jointly limited the terms on which they would license subsequent runs of their films in violation of Section 1 of the Sherman Act. However, there was no evidence of any direct agreement among the eight *distributors* ; in fact, the evidence showed that the *exhibitors* had made the initial request (and it was their interests in limiting competition from subsequent runs in the Texas market which were served by the contract modifications [11]). In upholding the district court's finding that there had in fact been an agreement among the distributors, the Supreme Court relied on four factors: (1) Because one exhibitor had made its request in a letter addressed to all distributors, each distributor knew that all were being asked to make the same changes in the contract; that is, each defendant knew that the same "offer" had been communicated to the others. (2) Substantially identical alterations were in fact made in each contract and the modifications were complex; these changes were no coincidence. (3) The changes were major (especially in comparison with the price increase) and could be effected only if all agreed to them; and

11. By raising the price of subsequent run films—the contract modifications required a 25 cents minimum price in such theaters and prohibited their inclusion in double features—the exhibitors were seeking to limit the attractiveness of such films as substitutes to their first run offerings.

the initial communication assured that each of the distributors understood this. (4) The failure of the defendants to call their top officers as witnesses to deny the existence of an agreement suggested that the testimony of the latter would have proved unfavorable.

While *Interstate Circuit* is famous for its dicta that an agreement need not be shown ("It was enough that, knowing that concerted action was contemplated and invited, the distributors gave their adherence to the scheme and participated in it."),[12] the case is also significant for the criteria which it suggests may be applied to determine whether the evidence supports an inference of a conspiracy under the antitrust laws. Overt communications among the conspiring distributors was not required; the failure to offer an innocent explanation further supported the district court's findings based on circumstantial evidence. This holding was reinforced by the decision in American Tobacco Co. v. United States, 328 U.S. 781 (1946), where the Court apparently held that several firms could be enjoined from joint monopolization in violation of Section 2 of the Sherman Act even though no agreement among them had been shown.

But in Theatre Enterprises, Inc. v. Paramount Film Distributing Corp., 346 U.S. 537 (1954), (a private treble damage action tried before a jury), the Court upheld a verdict that distributors of first

12. See p. 267 infra.

run films had not conspired to deny a suburban exhibitor first run rights. The Court there relied upon the fact that several traditional elements of a conspiracy had not been shown: (1) There existed sound economic reasons which independently supported each distributor's action; licensing the plaintiff would have reduced revenues from competing downtown theaters; and the plaintiff's offer did not appear genuine. (2) There was no evidence that all defendants knew that the others had received or turned down the first-run offer; prior antitrust convictions did not constitute evidence of misconduct in this instance. (3) The distributors' responsible officers specifically denied any collaboration. Also in response to the overdrawn reaction to its earlier dicta in *Interstate Circuit,* the Court now pronounced (in equally famous language): "Circumstantial evidence of consciously parallel behavior may have made heavy inroads into the traditional judicial attitude toward conspiracy; but 'conscious parallelism' has not yet read conspiracy out of the Sherman Act entirely."

The divergent results in *Interstate Circuit* and *Theatre Enterprise* can also be explained by the procedural posture of the two cases. In both instances the Court upheld a lower court decision; and *Interstate Circuit's* seemingly radical departure from previous thinking may have been in part the result of judicial reluctance to overturn a decision where purpose is significant and where the trial court's proximity to the witnesses was undoubtedly of influence. Cf. Poller v. Columbia Broadcasting System, Inc., 368 U.S. 464, 473 (1962) ("summary procedures should be used sparingly in complex antitrust litigation where motive and intent play leading roles, the proof is largely in the hands of the alleged conspirators, and hostile witnesses thicken the plot").

While circumstantial evidence can support an inference of conspiracy, this evidence will be closely scrutinized. For example, if the factual context of a case makes an antitrust violation implausible—especially where it makes no economic sense—the claimant must provide particularly persuasive evidence that a conspiracy in fact occurred. See First National Bank of Arizona v. Cities Service Co., 391 U.S. 253, 277–80 (1968). Similarly, a plaintiff seeking to prove a conspiracy must present evidence "that tends to exclude the possibility of" independent action. See Monsanto Co. v. Spray-Rite Service Corp., 465 U.S. 752, 764 (1984), discussed p. 307 infra. Thus, in Matsushita Elec. Indus. Co. v. Zenith Radio Corp., 106 S.Ct. 1348 (1986), the Court held that the conspirators in a predatory pricing scheme must have a reasonable expectation of recoverying monopoly profits in the future to recoup the losses resulting from the alleged agreement to fix prices below the competitive level. Without such evidence, "[t]he alleged conspiracy's failure to achieve its ends in the two decades of its asserted operation is strong evidence that the conspiracy does not exist." The Court was impressed that the two leading sellers of television sets in the U.S. were admittedly not participants in the alleged conspiracy by foreign producers to monopolize the sale of tv sets and thus were unlikely to participate in the predators' program of first cutting and then raising prices. Without their cooperation, the alleged conspiracy seemingly had no chance to succeed.

CHAPTER VII

THE OLIGOPOLY PROBLEM

Earlier we briefly examined the economic theory of oligopoly which predicts that where a few sellers have a dominant share of the market, monopoly pricing will occur even though the dominant sellers neither expressly agree on prices nor communicate with each other about prices or marketing strategies. (See pp. 78–85 supra.) Oligopoly theory maintains that these sellers will recognize their mutual dependence and act accordingly; that each will take into account the reactions of his competitors when making output or pricing decisions. Its limitations (like those of monopoly theory) are also significant: it neither explains how a few sellers gain a dominant share of the market nor includes an analysis of conditions of entry which seemingly would affect the significance of the firms' market shares.

The legal rules applicable to pricing by oligopolists are even less clear than other areas of antitrust, or for that matter, of economic theory. A traditional interpretation of the Sherman Act would seemingly render noncollusive interdependent pricing by oligopolists immune from antitrust attack under Section 1 because no facial agreement exists.[1] There is neither direct nor circumstantial evidence of a "meeting of the minds."

1. And Section 2 also seems inapplicable since one firm does not have monopoly power. See pp. 115–21 supra.

It is here, however, that the dicta of *Interstate Circuit* and *Theatre Enterprises* (see pp. 260–64 supra) become significant. In *Interstate Circuit*, after concluding that the district court was justified in finding an agreement among the distributors, the Court also said that, "in the circumstances of this case such agreement . . . was not a prerequisite to an unlawful conspiracy. It was enough that, knowing that concerted action was contemplated and invited, the distributors gave their adherence to the scheme and participated in it." This language, it has been suggested, indicates that oligopoly pricing might be attacked under Section 1 because each seller knows that his competitors must take his reactions into account (and vice versa) and that oligopoly pricing succeeds only if all sellers "participate" by selling above their marginal costs. Moreover, it otherwise would be difficult to explain the Court's statement of this alternative ground for the decision since, as the Court itself acknowledged, the circumstantial evidence of agreement adequately justified the lower court's finding of a conspiracy. Before carrying this analysis too far, it should be noted that *Interstate Circuit* is an early case (decided in 1939, one year before *Madison Oil*) and in fact preceded most economic theory and empirical study of oligopoly markets.

In any event, some 15 years later the Court seemingly reversed direction when in *Theatre Enterprises* it trenchantly observed:

To be sure, business behavior is admissible circumstantial evidence from which the fact finder may infer agreement . . . . But this Court has never held that proof of parallel business behavior conclusively establishes agreement or, phrased differently, that such behavior itself constitutes a Sherman Act offense. Circumstantial evidence of consciously parallel behavior may have made heavy inroads into the traditional judicial attitude towards conspiracy; but "conscious parallelism" has not yet read conspiracy out of the Sherman Act entirely.

Of course, one can distinguish the cases on procedural grounds (see p. 263 supra) as well as parse the Court's language in these and other cases to find some support in the precedents for applying Section 1 to oligopoly conduct even though no agreement is found. But it is perhaps more accurate to observe that a shift in legal analysis occurred in these two cases. On the other hand, other cases indicate continuing judicial acceptance of basic oligopoly theory, although in general these cases have not also posed difficult problems in finding an agreement.[2]

2. See, e.g., United States v. Container Corp. of America, 393 U.S. 333 (1969) (information exchange); United States v. Philadelphia Nat'l Bank, 374 U.S. 321 (1963) (merger); United States v. United States Gypsum Co., 438 U.S. 422 (1978). Most of these cases, however, generally antedate powerful new criticism of what was once generally accepted empirical evidence supporting oligopoly theory. For a collection of recent materials on the current debate, see *Industrial Concentration: The New Learning* (eds. H. Goldschmid, H. Mann & J. Weston 1974); see also Brozen, *The Concentration-Collusion Doctrine*, 46 Antitr.

Whether the Sherman Act can be so interpreted as to apply to oligopoly behavior has been the subject of imaginative and finely honed analysis. Arguing that interdependent behavior should not be interpreted as an illegal conspiracy and that in any case no effective remedy for such behavior is available under Section 1, Donald F. Turner (formerly a law professor at the Harvard Law School) would continue the dicta of *Theatre Enterprises.* Turner, *The Definition of Agreement Under the Sherman Act: Conscious Parallelism and Refusals to Deal,* 75 Harv.L.Rev. 655 (1962). Turner's argument begins with the observation that an oligopolist behaves in exactly the same way as a seller in a competitive industry except that the oligopolist takes an additional factor into account (i.e., his rivals' reactions); and that the Sherman Act cannot be so unreasonably interpreted as to condemn rational and unavoidable behavior. "If monopoly and monopoly pricing are not unlawful per se, neither should oligopoly and oligopoly pricing, absent agreement of the usual sort, be unlawful per se." Id. at 667–68.

Moreover, Turner concludes that even if oligopoly behavior were held illegal no remedy available under Section 1 would prove effective. Injunctive relief would be anomalous in that it would order defendants to make irrational price and output

L.J. 826 (1977); Scherer, *Structure-Performance Relationships and Antitrust Policy,* id. at 864; Weston and Ornstein, *Efficiency Considerations in Joint Ventures,* 53 Antitr.L.J. 85, 92–94 (1984).

decisions; full compliance therefore appears impossible. Alternatively, ordering the defendants to price their goods at their marginal costs (i.e., as if the market were competitive) would involve the courts in continuous regulation for which they are ill-equipped. Cf. United States v. Aluminum Co. of America, 148 F.2d 416, 445 (2d Cir.1945). Nor would dissolution or other structural solution seem appropriate since the essence of the offense under Section 1 is the interdependence theory and this relies on the seller's conduct (i.e., interdependent pricing) rather than the market's structure as being fundamentally responsible for the result. Consequently, Turner contends that if concentration is undesirable (as he believes it to be) the only appropriate remedy is to deconcentrate such markets by breaking up the oligopolistic firms into smaller units, either by charging the oligopolists with joint monopolization in violation of Section 2 [3] or by adopting special legislation. See Turner, *The Scope of Antitrust and Other Economic Regulatory Policies*, 82 Harv.L.Rev. 1207, 1217–31 (1969).

That these analytical difficulties might be overcome by an alternative theory is suggested by Judge Richard A. Posner (formerly a law teacher at the University of Chicago Law School) in *Oligopoly and the Antitrust Laws: A Suggested Approach*, 21 Stan.L.Rev. 1562 (1969). First he points out that oligopoly markets involve concerted action in

3. See American Tobacco Co. v. United States, discussed at p. 149 n. 23 supra.

that they manifest a tacit output agreement among
the sellers, or stated another way, it takes voluntary actions by sellers in a concentrated market to
translate that structure and their mutual dependence into oligopoly prices. This boils down to a
meeting of the minds among sellers even though
there is no overt communication between them.
Each seller communicates his offer to the others by
restricting output (and thereby maintains his
prices above marginal cost); and if oligopoly pricing is to be successful, his rivals must cooperate by
also restricting their output. Therefore Posner
argues that since "tacit collusion or non-competi-
tive pricing is not inherent in an oligopolist market
structure but, like conventional cartelizing, requires additional, voluntary behavior by the sellers," it violates the legal requirements of Section 1.
Id. at 1578.

Nor does he find the problem of formulating an
effective remedy under Section 1 insoluble. Such
tacit collusion is not significantly different from
formal cartel arrangements supported by an express agreement—other than it is easier to conceal.
He contends that simple remedies can be suggested
to increase the costs of tacit collusion. Oligopoly
behavior is avoidable; in fact, fearing that rivals
will cheat or otherwise not react "rationally,"
firms in such markets constantly face a choice of
whether to participate or not whenever they make
output and pricing decisions. Consequently, injunctive relief would not be unwieldy or impracti-

cal. Oligopoly compliance could be tested by the seller's rate of return as compared with the risk and return in other markets. As this suggests, and as Posner concedes, the more difficult question is what proof establishes tacit collusion which violates Section 1 since, by definition, evidence of explicit communication will not be available.

Applications of the antitrust laws to oligopoly practices, however, are still scattered and rudimentary and therefore only suggestive of future possibilities. In FTC v. Cement Institute, 333 U.S. 683 (1948), the Supreme Court upheld an FTC order barring cement producers from using base-point pricing.[4] While the Court ruled that there was substantial evidence in the record to support the Commission's conclusion that cement sellers had in fact agreed with each other to establish this system for fostering monopoly pricing, it also observed (in footnote 19) that this "does not mean that existence of a 'combination' is an indispensable ingredient of an 'unfair method of competition' under the Trade Commission Act."[5] Occasional FTC

---

4. Base-point pricing is the establishment of a delivered price which includes transportation figured from a standard point (which often is not where the goods were made and shipped). It permits sellers to quote identical prices regardless of the buyers' location (thereby facilitating price-fixing) and to distribute cartel profits among its participants equitably. See Kaysen, *Basing Point Pricing and Public Policy*, 63 Q.J.Econ. 289 (1949); G. Stigler, *The Organization of Industry* 147–64 (1968). Recent analysis suggests that base point pricing is not necessarily inconsistent with marketplace competition. See note 3, p. 237 supra.

5. As noted earlier, the FTC does not have specific jurisdiction to enforce the Sherman Act. However, its authority under

prosecutions and pronouncements have adopted the view that mere conscious parallelism violates Section 5, but this authority has not been pressed successfully. And except for isolated cases such as the Supreme Court's *American Tobacco* ruling in 1946 (discussed p. 149 n. 22 supra), "shared monopoly" has not as such been held to be covered by Section 2 of the Sherman Act's monopolization provision.

Occasional cases continue to test possible approaches. During the Carter presidency, the Justice Department announced that it would investigate "shared monopoly" practices as possible violations of the Sherman Act; but no actions were filed. Similarly, in the early 1970's the FTC charged leading makers of ready-to-eat cereals and the major oil companies with the collective possession of monopoly power and exclusionary activity in violation of Section 5; but after years of preliminary skirmishing, the cases were dismissed before trial. E.g., Kellogg Co., 99 F.T.C. 8 (1982). Reflecting a very different perspective on antitrust enforcement, the leaders of three government agencies no longer accepted the application of the antitrust laws against oligopoly practices where an express agreement was not shown.

Section 5 of the FTC Act is even broader than the Sherman Act because the FTC can prosecute violations of the Sherman Act as violations of the FTC Act's prohibition of unfair methods of competition, without some of the limitations of the Sherman Act. See also FTC v. Sperry & Hutchinson Co., 405 U.S. 233, 244–45 n. 5 (1972); FTC v. Brown Shoe Co., 384 U.S. 316, 320–22 (1966).

Recent cases touching this area tend to reflect a similar caution, although there are some exceptions. In Boise Cascade v. FTC, 637 F.2d 573 (9th Cir.1980), the Ninth Circuit ruled that an industry-wide basing-point scheme among plywood sellers did not violate Section 5 of the FTC Act where there was no evidence of an express conspiracy. There must, the court said, be evidence either of an "overt agreement" to engage in basing-point pricing or that the scheme "actually had the effect of fixing or stabilizing prices." On the other hand, the Fifth Circuit condemned the very same practice when ruling in a companion private treble damage action (under the Sherman Act) that evidence of identical practices *plus* contacts among the participants showing they had an opportunity to conspire was enough to allow a jury to find an agreement. In re Plywood Antitrust Litigation, 655 F.2d 627 (5th Cir.1981), cert. dismissed sub nom., Weyerhaeuser Co. v. Lyman Lamb Co., 462 U.S. 1125 (1983). The significance of this ruling is limited by the fact that the Justice Department had filed an amicus brief in the Supreme Court arguing that additional evidence was necessary before mere tacit collusion could support the finding of a conspiracy (for example, that the action was against the self-interest of the participants unless all went along) and the parties settled so the writ was dismissed.

The issue of whether "facilitating practices" uniformly undertaken by the four manufacturers of gasoline antiknock compounds violated Section 5 of the FTC Act was presented in Ethyl Corp., 101 F.T.C. 425 (1983), reversed sub nom., E.I. duPont de Nemours & Co., 729 F.2d 128 (2d Cir.1984). The practices included 30-day advance announcements of price changes, "most favored nation" clauses in sales contracts assuring buyers the benefit of subsequent price cuts, and uniform delivered prices. Although each practice was apparently adopted "independently and unilaterally" by the four firms, the Commission concluded that by removing some uncertainty from the market, they had the effect of facilitating parallel prices at noncompetitive levels higher than they otherwise might have been. The Second Circuit, however, reversed because Section 5 could not be "violated by noncollusive, nonpredatory and independent conduct of a nonartificial nature." The missing element of oppressiveness before a practice can be labelled "unfair" (under Section 5's equivalence of agreement) could be inferred only from "(1) evidence of an anticompetitive intent or purpose on the part of the producer charged, or (2) the absence of an independent legitimate business reason for the conduct." Thus, the court held that "[t]he mere existence of an oligopolistic market structure in which a small group of manufacturers engage in consciously parallel pricing of an identical product does not violate the antitrust laws."

Another strategy receiving sporadic legislative attention is the set of proposals for new legislation which would require deconcentration of already concentrated industries,[6] bar mergers by large firms in concentrated industries, or directly attack persistent monopoly. (See p. 149, n. 22 supra, for a description of a proposals to attack on persistent monopoly.) While several approaches have been offered, in general their aim is to break up oligopolistic industries unless they are merely the result of lawful patents or unless dissolution would cause the loss of substantial economies of scale. With the economic evidence of the adverse effects of concentration so much in dispute and the economy in this country and elsewhere so unstable, it seems unlikely that such legislation will be adopted in the immediate future. Serious questions can be raised about each of the legislative models. The defense of efficiency would substantially raise the cost of litigation, yet the general remedy of dissolution is undesirable and likely to be ineffective if efficiency is not a defense (i.e., profit incentives will lead firms in the newly deconcentrated industry to seek these same efficiencies by returning to their former size). To the extent that the threat of dissolution is substantial it operates as a serious disincentive to firms whose market power approaches the statutory standard—yet it seems absurd for legislative policy to encourage higher prices, lower efficiency, reduce productivity, etc. These and similar questions have focused attention on alternative proposals in recent years that would

6. Anti-merger laws, which are the focus of Chapter 9 infra, would be relied upon to break up oligopolies created by mergers.

narrow rather than expand the reach of the anti-trust laws.[7] Recent history suggests that they are unlikely to be acted upon quickly.

7. See, e.g., Reagan Administration Package to Congress for Revision of Federal Antitrust Laws, 50 BNA, Antitr. & Trade Reg.Rep. No. 1253 (Spec.Supp. Feb. 20, 1986).

CHAPTER VIII

VERTICAL RESTRAINTS

Thus far this text, in examining agreements among firms, considered only those agreements of competitors which restrain competition among sellers (or buyers) at the same level of distribution. These arrangements have generally involved horizontal cartels seeking to fix prices, to allocate territories, or to boycott mavericks. Our focus now shifts to restraints imposed by the seller on the buyer (or vice versa) or on what is called the vertical relationship. For example, a car manufacturer usually confines his operations to one level—production. He sells the cars he manufactures to dealers; they, in turn, sell them to consumers at the retail level. This chapter in general is devoted to an examination of the application of antitrust law to vertical arrangements. It is not restricted, however, to situations where firms operate only at one established level. Some industries—petroleum firms for example—are vertically integrated. That is, these oil companies not only produce and refine crude oil, but they also distribute it to consumers through franchised service stations. Their dealings with agents, buyers and suppliers are likewise frequently affected by the antitrust laws.

Before considering the various restrictions which have been developed in the course of vertical dealings between manufacturer and dealer, it is useful to consider why a seller chooses to operate at one or more distribution levels.[1] Whether or not a firm integrates vertically usually depends upon relative operating costs or efficiencies. If internal integration proves cheaper or simpler, the firm will tend to integrate and operate at both the manufacturing and retailing levels; on the other hand, the firm will operate at only one level and will not expand vertically if present market transactions are convenient and the existing process is not costlier. See generally Coase, *The Nature of the Firms*, 4 Economics (n.s.) 386 (1937). See also O. Williamson, *Markets and Hierarchies* 11–13 (1975) (vertical integration is preponderantly a transaction cost issue). This suggests an important consideration sometimes not observed in antitrust decisions, namely that a primary motivation for vertical integration by a firm is the achievement of efficiencies—i.e., lower costs—not available to it with existing market arrangements. Other reasons may also exist, some of which will be noted later, but they are not as likely to be controlling.

Undoubtedly similar opportunities are often also sought by firms which integrate vertically on a less formal basis—that is, those seeking the advantages of internal integration through contractual arrangements. A firm may seek a stable supply or

---

1. While this discussion emphasizes a two-level distribution scheme (manufacturer and retailer), it should be recognized that others exist including wholesalers, jobbers, distributors, etc.

output through arranging a long-term exclusive
dealing agreement or by requiring that dealers
purchasing its product for resale concentrate their
sales and advertising effort within assigned territories. On the other hand, it is possible that such
restraints—especially where they seek to restrict
the price at which the dealer may resell the product—may merely camouflage efforts by dealers or
manufacturers to fix prices on a horizontal basis.
Or the manufacturer may be attempting to extract
a monopoly price at the retail level because it
cannot do so at the manufacturing point.

Which rationale best supports vertical integration by contract cannot be assessed in advance, nor
do empirical studies support any particular view.
An examination of the facts of antitrust cases
involving vertical contract relations suggests that
most such arrangements could serve only to increase a firm's efficiency. Occasionally they may
be part of an effort to enhance a firm's market
power; while others lie somewhere between these
polar positions. Until 1977, antitrust case law did
not focus on this issue. More often than not the
legality of vertical restraints had been determined
through application of rules governing similar conduct in a horizontal context. In other words, vertical price-fixing and territorial restraints (the latter
until 1977) were generally condemned under a per
se-type rule. However, one firm is usually not
obligated to deal with another (a refusal to deal is
not itself illegal) and long-term supply and output

contracts are judged under a rule of reason approach. The reasonableness standard now applies to territorial and customer location clauses also. All this will be examined in greater detail in this chapter.

The vertical "restraints" considered here can be classified into two categories: those restricting the distribution of a product and those excluding or foreclosing competing firms (i.e., cartel type arrangements creating monopoly power) from a market. Typical of the former are resale price maintenance systems in which a manufacturer specifies a minimum price at which its product can be resold to retail consumers. Examples of the latter are tying clauses in which the manufacturer's sale of one product is conditioned upon the buyer's purchase of a second product from him. Conceptually these practices are quite distinct, even though they are often lumped together in antitrust case law. Distribution restrictions are in essence agreements by firms to eliminate some of the competition among themselves; thus they are analogous to price or territorial cartels. Exclusionary practices, on the other hand, are attempts to exclude rivals, with the result being sought through agreement between buyer and seller rather than by a seller offering his products at lower prices. Many of the boycott cases already examined, therefore, fall within this category.

A. RESTRICTIONS ON DISTRIBUTION

1. RESALE PRICE MAINTENANCE (RPM)

Among the earliest cases of vertical restraint heard by antitrust courts were those involving efforts by manufacturers to set the prices below which retailers could not subsequently resell their products. In the still leading case of Dr. Miles Medical Co. v. John D. Park & Sons Co., 220 U.S. 373 (1911), a manufacturer of a proprietary medicine (produced according to a secret, but unpatented, formula) sued a wholesaler on the ground that the latter obtained the plaintiff's medicine at cut prices by inducing others to breach their price agreements with Dr. Miles. In turning aside the manufacturer's effort to enjoin breaches of his established resale prices, the Court ruled that a manufacturer who sells his medicine to a wholesaler is not entitled to restrict its resale through interference with the purchaser's pricing decisions. Relying on the common law's hostility towards equitable servitudes on chattels, the Court noted that "a general restraint upon alienation is ordinarily invalid" and where its purpose is to destroy competition by fixing prices the restraint is "injurious to the public interest and void." While this analysis of the common law's protection of the alienation of property can be challenged,[2] the im-

---

2. The resale price requirement does not in fact prevent alienation in that it merely limits pricing opportunities, not

portance of the case from an antitrust viewpoint lies in its formalistic reliance on property law doctrines in deciding whether a vertical restraint violates the Sherman Act. The Court seemingly ignored the economic purpose of the arrangement and its effect on consumer welfare, except indirectly in its assertion that once a product has been sold (and title passed) "the public is entitled to whatever advantage may be derived from competition in the subsequent traffic." Other cases applied an identical rule to forbid resale price maintenance of patented or copyrighted items.

The soundness of this rule, which automatically condemns RPM agreements as a matter of policy, is vigorously debated. (And despite the established character of this rule—reiterated by the Supreme Court in California Retail Liquor Dealers Ass'n v. Midcal Aluminum, Inc., 445 U.S. 97, 102–03 (1980); but see Monsanto v. Spray-Rite Service Corp., 465 U.S. 752 (1984)—it is still worth discussing since it is the foundation of other antitrust issues involving vertical transactions, many of which are still open questions.)

Resale price maintenance agreements between a manufacturer and his dealers may serve several

resale. Moreover, equivalent common law protections are still available to limit the purchaser's "freedom"—namely, the purchaser cannot disparage the goods and he is also liable to his customers for any defects even though the latter were the result of defective design or manufacture. Finally, even under the common law the legality of a trade restraint usually depended upon its reasonableness (see p. 8 supra), and the Court in *Dr. Miles* made no effort to assess the interests promoted by resale price maintenance or its effects.

functions. Most antitrust decisions have focused on their likely harm. For example, retailers may have formed a cartel fixing the prices at which they would sell the product and (because of the legal difficulty of enforcing that agreement) have pressured the manufacturer to enforce it for them. Or RPM may have been imposed by the manufacturer on his dealers in order to assure adherence to a price-fixing conspiracy (or tacit oligopolistic collusion) among the manufacturers; with industry-wide RPM, a manufacturer seeking to cheat on the cartel would gain no advantage through shading prices to his dealer since increased sales would not result.

If these represented the only reasons for a manufacturer to participate in an RPM agreement, the result (although not the reasoning) in *Dr. Miles* would be unassailable. On the face of it, in fact, it seems questionable whether RPM agreements could benefit the manufacturer since the effect of setting a *minimum* resale price above the competitive level is to place a floor on retail prices, while setting the resale price below the competitive price would render the RPM agreement superfluous. Recalling our earlier analysis that when price goes up demand is necessarily reduced (see pp. 49–51 and Figure 1, p. 49, supra), the impact of RPM seemingly is to reduce a manufacturer's sales and correspondingly his profits, for without the RPM price retailers would sell more at a lower retail price—but pay the same wholesale price.

There are, however, other possible reasons for a manufacturer to seek an RPM arrangement with his dealers. It may be to a manufacturer's advantage that the retailers provide effective service to their customers (e.g., color television) or that the product be better promoted throughout a sales area in order to attract buyers (e.g., cosmetics and other drug store items). Through creation of an effective minimum retail price, dealers are induced to compete on a nonprice basis—that is, competition among retailers will bring additional rivalry in service (repairs, returns, credit) and promotion (advertising). Such nonprice competition would increase each seller's costs until, in a competitive retail market, the dealers' marginal cost equalled the RPM price. Figure 11 illustrates this effect.

To explain. Initially, the RPM price (P_{rpm}) will intersect with the demand curve (D_1) and clear the market at a level (Point A) substantially above the retailer's marginal cost (MC_1); resulting in consumers demanding the limited quantity (q_1) with the retailer's supracompetitive return equalling the shaded area. But such supranormal returns would quickly dissipate under the pressure of nonprice competition. A new and larger demand (D_2) would occur because increased service and promotion would make the product more valuable to an expanded group. Marginal cost would increase (MC_2) as dealers competed with each other by service and promotion, and the new equilibrium (Point B) would eliminate the "excess" profits as output increased (to q_2).

FIGURE 11: RIVALRY AMONG DEALERS UNDER RPM

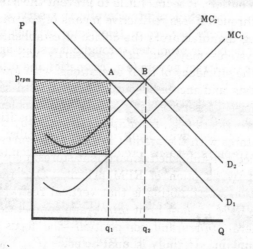

Whether RPM agreements are desirable even from an efficiency viewpoint is debatable, of course. Lack of competition among retailers may protect supranormal returns for the dealers until "corrected" by new entrants. In any case, customers are denied the option of buying the product at a lower price through foregoing service or advertising. Still, manufacturers are usually permitted to select the price and service levels at which their products are sold. Presumably, if consumers desired the options of lower-priced non-serviced goods, manufacturers would make them available (e.g., as with separate service contracts now available for large household appliances) or there would be new entrants to satisfy this demand. And since a manufacturer is free to integrate vertically forward and to impose similar conditions on sales in his own outlets, it seems futile to prevent the same result through a less restrictive means of contract. Allowing manufacturers the choice of establishing RPM systems may (but not necessarily will) enhance the efficiency of their operations, with lower total costs and increased output. That is to say, efficiencies of service may result and problems from free riders (e.g., from appliance sales by discount stores with the product returned for warranty service to established department stores) may be avoided by adoption of RPM pricing. One final distinction worth noting is that vertical restraints such as RPM at most limit *intra*brand competition. In general, *inter*brand competition—the focus of horizontal price-fixing—is unaffected.

All this does not mean that the result in *Dr. Miles,* and later cases condemning resale price maintenance, is always erroneous. It does suggest, however, that unless substantial evidence demonstrates that RPM is likely to result in restricted output, higher prices, or oligopoly coordination, the antitrust legality of RPM should be measured by the rule of reason, on a case-by-case basis. And few convincing studies showing the effect of RPM exist. Despite the per se condemnation of RPM by the Supreme Court in *Dr. Miles,* such pricing was permitted in several states which adopted "fair trade" laws under an exception authorized by Congress (but which Congress repealed in 1975).

This generally rigid rule against vertical price-fixing was extended from minimum to maximum prices in Albrecht v. Herald Co., 390 U.S. 145 (1968).[3] Again, analysis suggests that such vertical price-fixing may enhance distributional efficiency and increase interbrand competition. But the Court's reluctance to approve any form of price-fixing and its concern over the possibility of larger manufacturers using maximum price agreements to coerce smaller dealers led it to condemn the arrangement. See also Arizona v. Maricopa County Medical Soc'y, 457 U.S. 332 (1982) (horizontal maximum price fixing condemned as per se illegal) discussed pp. 183–85 supra.

Moreover, the Court's analysis in Continental T.V., Inc. v. GTE Sylvania Inc., 433 U.S. 36, 51 n. 18 (1977), which justified a continuation of the *Dr. Miles* rule against vertical price-fixing primarily because of its stablizing effect on retail prices, may signal the end of the rule declaring maximum price-fixing illegal per se. Such an automatic prohibition now seems inconsistent with the result of *Sylvania,* under which dealers can be granted legally exclusive territories; by thus protecting dealers against intrabrand competition, courts may find it more desirable to allow manufacturers the authority to control the maximum price their dealers charge. And in Monsanto Co. v. Spray-Rite

3. The defendant newspaper violated Section 1 of the Sherman Act by refusing to sell to the plaintiff-distributor when the latter resold the papers to customers at more than the suggested retail price.

Serv. Corp., 465 U.S. 752 (1984) the Court made clear that the per se rule of *Dr. Miles* is the exception to the principle that manufacturers and dealers are free to establish the best arrangement for marketing their product. This conclusion is reinforced by the Court's strong endorsement of *Colgate* (and its rule that a manufacturer is free to decide with whom and on what terms it will deal with others, discussed pp. 308–13 infra). On the other hand, the Court declined to consider whether *Dr. Miles* should be overturned even though urged to do so by the Solicitor General and others. Its opinion seemed to invite another challenge where the record would better support a re-examination of whether vertical price fixing should remain illegal per se. The inconsistency between *Dr. Miles* and *Sylvania* is disconcerting and breeds litigation such as *Monsanto*. But the felt need to protect smaller dealers and consumers from RPM—and its supposedly higher prices—remains strong. Congress reflects this sentiment in its repeated condemnation of efforts to overturn or question *Dr. Miles*. (It went so far as to bar the head of the Antitrust Division from arguing to the Supreme Court in *Monsanto* for a more lenient rule.) Whether the Court will challenge these popular views is uncertain; for now it has managed to avoid taking any position.

2. CONSIGNMENTS AND DISTRIBUTION THROUGH AGENTS

Dr. Miles applied the rule against price-fixing to sales by a manufacturer to a dealer on the grounds that the resale price restraint denied the retailer-purchaser his common law "right" to resell (i.e., alienate) his property. Under this analysis, the critical points were apparently that the purchaser was a separate legal and economic entity and that he had purchased and taken title to the product.

The question then arose as to whether this vertical rule against price-fixing applied where the retailer was the manufacturer's agent and, instead of taking title to the products, received them on consignment. Could the manufacturer then set the resale price? In United States v. General Elec. Co., 272 U.S. 476 (1926), the Court answered that where it is clear that the arrangement is legitimate and that the manufacturer both retains title and bears substantial risks of ownership (e.g., losses from acts of God, obsolescence, possible price declines), the antitrust laws do not prevent him from dictating the terms of sale—including retail prices. In this circumstance price-fixing is not illegal. Under *GE,* then, a manufacturer can avoid the limitations imposed under *Dr. Miles* by appointing retailers as his agents and by arranging for sales to them under a consignment agreement.[4]

4. In fact, it seems likely that GE adopted this arrangement for other reasons such as to divide its sales and prices between two markets—industrial and retail. That is, the usual ratio-

GE, in other words, continued the formalism of *Dr. Miles* while reaching a contrary result. Despite this opposition, analytically *GE* seems equally unsatisfactory. Although GE had an agency rather than a sales relationship with its retailers, GE and its retailers were separate legal entities and the agreements between them were seemingly designed to restrain trade—with the same effect as resulted under RPM agreements condemned in *Dr. Miles.* To be sure, once the rule against resale price agreements is adopted, a line must be drawn somewhere which recognizes and upholds the authority of a manufacturer who is vertically integrated to set the prices of his retail outlets. But neither distributional efficiency nor logic support the drawing of the line at the agency relation—except that it is somewhat consistent with the property law rule and rationale applied by the Court in *Dr. Miles.* (And consistency for the wrong reason hardly seems a persuasive argument.) It should be noted that the focus under *GE* is on the *method* of the manufacturer's control over the resale price and not on its *effect* on competition or consumer welfare.

Not surprisingly, the history following *GE* is characterized by a consistent judicial retreat from the rule as well as an unrequited search for a

nale for RPM seemed absent. What GE apparently sought was to discriminate in the prices charged to industrial and to retail customers; it wanted to prevent industrial customers from purchasing electric lamps at lower prices and then reselling them to retail consumers in competition with GE but at a lower price.

reasonable rationale justifying the result. Occasional cases attacked the legitimacy of the consignment, the question being whether the retailers were in fact the manufacturer's agents. See United States v. Masonite Corp., 316 U.S. 265, 279 (1942). And then in a quixotic opinion by Justice Douglas in Simpson v. Union Oil Co., 377 U.S. 13 (1964), the Court inconsistently ruled that Union Oil violated the Sherman Act by fixing the prices charged by its service station-consignees to retail customers. But the Court's opinion in *Simpson* did not overrule *GE.* (*GE* was distinguished on the ground that a patentee was entitled to restrict its licensee's prices—although Justice Stewart's dissent correctly noted that this argument related to a wholly separate ruling in *GE,* see p. 391 infra.) Nor could it effectively distinguish the legitimacy of the agency relation. About the only reason which the Court offered for invalidating the vertical price restraint was that Union Oil used it as a device to "coerce" nominal agents "who are in reality small struggling competitors seeking retail gas customers."

The difficulties with the *Simpson* analysis are manifold: by implication it suggested that dealer imposed price restraints would be upheld, but this is inconsistent with horizontal price-fixing case law; nor was the Court presented with any evidence that Union Oil in fact held substantial market power vis-a-vis its retailers. The Court used the antitrust laws to redress what was to it an apparent inequity in the bargaining power of an oil company with its retail service stations, but without any consideration of the costs which this action imposes on distributional efficiency. In addition, if those savings are substantial, then it would seem likely that the oil company will integrate forward and establish company-owned retail outlets—which is hardly supportive of the retailers the Court sought to protect.[5]

Whether vertical price-fixing by contract except where the manufacturer clearly controls the retail outlet is now automatically condemned by *Simpson* remains uncertain. After 62 years the General Electric Co. abandoned its agency system in 1974. On the other hand, the legal distinction between ownership (or agency control) of goods and their resale, recognized in *Dr. Miles* and repeated since then, was not disturbed by *Sylvania's* change of course insofar as the Court had held that the owner of goods or his agent can set the price and other terms under which they are sold. Lower courts therefore will generally uphold good faith consignment arrangements to agents—at least when they are not part of a "giant" distribution system. See, e.g., Mesirow v. Pepperidge Farms,

5. As this has occurred, primarily in response to the OPEC boycott and the reduced opportunities to make profits through production and refining, state laws have been rewritten to protect service station dealers from the competition of company-owned stations. These laws have been upheld against both constitutional and federal antitrust attack. Exxon Corp. v. Governor of Maryland, 437 U.S. 117 (1978); Cf. New Motor Vehicle Bd. of California v. Orrin W. Fox Co., 439 U.S. 96 (1978).

Inc., 703 F.2d 339 (9th Cir.1983), cert. denied, 464 U.S. 820 (1983).

3.   TERRITORIAL AND CUSTOMER RESTRICTIONS

With the opportunity for vertical price restrictions first narrowed in *Dr. Miles* and then seemingly foreclosed in *Simpson,* attention shifted to less-inclusive restraints such as manufacturer limitations on dealer territories and customers by which similar or additional distributional advantages could be obtained.   Judicial concern with the "costs" of such restrictions on competitive price and output levels sharply limited vertical restraints on distribution until, in 1967, the Court ruled in *Schwinn* (discussed p. 294 infra) that territorial or customer restrictions on the resale of goods were per se illegal.   The ruling raised a storm of criticism for its archaic legal analysis. New economic insights into vertical distribution arrangements and their purposes further undermined this rigid rule.   Thus, only a decade after its per se ruling—in a major shift that has already affected other areas of antitrust as well—the Supreme Court reversed direction in *Sylvania* (discussed p. 302 infra), overturned its 1967 ruling, and set forth a rule of reason standard for nonprice vertical distribution arrangements.   A closer look at these arrangements is a prerequisite to understanding their legal control.

In making arrangements for the distribution of his products, a manufacturer may wish to insulate appointed dealers from competition from others also selling his product. Where the manufacturer relies on the dealer to promote his products by local advertising, dealer protection from intrabrand competition is likely to be the sine qua non of the latter's efforts. (See pp. 205–11, supra discussing *Sealy* and *Topco* and the "free rider" problem in a horizontal context.) Likewise the manufacturer may already have developed sales contacts in the dealer's territory and thus be unwilling to appoint a dealer who might capture such sales. Consequently customer limitations are also commonly included in dealer franchise agreements.[6]

Manufacturers argue that retail dealers need protection from intrabrand competition in order to

6. Some of the reasons for these limitations are not dissimilar to justifications already rejected by the Supreme Court in overruling resale price maintenance arrangements. There is, perhaps, a basic difference between RPM and territorial restraints in the type of products involved and the manufacturer's interest in forming such agreements. Typically RPM agreements involve convenience goods such as proprietary drugs where the manufacturer seeks to assure that the branded goods are available even through low volume outlets. On the other hand, nonprice restrictions on distribution are normally applied to larger specialty items, such as cars or bicycles, where dealer promotion of the manufacturer's brand is of signal importance. Customers generally shop for the latter products and the manufacturer's desire is that they be attracted to his product by the intensive sales and service efforts of his dealers. The dealer's greater investment in promoting the specialty goods may suggest why courts have generally been more receptive to non-price vertical restraints.

support desired activities and, sometimes, to obtain a greater return on investment. In this way superior dealers are attracted, they are responsive to manufacturer suggestions, they will carry larger inventories (and thus better satisfy customer needs), they will increase market penetration through greater use of advertising and sales efforts, and they will provide higher quality maintenance and repair, which is important for continued sales of complex durable goods. Dealer justifications are often the other side of the same coin. Dealers contend that, freed from intrabrand competition they can exploit the product more fully through specialization in sales and service; they can assure greater promotional and service efforts since they are protected against invasions by free riders; they can reduce their investment risk; and they can increase the scope of those investments.

Whether these arguments are persuasive depends on several unanswered questions. If *inter*brand competition is vigorous, it would seem of little consequence what restraints a manufacturer or retailer imposes on the other—as long as it is not a cover for a horizontal price or territorial cartel. Unless vertical integration—at least by internal growth—is restricted, and that is generally *not* the case, then a manufacturer's choice of distribution techniques seemingly should go unobstructed; such techniques probably are designed to increase his productive efficiency, ultimately lowering prices and increasing output. And barring

integration by contract may only force the manufacturer to select a less efficient means—namely,
internal expansion or merger. In fact, by allowing
a manufacturer the opportunity to design his own
distribution system, interbrand competition should
be invigorated and new entry facilitated—especially since smaller scale enterprises can be designed;
that is, the alternative of forward vertical integration is likely to require greater capital investment.

Perhaps an example will make this point clearer.
Assume for a moment that you are a manufacturer
of bicycles seeking to compete with Sears and other
large sellers. By assuring your dealers that they
will not face competition from other sellers of your
bikes, the dealers will be willing to advertise your
brand in their territory, to service your bikes to
gain repeat business, etc. And in this way your
capital investment can be limited to that necessary
for the manufacture of bicycles; it will not need to
include the establishment and continuance of numerous retail outlets.

This analysis suggests that whether vertical restraints on distribution by customer and territorial
devices should be allowed is unrelated to whether
the manufacturer retains title or whether the dealer is his agent. Rather it would seem to invite a
rule of reason approach, weighing the potential
harms against the benefits (and possibly the less
restrictive alternatives), unless it can be shown
that in the vast majority of instances the costs of
such restrictions substantially outweigh the bene-

fits. This appeared to be the Supreme Court's approach when it first considered the issue in White Motor Co. v. United States, 372 U.S. 253 (1963).

Seemingly overturning the Justice Department's long-standing contention (since 1948) that vertical territorial allocations were illegal per se, the Court in *White Motor* reversed the lower court's grant of summary judgment for the government. White Motor sold its trucks to dealers who agreed to resell them only to customers not otherwise reserved to the manufacturer and who had a place of business or purchasing headquarters within the assigned territory. Because of the meager record and the Court's own inexperience with franchise limitations, the Court concluded that it did not "know enough of the economic and business stuff out of which these arrangements emerge" to be certain whether they stifle or invigorate competition.

Despite widespread interpretation of this decision as adopting a rule of reason approach to vertical limitations—especially since three dissenters called for a per se rule—the Court in fact noted that "[w]e only hold that the legality of the territorial and customer limitations should be determined only after a trial." Shortly thereafter lower courts assessed territorial restrictions on a rule of reason basis, evaluating their purpose, power and effect, and usually upholding the particular schemes. See, e.g., Sandura Co. v. FTC, 339 F.2d 847 (6th Cir. 1964). Note, in none of these decisions did the courts pay any notice to the rationale of *Dr. Miles* and *Simpson:* namely, whether there were restrictions on the alienation of property, or whether title had passed to the dealer.

This suggestion that antitrust analysis of vertical restraints was moving to a more rational ground proved a vain hope, however, when in United States v. Arnold, Schwinn & Co., 388 U.S. 365 (1967), the Court examined, on its merits, Schwinn's scheme for distributing its bicycles. Schwinn, once the leading manufacturer of bicycles in the United States, had seen its market share almost halved in the preceding decade as competitors selling to Sears and other mass merchandisers captured an increasing share of the market. Schwinn distributed most of its bicycles in two ways: through sale to wholesale distributors who resold them to franchised distributors (for resale to the public); and under the "Schwinn Plan," by direct sale to franchised retailers after paying commissions to the wholesalers who placed the orders. The "Schwinn Plan" was, in other words, a consignment arrangement whereby the bicycles were shipped directly to franchised retailers. Distributors and retailers were restricted as to the class of persons to whom they could sell: distributors could sell only to retailers within their exclusive territory, and retailers could sell only to ultimate customers and not to other unfranchised retailers.

The fundamental question, therefore, was whether the vertical territorial restrictions on the distributors and retailers were lawful—and whether they would be tested on a rule of reason or a per se basis. Initially, in *Schwinn* the Court indicated that a rule of reason would apply when it stated that "[under *White Motor*] we must look to the specifics of the challenged practices and their impact upon the marketplace in order to make a judgment as to whether the restraint is or is not 'reasonable' . . . ." But only a few pages later in the same opinion the Court apparently announced a partial per se test, namely that where the manufacturer sells the product subject to territorial or other restrictions upon resale, he commits a violation of the Sherman Act. However, where title, dominion and risk are retained by the manufacturer and the distributor takes the goods on consignment, the territorial restriction will only violate Section 1 if the restraint on competition is unreasonable.

As noted, the decision in *Schwinn* was criticized from almost every corner, and not always fairly. An example of the latter was the charge that the Court had radically shifted direction in the space of four years, after having said it needed to learn more about the business basis of vertical territorial arrangements. That commentary, however, reflected only a shallow reading of the Court's opinion in *White Motor*. More serious was the complaint that, as in its ruling on vertical price-fixing, the Court had resolved a question of economic policy by resort to ancient property law rules governing restraints of alienation. As was frequently

and acidly noted, why the location of title and risk
was relevant in deciding whether a manufacturer
could control his retail sales was nowhere explained—and appeared unexplainable. The underlying policy question was whether these restraints
served to make product distribution more efficient
and interbrand rivalry more vigorous. And it is
here that the new economic learning—especially in
regard to the problem of free riders—was effective
in explaining the error of the *Schwinn* result. The
Schwinn rule also produced several anomalies.
For example, under the rule (of reason) applicable
to exclusive dealing (see p. 328 infra), a manufacturer could promise a purchasing retailer that the
former would not sell the product to a competing
retailer; but the same promise by a purchasing
retailer—not to resell to another retailer—was illegal per se under *Schwinn* even though the competitive impact in the two situations was obviously
indistinguishable.

Not surprisingly, manufacturers, distributors
and retailers found the rule in *Schwinn* difficult to
accept since it often imposed higher costs on them
depending on the form of organization or the character of the distribution transaction. They sought
to avoid its reach by alternative but similar devices
through assignments of "primary responsibility"
on dealers, inclusion of "location clauses" in franchise agreements, provisions for "profit passovers,"
and so forth. Lower courts often aided this process
by sharply limiting *Schwinn* to its facts or by

distinguishing its treatment of territorial allocations from these supposedly less inclusive alternatives. Faced with this two-pronged attack of direct
and indirect criticism, the Supreme Court, in the
next vertical distribution to reach its case docket,
reversed itself, overruled *Schwinn,* and announced
a rule of reason standard.

The decision in Continental TV, Inc. v. GTE
Sylvania Inc., 433 U.S. 36 (1977), is possibly the
most important antitrust case since *Madison Oil*
and *Alcoa* in the 1940's. It deserves close analysis.
As a manufacturer of television sets, Sylvania had
a miniscule share (1–2 percent) of the U.S. market
when compared to RCA (60–70 percent), Zenith and
Magnavox. Thus, in 1962 Sylvania decided to
abandon its saturation distribution through independent or company-owned wholesalers and moved
to sell directly to a smaller group of franchised
retailers. These dealers were free to sell and ship
their goods anywhere and to all classes of customers. But Sylvania reserved to itself the determination of how many retailers it would appoint in any
geographic area and required the dealers to agree
to operate only from approved locations. This new
marketing approach appeared to be successful and
within three years Sylvania's share of national
television set sales increased to 5 percent. However, a dispute arose with one of its franchisees when
Sylvania, dissatisfied with overall San Francisco
sales of its television sets, appointed an additional
dealer to serve that area. The plaintiff, a nearby

Sylvania dealer, objected and, after being unable to reach an understanding with Sylvania, moved its store to Sacramento contrary to the provisions of the franchise agreement. Sylvania terminated the franchise and this suit followed which, when it reached the Supreme Court, focused on whether the location clause in the franchise agreement was permissible, or was per se illegal as ruled by the trial court.[7] After a careful review of the *Schwinn* opinion, its analytical base, and the economic criticisms of its approach, the Court endorsed a case-by-case balancing of competitive effects for testing nonprice vertical restraints. Although *Sylvania* involved location clauses often said to be less inclusive and therefore not as restrictive as the territorial limitation tested in *Schwinn,* the Court concluded that there was no basis for distinguishing the two restraints since both involved franchise systems that effectively foreclosed significant *intra*brand competition.

In holding that vertically imposed nonprice territorial restraints should be tested under a reasonableness standard even though intrabrand competition was necessarily lessened if not practically eliminated, the Supreme Court's new analysis emphasized the redeeming purposes and possible beneficial effects of the arrangement. Sylvania was, in other words, allowed to seek a more efficient

7. One interesting sidelight is that the trial judge in *Sylvania* was retired Supreme Court Justice Tom Clark, sitting by designation. He had served on the Court in 1967 when *Schwinn* was decided but had not participated in that case.

method of distribution on the ground that *inter*-brand rivalry—competition among different television set manufacturers—would thereby be enhanced. And, as long as competition was present at the *inter*brand level, these benefits would probably outweigh the necessarily less significant limitation of *intra*brand rivalry—competition among dealers of Sylvania television sets.

The Court relied on economic theory to demonstrate that the location clause would benefit Sylvania's effort to compete against other manufacturers at the retail level. That is, assuring dealers of Sylvania sets some protection from other Sylvania dealers would induce competitive and aggressive dealer activity in advertising the product and providing customer services; that is, the location clauses protected dealers from other "free-riding" dealers who might seek to cash-in on the benefits of these activities—and thereby discourage the initial dealer effort to advance the manufacturer's product. Furthermore, the Court argued that consumers will be protected from excessive prices or services because of the competition offered by other non-Sylvania television set sellers and because each manufacturer has an independent interest in maintaining as much intrabrand competition as is consistent with efficient distribution. Thus the Court concluded that, on balance, nonprice restrictions in vertical distribution arrangements possess sufficient economic benefits to warrant their testing under a rule of reason standard.

Sylvania is an important doctrinal reversal involving an explicit adoption of price theory analysis as the foundation of its decision. Many questions were left undecided, however. The Court did "not foreclose the possibility that particular applications of vertical restrictions might justify per se prohibition," although it did emphasize that any "departure from the rule of reason standard must be based upon demonstrable economic effect rather than—as in *Schwinn*—upon formalistic line drawing." Nor did it make clear how the rule of reason was to be applied, who was to bear the burden of persuasion on measuring intra- and interbrand effects, or which justifications deserved special consideration. Subsequent lower court decisions have focused on these two criteria identified by Justice Powell in *Sylvania* in determining whether the rule of reason standard has been satisfied. They are: (1) whether the arrangement is likely to have a "permanent effect" on interbrand competition, and (2) whether the restraint has "redeeming virtues." [8] Several cases now suggest the first criterion requires a showing that the manufacturer imposing the restraint had a substantial share, e.g., Valley Liquors, Inc. v. Penfield Importers, Ltd., 678 F.2d 742 (7th Cir.1982) (Posner, J.); Graphic Prods. Distrib. v. Itek Corp., 717 F.2d 1560 (11th Cir.1983), and that there be a convincing business rationale for the restraint, e.g., Beltone Electronics Corp.,

---

8. For a review of the cases, see Gellhorn & Tatham, *Making Sense Out of the Rule of Reason,* 35 Case Wes.L.Rev. 155, 170–77 (1984–85).

100 F.T.C. 68 (1982). By effectively placing the burden of demonstrating possible anticompetitive effects of the restraints on the plaintiff, nonprice vertical restraints now generally pass the rule of reason test. It is not enough for the complaining dealer to demonstrate that it cut prices or was otherwise a maverick dealer. Nonprice vertical restraints are by their nature designed to obtain uniformity in distribution and increased attention to promotion and service. The case law, however, still concentrates on proxies for market effects— i.e., the market power of the manufacturer and justifications for the restraint—rather on direct evidence of reduced output or higher market price effects.[9]

Another issue that divided the lower courts is whether *Sylvania* protects a manufacturer who terminates a dealer as a result of pressure from a competing distributor seeking to escape the terminated dealer's price competition. Here the question is whether the manufacturer's action is tested under the per se standard for horizontal conspiracies or rule of reason for vertical restraints. Illustrative are the approaches in Oreck Corp. v. Whirlpool Corp., 579 F.2d 126 (2d Cir.1978) (en banc), cert. denied, 439 U.S. 946 (1978); Cernuto Inc. v. United Cabinet Corp., 595 F.2d 164 (3d Cir.1979). *Oreck* viewed the manufacturer as implementing

9. For additional efforts to use market concentration and other measures as filters for prosecutorial discretion, U.S. Dep't of Justice, Vertical Restraints Guidelines (Jan. 23, 1985), reprinted 48 BNA Antitrust & Trade Reg.Rep. 193; Easterbrook, *The Limits of Antitrust,* 63 Tex.L.Rev. 1 (1984).

its vertical territorial program, justifying a rule of reason approach; *Cernuto* focused on the exclusionary effect of dealer complaints, concluding that the manufacturer's action did not alter its horizontal, interdealer character.

The Supreme Court provided some clarification in Monsanto Co. v. Spray-Rite Service Co., 465 U.S. 752 (1984) where a herbicide manufacturer terminated a cut-rate distributor for failure to comply with various service requirements after also receiving price complaints from other distributors. The lower appellate court had upheld a jury finding of a price conspiracy from "proof of termination following competitor complaints." This was not enough for the Supreme Court. It observed that manufacturers and distributors are naturally in constant communication about prices and market strategies. Thus, before a conspiracy to fix prices can be found, there must be evidence that tends to exclude the possibility of independent action by the manufacturer and distributor.[10] While the Court in fact found such evidence in *Monsanto* on highly ambiguous evidence (see Easterbrook, *Vertical Arrangements and the Rule of Reason,* 53 Antitr.L.J. 135, 171–72 (1984)), subsequent cases reflect considerable judicial skepticism that price fixing was the manufacturer's purpose.

10. There must, the Court said, be "direct or circumstantial evidence that reasonably tends to prove that the manufacturer and others had a conscious commitment to a common scheme designed to achieve an unlawful objective" before the per se rule will apply. 465 U.S. at 753.

B. LIMITS ON SUPPLIER POWER: EXCLUSIONARY PRACTICES

1. REFUSALS TO DEAL

Earlier we explored concerted refusals to deal (under the pejorative name of group boycotts) which were scrutinized with varying degrees of strictness according to the comparative dangers presented by their means and ends. A wholly different approach is applied where individual decisions as to whether to deal with another are involved. Traditional concepts of "freedom of contract" are followed when a manufacturer unilaterally decides that he will no longer deal with a particular retailer. At least that is the basic theory. But reality is seldom so simple and many cases have questioned whether a particular manufacturer's actions were unilateral or constituted an exclusionary agreement with some of his dealers (to the detriment of others).

The leading and still much debated case is United States v. Colgate & Co., 250 U.S. 300 (1919).[11] Bound by the trial court's interpretation of a criminal indictment which charged Colgate only with refusing to sell to a dealer (but not pursuant to a resale price agreement), the Court ruled that a manufacturer's mere advance announcement that he would not sell to price-cutters was not a violation of the Sherman Act. In the Court's view, the

11. See Pitofsky & Dam, *Is The Colgate Doctrine Dead?*, 37 Antitr.L.J. 772 (1968).

missing element was that no agreement existed between Colgate and its other dealers (who adhered to the announced RPM plan). "In the absence of any purpose to create or maintain a monopoly, the act does not restrict the long recognized right of trader or manufacturer engaged in an entirely private business, freely to exercise his own independent discretion as to parties with whom he will deal."

The rule seems at once both necessary and illogical. On the one hand, a competitive market relies on the individual manufacturer's choice of how best to distribute his products as an essential element of productive efficiency. As a practical matter the case also may have great significance in limiting specious treble damage claims by private antitrust plaintiffs. *Colgate* is not important in upholding the manufacturer's freedom to suggest prices [12] because its facts are limited to Colgate's action to cease supplying the dealer. But without the *Colgate* rule a manufacturer's termination of a dealer for inadequate sales, etc. would be perilous. That is, citing *Dr. Miles* (and *Interstate Circuit*) the terminated dealer could file a private antitrust action seeking treble damages claiming that the termination violated Section 1 by seeking to enforce an illegal resale price system. Because of *Colgate* the terminated dealer must show that an agreement exists between the manufacturer and

12. Indeed, some legislation even requires dealers to display a manufacturer's suggested retail price. E.g., 15 U.S.C.A. §§ 1231–33 (1958 Automobile Information Disclosure Act).

one of his dealers to enforce the RPM or some other restrictive plan. See Monsanto Co. v. Spray-Rite Serv. Co., 465 U.S. 752 (1984) (reaffirming *Colgate* doctrine).

The rule in *Colgate* is, it should be noted, limited to those situations where the person refusing to sell does not have a "purpose to create or maintain a monopoly." Although seldom noted or analyzed, this limitation is consistent with other rules in antitrust imposing an obligation on a monopolist not to act discriminatorily (see pp. 141, 147–49 supra) or in common law imposing special obligations of reasonable care and strict liability on a common carrier or other person in a monopoly position. Where the buyer has no other readily available source, the seller may be deprived of his freedom to choose not to deal, at least insofar as he cannot show a basis for any refusal. In this limited circumstance, the balance may weigh in favor of the purchaser. However, where the monopolist can establish a basis for the refusal or where no monopoly exists and the buyer has alternatives for the seller's product or service, an individual refusal to deal may still be upheld. Thus, in Official Airline Guides, Inc. v. FTC, 630 F.2d 920 (2d Cir. 1980), cert. denied, 450 U.S. 917 (1981), the Court ruled that a monopoly publisher's refusal to publish commuter flight schedules was not illegal. The FTC had to show that the respondent sought to exclude the commuter airlines or otherwise was seeking to enlarge or entrench its monopoly (or that of its customers).

The illogic of Colgate, though, is its apparent inconsistency with *Dr. Miles*, its formalism and unreality, and the narrowness with which it interprets the meaning of agreement under the Sherman Act. *Dr. Miles* struck at vertical price-fixing accomplished by direct agreement; but *Colgate* seemingly permits a manufacturer to achieve the same end result (for that was Colgate's admitted purpose), though indirectly, by allowing Colgate to announce an RPM policy and then to take unilateral action to enforce it. It seems unsurprising, therefore, that after *Colgate* the resale price policies urged by manufacturers were invariably followed by retailers. The rationale of *Colgate* seems equally unsatisfactory. Relying on the fact that Colgate's dealers were under no formal constraint and could sell the product at any price without fear of suit for a breach of contract, the Court found that no agreement existed and hence there was no violation of the Sherman Act. Again this formalism ignores apparent reality.

Not surprisingly, *Colgate* has been questioned since its inception and its subsequent history is one of limitation and exception. Almost immediately the Court itself found that the ruling was "misapprehended" and distinguished it to invalidate an RPM system enforced by a "course of conduct" or "tacit understandings." E.g., FTC v. Beech-Nut Packing Co., 257 U.S. 441, 452 (1922). In United States v. Parke, Davis & Co., 362 U.S. 29 (1960), a manufacturer of drug products sought to obtain adherence to its RPM plan by bargaining and mediating with retailers in order to obtain their adherence and trade. In effect the drug manufacturer sought and received promises of future compliance. Without here reviewing each factual distinction, the goal and primary effort of Parke, Davis was indistinguishable from that of Colgate: the only difference seemingly was that the dealer in *Colgate* did not comply so it was cut off, whereas in *Parke, Davis* the manufacturer was successful and did not need to terminate the dealer.[13] While *Colgate* is still cited with approval, unilateral refusals to deal with retailers in support of a manufacturer's announced policy are lawful only if the facts are "of such Doric simplicity as to be somewhat rare in this day of complex business enterprise." George W. Warner & Co. v. Black & Decker Mfg. Co., 277 F.2d 787, 790 (2d Cir.1960). Professor Sullivan has aptly summarized the cases as follows: "[I]f a manufacturer seeks to achieve resale price maintenance or any other unlawful vertical restraint through the exercise of its right to refuse to deal and a prior announcement of policy, the manufacturer's conduct remains lawful only so long as no step in addition to announcement of policy and withdrawal of trade from violators is taken by the manufacturer." L. Sullivan, *Antitrust* 393 (1977).

The strong reaffirmation of *Colgate* by the Supreme Court in *Monsanto* seems to assure that

---

13. Subsequent cases such as Albrecht v. Herald Co., 390 U.S. 145 (1968), remove even this distinction, finding an agreement whenever a dealer succumbs to manufacturer pressure or other dealers adhere to the manufacturer's announced policy— even though no express understanding is demonstrated.

unilateral refusals to deal will be protected from antitrust challenge. What is unclear—and vigorously debated—is whether the per se prohibition on resale price maintenance will continue. *Monsanto* seems to invite further challenge. How a later Court will rule is, of course, unknown.

2. TYING ARRANGEMENTS [14]

A tying contract describes the situation where the seller of a product, such as a copying machine, conditions the sale of the copier upon the buyer's agreement to purchase all the paper used in the machine from the seller. That is, the seller of the copier ties the sale of a *tying* product (the copier) to the buyer's purchase of the *tied* product (the paper). Whether such an arrangement is permitted under the antitrust laws depends on many factors, often including the business purpose or effect of the arrangement. And these are highly diverse. As a consequence this discussion is even more selective than heretofore encountered in this text, and particularly useful references presenting in greater detail the economic and antitrust issues involved are noted in the margin.[15]

14. Tie-ins are not dissimilar to package transactions, franchise dealer sales programs (e.g., tires, batteries and accessories, known as the "TBA" cases) and reciprocal trading. None of these is dealt with directly in this text. Each involves an alleged problem of leverage; the judicial results are not dissimilar to the rules applied to tie-ins.

15. See, e.g., Baker, *The Supreme Court and the Per Se Tying Rule: Cutting the Gordian Knot,* 65 Va.L.Rev. 1233 (1980); Posner, *Exclusionary Practices and the Antitrust Laws,* 41 U.Chi.L.Rev. 506 (1974); Markovits, *Tie-ins, Reciprocity, and the Leverage Theory,* 76 Yale L.J. 1397 (1967); Burstein, *A Theory of*

Initial efforts to exercise legal control over tie-ins involved patent laws and efforts by the owner of a patented product to assert a right (under the patent grant) to tie a second, usually unpatented article to the tying product. For example, in *Motion Picture Patents Co. v. Universal Film Mfg. Co.*, 243 U.S. 502 (1917), the patentee of a motion picture projector sold it on the condition that it would be used only to project the films of the patentee. When a licensee used the projector to show other films the patentee sued for contributory infringement—an invasion of the patentee's rights under the patent grant. In denying the patentee's claim for infringement, the Court ruled that the patent grant did not give the patentee the right to restrict the use of the machine to particular materials; the Court expressed its concern with any attempt to extend the monopoly grant of the patent.[16] The tying arrangement, in other words, was condemned because the holder of a legal monopoly in one market (projectors) was using that leverage to monopolize another market (films).

Full-Line Forcing, 55 Nw.U.L.Rev. 62 (1960); Turner, *The Validity of Tying Arrangements Under the Antitrust Laws,* 72 Harv.L.Rev. 50 (1958); Bowman, *Tying Arrangements and the Leverage Problem,* 67 Yale L.J. 19 (1957). For an effort to resurrect the leverage thesis, see Kaplow, *Extension of Monopoly Power Through Leverage,* 85 Colum.L.Rev. 515 (1985).

16. Tying provisions in a patent license constitute patent misuse (as a matter of patent law) and will operate to deny the patentee relief for infringement of the tying clause and of the patent itself. Note, the doctrine of patent misuse may have a somewhat broader scope than an antitrust violation since the former does not depend on a showing of anticompetitive effect.

While the precise holding of the Court involved only a ruling that the mere existence of a patent does not entitle the patentee to impose a tie-in on the purchaser of a patented product, the "leverage" rationale relied upon by the Court suggested that tying arrangements would be vulnerable to attack under the antitrust laws.

This reasoning was first applied to tying arrangements under Section 3 of the Clayton Act which makes it unlawful to lease or sell

> goods, wares, merchandise, machinery, supplies, or other commodities, whether patented or unpatented, . . . on the condition . . . that the lessee or purchaser thereof shall not use or deal in the goods [etc.] . . . of a competitor or competitors of the lessor or seller, where the effect of . . . such condition . . . , may be to substantially lessen competition or tend to create a monopoly in any line of commerce.

Thus in International Business Machines v. United States, 298 U.S. 131 (1936) (*IBM*), the two leading makers of business machines were enjoined from leasing their machines with the condition that their lessees purchase unpatented tabulating cards exclusively from the lessors. Since the machines of IBM and Remington Rand were the only ones in the market capable of performing mechanical tabulations and computations without intervening manual operation, the Court apparently concluded that the companies possessed monopoly power in the tying (business machine) market and that they were using this power to eliminate competition and to monopolize the manufacture and sale of tabulating cards. Looking at IBM's business alone, the commerce in the tied product (tabulating cards) was substantial—sales of over three billion cards involving more than $3 million annually; therefore the Court concluded that the effect of the condition "may be to substantially lessen competition." The Court was, moreover, unimpressed by the defense's argument that each manufacturer's cards were specially made for his machines and that other cards might cause the machines to malfunction and therefore damage the machine manufacturers' business reputations. Others were capable of manufacturing suitable cards for use in the machines, just as the Government had done for the machines it leased (at a 15 percent higher lease price). There was a less restrictive alternative available: neither company was "prevented from proclaiming the virtues of its own cards or warning against the danger of using, in its machines, cards which do not conform to the necessary specifications, or even from making its leases conditional upon the use of cards which conform to them."

In *IBM* the Court was, in other words, apparently following a rule of reason approach in deciding whether a tie-in condition covered by Section 3 adversely affected competition. First it examined whether the seller (or lessor) had power in the tying product—since without such market power the tie-in could have no effect on the tied product. Then it considered, if only briefly, the quantitative effect of the tie-in on sales in the tied market. And in reviewing defenses that the condition imposed by the machine manufacturers was necessary for the efficient distribution of the tying product, the Court held that such defenses would apply only if no other reasonable and less harmful alternatives were available.

However, a more rigorous legal standard was applied in International Salt Co. v. United States, 332 U.S. 392 (1947). There International Salt, the largest producer of salt for commercial use, tied the lease of two patented machines (one for dissolving rock salt into brine for use in industrial processes, and the other for injecting salt into canned products) to the lessee's purchase from it of all the salt used in operating the machines. In finding that these leases violated Section 3 of the Clayton Act, the Court relied on International Salt's patents as establishing its market power in the tying product's (the machines') market and on the substantial dollar volume of business in the tied product which was foreclosed to competitors (here about $500,000 per year) as establishing the requisite competitive effect. That is, once these minimum threshold elements were shown, the Court held that a violation was established:

> We think the admitted facts left no genuine issue. Not only is price-fixing unreasonable, per se, but also it is unreasonable, per se, to foreclose

competitors from any substantial market. The volume of business affected by these contracts cannot be said to be insignificant or insubstantial and the tendency of the arrangement to accomplishment of monopoly seems obvious. Id. at 396.

Once again the defense that the condition was necessary was rejected: "But it is not pleaded, nor is it argued, that the machine is allergic to salt of equal quality produced by anyone except International."

Because *IBM* and *International Salt* form the foundation of later applications of the antitrust laws to tie-ins and because the Court's legal standard in *International Salt* amounts to a per se-type ruling (i.e., anticompetitive effects are presumed from foreclosure of a certain dollar volume), the cases and the standard deserve close analysis. Both cases rely on the leverage theory that by use of the tying arrangement the firms were in effect extending monopoly power from one product market to another. However, neither the factual analysis nor the theory seems fully persuasive. For example, it does not follow that International Salt's patents on salt dispensing machines necessarily gave it a monopoly in that (the tying product) field. The Court did not consider how many other machines were available, what International Salt's market share was, or the alternatives available to users of brine and to canners. More importantly, the leverage theory itself seems faulty. It

is probably true that, due to the extent that IBM
(and Remington Rand) occupied the tabulating machine market, they also obtained a monopoly in the
sale of tabulating cards—at least for use in tabulating machines. But it does not follow, as the Court
further assumed, that the firms obtained monopoly
profits in the second market. Since the two products (machines and cards) were complementary,
and therefore both were necessary for any tabulating service, the firm that monopolized either product could extract the full monopoly profit obtainable from the monopolization of the entire service.
Here IBM's lawful patent on tabulating machines
justified its extraction of monopoly profits from the
tabulating service, and whether it extracted that
profit through the rental price of the machines or
through the sale of punch cards seems unrelated to
the Court's expressed leverage theory.

But this raises the question of why sophisticated
firms such as IBM and International Salt would
impose tying conditions when they could lawfully
obtain monopoly profits on the sale or lease of the
tying product. One reason offered by economists is
that these conditions enable a manufacturer to
discriminate among users in relation to the intensity of the latter's use of the product—that is, to
charge users different prices according to their use
of the machines. By tying card purchases to the
rental of the machine, IBM was thus able to meter
the degree of use and then price the service so that
low as well as high intensity users would find it

economical. Nor is it conclusive that the tying provision forecloses competing sellers of cards from entering the market. Since IBM's interest lies in obtaining the monopoly profit on the tabulating service, it will either manufacture the cards itself or buy them from others depending on which alternative offers the lower price; that is, IBM has no incentive to disturb the market structure of the tied product except to keep it competitive. This further suggests that concerns that tying arrangements create entry barriers because they force competing producers of tabulating machines to enter a second market, and thereby increase their capital costs, are dubious; it seems more likely that these others would use the same suppliers of tabulating cards.[17]

Because the Clayton Act's application is limited to the sale or lease of commodities, tie-ins have also been judged under Sherman Act standards, and for a time these standards appeared to be somewhat different. For example, in Times-Picayune Publ. Co. v. United States, 345 U.S. 594 (1953) a publisher of both a morning and evening newspaper faced competition from only one other evening paper. The government challenged, as a Sherman

---

17. Not all such explanations are benign, however. The tie in *International Salt* required the user to take International Salt unless some other firm's salt was cheaper. One purpose may have been to find out the prices being charged by its rivals. This information could be crucial in enforcing a cartel among salt producers. See Peterman, *The International Salt Case,* 22 J.L. & Econ. 351 (1979). However, if this analysis is correct, the objection should be with the cartel, not the tie-in, unless one concludes that tie-ins serve no legitimate purpose.

Act violation, the defendant's "unit plan" which required advertisers to take space in both morning and evening papers, and not in either separately.[18] It contended, inter alia, that this tie-in foreclosed the competing afternoon newspaper from advertising lineage. While concluding that the defendant did not in fact occupy a "dominant" position in the tying product—and therefore could not have foreclosed advertising markets to competitors—the Court also expressed the view that under the Sherman Act the plaintiff must show both a monopolistic position in the tying product and that a substantial volume of commerce in the tied product was restrained.[19]

The case seemed significant for several reasons. The Sherman Act standard was less likely to hold tie-ins illegal. Here, not only must power in the tying product be present, but competitive effects must be shown. And neither was presumed from minimal evidence as in *International Salt*. Mere market power such as that indicated by a patent for the tying product was insufficient; dominance or overwhelming power was also required. Likewise competitive effect in the tied product could not be presumed from dollar volume; rather actual market effects had to be demonstrated. In addi-

18. The government had not sued under the Clayton Act, relying on an earlier informal opinion of the FTC that advertising space was not a "commodity."

19. Whereas, according to the Court in *Times-Picayune,* the rule of *International Salt* found a Clayton Act § 3 violation if *either* ingredient was present.

tion, the Court dwelt at length on the legitimate business aims which motivated the unit price offering, including the overhead savings and other efficiencies secured by eliminating repetition of 30 separate steps in the publishing operation. Finally, the Court refused to consider this a real tie-in case since only one product (readership of newspaper advertising in the New Orleans market), and not two separate products, was involved and there was as a consequence no tying of one product to another.

This rule of reason approach to tie-ins under the Sherman Act proved short-lived as the Court moved toward a per se-type rule (similar to that explored in connection with boycotts, pp. 215–22 supra). First, in Northern Pac. Ry. Co. v. United States, 356 U.S. 1 (1958), the Court applied Section 1 of the Sherman Act to condemn the defendant's sales (and leases) of land adjoining its rail lines because the contracts contained preferential routing clauses requiring the purchasers to ship commodities produced on such land over Northern Pacific's rails.[20] Several aspects of the Court's analysis stand out. The rule of *International Salt* was expressly labeled a per se test and its standard was restated as requiring a showing that "a party has sufficient economic power . . . to appreciably restrain free competition in the market for the tied product" and a showing that "a 'not insubstantial'

---

20. Again note that Clayton Act § 3 did not apply since the tying product was land, which is not a commodity.

amount of interstate commerce was and is affected" in the tied product. That standard was then held fully applicable to Sherman Act cases. That is, despite the Court's faint efforts at reconciliation, it seemed clear that the Court was abandoning the view in *Times-Picayune* that the Clayton and Sherman Acts applied different standards of legality. And without requiring any specific proof of substantial market power in the tying product (the Court assumed such existed on the basis of vastness of NP's land holdings and on the fact that without power the tie-in would be of no benefit to NP) the Court held that the arrangement was unreasonable. Consequently it upheld the district court's grant of summary judgment for the government. Whether any defenses would have been permitted was unclear, however, since no business justification for the tie-ins (as shown in *Times-Picayune*) was offered.[21]

21. Whether it would have been accepted by an antitrust court seems doubtful, but the primary justification which may partly explain the tying arrangement was that Northern Pacific could thereby avoid the price controls imposed by the Interstate Commerce Commission. See F. Scherer, *Industrial Market Structure and Economic Performance* 583 (2d ed. 1980): "Finally, tying contracts may be employed to evade governmental price controls—i.e., when a firm supplying some commodity such as gas or telephone service whose price is regulated requires customers to buy from it fixtures and attachments whose prices are not effectively controlled." See, e.g., Litton Systems, Inc. v. American Tel. & Tel. Co., 700 F.2d 785, 790–91 (2d Cir. 1983), cert. denied, 464 U.S. 1073 (1983).

An intriguing study suggests that Northern Pacific's tying contracts probably were part of an effort to police price-fixing agreements among railroads. That is, the competitive conditions clause in the tie-in required a buyer or lessee not using the

A similarly rigid per se approach, presuming economic power in this case from the copyright of popular films, was applied to bar block booking in United States v. Loew's, Inc., 371 U.S. 38 (1962). There the Court objected to the selling of a package of motion pictures to television where the buyers were "coerced" into taking bad as well as good pictures in the sale. Several explanations have been offered for this practice, including a reduction in the costs of information and simulated price discrimination. See Kenney & Klein, *The Economics of Block Booking*, J.L. & Econ. 497 (1983); Stigler, *United States v. Loew's, Inc.: A Note on Block-Booking*, 1963 Sup.Ct.Rev. 152. Whatever the explanation, there seems little economic basis for condemning the transaction where many competing films and other programs were available for sale to television. It is often a way of putting things together and selling them cheaper, hardly something to be suspicious about.

An even stricter per se approach to tying agreements was revealed in Fortner Enterprises, Inc. v. United States Steel Corp., 394 U.S. 495 (1969) (*Fortner I*). U.S. Steel tied its offer of attractive credit services for home builders to their purchase from U.S. Steel of its prefabricated houses which the plaintiff claimed were over-priced and defective. The defendant's special credit terms, such as

NP line to disclose the lower rate or service available elsewhere. Cummings & Ruhter, *The Northern Pacific Case*, 22 J.L. & Econ. 329, 342 (1979). If correct, the decision in *Northern Pacific* reached the right result, albeit for the wrong reasons.

100 percent financing at rates below market levels, were said to be unique, thus demonstrating U.S. Steel's special economic power in the credit market; and sales of more than $9 million of prefabricated houses by U.S. Steel in three years across the country, allegedly foreclosed by the tying arrangements, were not an insubstantial effect. The Court curtly rejected U.S. Steel's argument that the tie-in was, in effect, a competitive price cut made possible through scale economies resulting from both the tie-in and avoided costs, such as credit controls otherwise imposed on lenders. U.S. Steel had contended that its tying arrangement was a method of passing efficiencies along to consumers in the form of lower prices and increased rivalry. The Court, however, ignored the point and responded by asserting that the tied product should then have been offered at a lower price. Still, the case was before the Court on review of the trial court's grant of summary judgment. The decision therefore only established a violation of the Sherman Act if the plaintiff could prove that U.S. Steel had economic power in the credit (tying product) market. Thus, the case was remanded to the trial court for further evidence.

Eight years later the matter returned to the Supreme Court in United States Steel Corp. v. Fortner Enterprises, Inc., 429 U.S. 610 (1977) (*Fortner II*). Technically it now involved only a review of the lower court's decision that U.S. Steel indeed did have economic power in credit. On this question the Supreme Court read its earlier standard narrowly and ruled that plaintiff's evidence was insufficient. That is, there was no evidence that U.S. Steel had "significant" economic power in the credit market. In reaching this result, the Court appeared to be moving away from its previously rigid rule against tying arrangements. To be sure, bound by the law of the case, it restated the per se rule, possibly in even more sweeping terms. But its approach to plaintiff's evidence suggested a new direction. It seemed to reflect a "partial per se" test similar to that applied to group boycotts. The Court now interpreted the evidence as showing only that the purchase requirement was part of the price of the loan—and nothing else. Fortner was not coerced into accepting its advantageous terms; rather, they represented the best possible arrangement Fortner could make.

The Court recently had an opportunity to clarify the law in a case where the tie-in appeared to be a cheaper way of bundling and selling a package of services. In Jefferson Parish Hosp. Dist. No. 2 v. Hyde, 466 U.S. 2 (1984) a large acute-care hospital required patients wanting an operation to use the hospital's anesthesiologists. The hospital claimed that this bundling of services reduced costs and improved quality of care; an excluded anesthesiologist complained that the tie prevented him from obtaining privileges of practice. A unanimous Court upheld the arrangement but could not agree why. Five members of the Court said that the per se rule still applied generally to tie-ins, but then went into an elaborate inquiry to conclude that there were two separate products, that the hospital did not have sufficient market power to invoke the per se rule (since it attracted only 30 percent of the patients in its district), and that there had been no showing of an adverse effect on competition. As one observer has acidly noted: "about the only thing left of the per se rule against tying is the label." Four concurring justices urged the Court to adopt a rule of reason approach—and concluded that surgery and anesthesia were not separate products. The opinions betray the deep division on the Court and among antitrust practitioners over the likely harmfulness of vertical restraints. The Court's language and often its application reflect an increasing appreciation of economic analysis; but it continues to be difficult for the Court to abandon the partial per se rules and allow freer play to privately imposed trade restraints. Not surprisingly, lower courts have found the standard difficult to apply. See, e.g., Digidyne Corp. v. Data General Corp., 734 F.2d 1336 (9th Cir.1984), cert. denied, 105 S.Ct. 3534 (1985) (market power presumed from copyright; inadequate consideration of business justifications).

In any case, it seems likely that earlier cases holding that tie-ins could be justified as providing a necessary avenue for entry or as the only means of protecting the integrity of the tying product will be given a more expansive reading.[22]

22. See United States v. Jerrold Electronics Corp., 187 F.Supp. 545 (E.D.Pa.1960), aff'd per curiam, 365 U.S. 567 (1961);

3. EXCLUSIVE DEALING

Another means of securing vertical integration through contract is exclusive dealing, where instead of relying upon his economic power in the tying product to obtain sales of a second or tied product, the manufacturer offers a sales contract conditioned upon the agreement by the buyer not to deal in the goods of a competitor. That is, the dealer purchasing cars or gas from a manufacturer or refiner must promise to promote and market only the seller's brand of cars or gas; the dealer is "tied" to a particular supplier. Alternatively, the arrangement may reflect the buyer's desire to obtain an assured source of supply—he seeks the producer's agreement to provide him with the producer's entire output or at least his (the purchaser's) requirements. See also Marvel, *Exclusive Dealing*, 25 J.L. & Econ. 1 (1982) (creates property rights in customers and prevents free riding).

Exclusive dealing contracts are, in other words, simply another variant of partial vertical integration which has already been explored. They are designed to facilitate the distribution of products to the ultimate consumer. See O. Williamson, *Markets and Hierarchies* 82–131 (1975). They are different from tie-ins in that a second (tied) product is not involved, and from refusals to deal in that the primary focus is not on maintaining a selected

Dehydrating Process Co. v. A.O. Smith Corp., 292 F.2d 653 (1st Cir.1961), cert. denied, 368 U.S. 931.

resale price. But they all involve the use of economic power in the sale or purchase of one product as leverage to affect intrabrand sales and they have the common effect of foreclosing that particular opportunity to interbrand competitors. To state the point somewhat differently, when an oil company obtains exclusive dealing contracts from its service station operators, it "denies" these outlets to sellers of competing brands of gasoline, just as the tie-in in *International Salt* limited the sales opportunities of competing sellers of industrial salt.

Despite the similarity of these business situations, and their apparent economic effects, exclusive dealing arrangements have long been dealt with under a different, more lenient antitrust standard. They are viewed under a modified rule of reason rather than a per se approach, which has meant they are subject to a measure of *comparative substantiality* or to a comparison of the effect of foreclosure on competing sellers.

The leading precedent on exclusive dealing is still Standard Oil Co. of California v. United States, 337 U.S. 293 (1949) (*Standard Stations*), where the largest seller of gasoline in seven western states made exclusive dealing contracts with independent stations constituting 16 percent of all retail outlets, whose sales involved almost 7 percent (or $58 million) of all retail gas sales in the area. There was no question that the arrangement, attacked under Section 3 of the Clayton Act, met the "quantitative substantiality" test applied by the Court in *International Salt* (where foreclosure of $500,000 of salt sales violated Section 3). Nonetheless, the Court applied a different standard, one which considered but did not closely examine the economic effects of the foreclosure. It ruled that in measuring the impact of an exclusive dealing arrangement, the market in the foreclosed line of commerce (here retail gasoline sales in seven western states) should be reviewed. The Court noted that the market was concentrated since the seven largest firms, all of whom used exclusive dealing contracts, controlled 65 percent of the market and that entry was apparently restricted since market shares had stabilized after these contractual arrangements were introduced. In this setting the Court held that a violation of Section 3 had been established because the agreements relating to 7 percent of retail sales created a potential clog on competition which was "foreclosed in a substantial share" of the market.

Standard Stations, then, is significant for several reasons. It enunciates a different, "quantitative substantiality" test for Section 3 in exclusive dealing contracts rather than when it is applied to tying arrangements. Exclusive dealing is not presumptively anticompetitive. Thus, under *Standard Stations* adverse effects of exclusive dealing arrangements are not assumed merely from the dollar volume impact on competitor opportunities to make sales to the foreclosed retailers. It held that foreclosure of a substantial share of the retail market—here almost 7 percent—where the market is otherwise concentrated and entry is restricted, establishes a sufficient foundation from which a court can draw the inference that the arrangement may substantially lessen competition.

This "partial" per se ruling seems questionable from two perspectives. Although it treats exclusive dealing contracts more favorably, as having potentially beneficial effects, it operates from the doubtful assumption that they are somehow substantially different and less harmful than tying arrangements. The foundation of this view can be challenged as was indicated in the prior consideration of tie-ins. (See pp. 313–27 supra.) And this suggests, perhaps, that the legal standard applicable to partial vertical integration by contract should be more receptive to tying arrangements than it is—for as Justice Douglas noted in a separate opinion in *Standard Stations,* if the vertical arrangement reflects substantial gains in efficiency, denying firms this opportunity by contract will only force them to achieve these ends by acquiring the formerly independent outlets or, if that is prohibited by the anti-merger laws (see ch. 9 infra), by forward vertical (i.e., internal) expansion.

Second, the Court's sole reliance on market shares as demonstrating market foreclosure and competitive effect also seems misplaced. Whether an exclusive dealing contract can foreclose competitors depends not only on the number of outlets or the share of sales foreclosed but also on the duration of the agreement. If the agreement can be terminated on short notice, as in *Standard Stations,* and there are available outlets, the exclusionary effect is likely to be minimal because a competitor could obtain entry simply by offering the retailers better terms.

Subsequent cases have reflected a retreat from this position although they have not expressly altered the rule of *Standard Stations.* In Tampa Elec. Co. v. Nashville Coal Co., 365 U.S. 320 (1961), the Court was called upon by a coal supplier to rule that its agreement to fill an electric utility's "total requirements" for coal for 20 years was illegal under Section 3 and that the contract was therefore unenforceable. (The price of coal had jumped, making the arrangement less profitable for the coal company.) Upholding the contract, the Court's analysis of the economic impact of the arrangement was considerably more intensive, both as to the markets likely to be affected and as to the probable effect of the particular foreclosure, than that given in *Standard Stations.* The Court appeared to be moving toward a less rigid rule of reason balancing approach. Yet in FTC v. Brown Shoe Co., 384 U.S. 316 (1966), the Court upheld the Trade Commission's condemnation of a franchise plan where a shoe supplier's dealers were required to promise not to carry shoes competing with the franchisor's lines even though the record contained no evidence of the market share affected or of the extent to which competing shoe suppliers were foreclosed—and the agreements could be terminated at any time by the dealers. Relying on the broader reach of Section 5 of the FTC Act, the Court ruled that competitive effects did not have to be shown: "the Commission has power under § 5 to arrest trade restraints in their incipiency without proof that they amount to an outright violation of § 3 of the Clayton Act or other provisions of the antitrust laws."

An oft-criticized opinion because it seemed likely that Brown Shoe was using its franchise plan as an indirect method of price competition and because no shoe manufacturing company appeared to have market power, this precedent has not been further developed. But see United States v. American Cyanimede Co., 719 F.2d 558 (2d Cir.1983). Lower courts have generally followed *Tampa Electric's* more relaxed view of exclusive dealing. See, e.g., Satellite Television & Assoc. Resources, Inc. v. Continental Cablevision, 714 F.2d 351 (4th Cir.1983), cert. denied, 465 U.S. 1027 (1984). The 1984 Department of Justice Merger Guidelines, p. 353 infra, also reflect a more lenient approach to vertical acquisitions. They do not challenge such arrangements unless the market is highly concentrated and the foreclosure exceeds 25 percent. It seems likely that the law of exclusive dealing will reflect this approach in the future.

CHAPTER IX

MERGERS

Beyond the consideration of monopoly power and the limits placed on its use by the antitrust laws, this text has concentrated on contractual or similar arrangements between independent firms. Their purposes and effects have been examined to determine whether cartels were created or other firms were excluded from the market. Agreements between independent companies, especially direct competitors, have been viewed as dangerous to competition, since their likely impact is the restriction of output and consequently increased prices. Hence, the primary question has become one of whether these arrangements are so inimical to competition that they should be banned outright (through application of a per se rule) or whether justifications for these arrangements should be heard (under a rule of reason) before deciding whether the antitrust laws have been violated.

Consistency in approach would seem to forbid almost every merger—the formal and complete integration of one firm into another. Such arrangements are permanent; they are not subject to the limits of contractual conditions. Unlike cartels or boycotts (which are temporary and subject to internal pressures that ultimately force their disintegration), the inevitable effect of a merger is the elimination of competition between the merging firms. Thus, if the antitrust laws prohibiting cartels and other partial integration through contract are to be consistently applied to similar functional transactions, the merger law should be simple and straightforward—and most mergers should be condemned through a simple per se rule.

A closer examination of mergers between independent firms, however, suggests a more cautious approach. Just as legitimate business activities stimulating demand and seeking additional customers generally were not prohibited despite their similarities to actions of price-fixing cartels or the fact that they might lead to the acquisition of monopoly power, so mergers often (probably, generally) serve useful social ends without impairing competition. A merger may have no impact on the markets in which the firms operate; the merging firms may be too small or entry into their markets may be easily accomplished. More importantly, mergers often provide an opportunity for an owner to sell his business—to someone else already familiar with the business and market who would be in a better position to pay the highest price. Without a possible avenue for selling a business, it seems less likely that anyone would enter into a business—or, in any event, it would be less attractive. Allowing mergers, in other words, may have a positive effect on competition by facilitating entry and exit.

The task of antitrust merger law, therefore, has been to weed out those mergers whose adverse impact on competition was apt to be so substantial that the benefits from the mergers are outweighed by their probable adverse consequences. Since courts are generally hesitant to undo a merger which went unchallenged at its inception, application of the antitrust laws to mergers has required agencies and courts to forecast market trends and future effects. Thus merger cases examine past events or periods, not so much for evidence of misconduct, but to develop an understanding of the participating firms' position in their markets and of the merger's impact on others and competition therein. It is not surprising then, that in applying the merger law courts have often placed increasing reliance on a structural analysis of markets (are they oligopolistic or competitive?) and on developing rules which outline for businessmen in advance which mergers are likely to be challenged (primarily through examining the market shares of the merging firms). Yet despite these efforts to provide predictability, antitrust law in this area often is in a state of flux.

A. THE SHERMAN ACT AND MERGERS TENDING TO MONOPOLY

The starting point for a discussion of merger law is the application of the Sherman Act to railroad mergers near the turn of the century. Beginning with the celebrated *Northern Securities* case (where Justice Holmes issued his famous dictum: "Great cases like hard cases make bad law."),[1] the Su-

1. Northern Securities Co. v. United States, 193 U.S. 197, 400 (1904) discussed at 26,123 supra.

preme Court initially took the position that all mergers between directly competing firms constituted a combination in restraint of trade and therefore violated Section 1. The Court looked to the purpose and effect of the merger, namely, elimination of all competition between the merging railroads, and relied on its original interpretation that the Sherman Act's prohibition of "every" restraint [2] allowed no exceptions. Subsequent cases applied the same rigid, per se test. See, e.g., United States v. Union Pac. R.R. Co., 226 U.S. 61, 96 (1912).

On the other hand, many mergers—indeed, thousands—were never challenged, and others were upheld under the Sherman Act. In 1911 the Supreme Court appeared to substitute a not-too-stringent rule of reason approach by which mergers leading to monopoly (as well as combinations establishing cartels) were to be tested. In *Standard Oil (N.J.)* it limited the earlier case law to railroad mergers.[3] Thus in applying this rule of reason standard in United States v. United States Steel Corp., 251 U.S. 417 (1920), the Court held that a consolidation of most of the steel industry

2. See United States v. Trans-Missouri Freight Ass'n, 166 U.S. 290 (1897) discussed at pp. 165–66 supra.

3. See Standard Oil Co. of New Jersey v. United States, 221 U.S. 1, 64–65 (1911) discussed at pp. 169–70 supra. Within a decade railroad mergers were also freed from antitrust attack when the Transportation Act of 1920 exempted railroad mergers from the jurisdiction of the antitrust laws. See also United States v. ICC (*Northern Lines*), 396 U.S. 491 (1970), upholding ICC approval of the railroad merger rejected on Sherman Act grounds by the Court in 1904 in *Northern Securities*.

into one firm possessing 80 to 90 percent of capacity in some basic lines did not violate either Section 1 or Section 2 of the Sherman Act. Even though the Court found that the mergers were undertaken for the purpose of gaining monopoly control, it concluded that U.S. Steel had not in fact achieved monopoly power and that the company had then abandoned its original goal.

The Sherman Act, as a means of preventing mergers which might create monopoly power or impair competition, appeared moribund if not dead. One last effort to revive its application to mergers was made after the price-fixing (e.g., *Madison Oil*), boycott (e.g., *FOGA*) and monopolization (e.g., *Alcoa*) cases of the 1940's indicated that the Supreme Court might be willing to apply a more rigorous standard against large acquisitions. Thus, in United States v. Columbia Steel Co., 334 U.S. 495 (1948), the government challenged U.S. Steel's acquisition of Consolidated Steel, a competitor in steel fabrication. Viewing the relevant geographic market as the eleven western states in which Consolidated sold all of its output, the market shares of the merging firms were 13 and 11 percent. In holding that the merger did not violate the Sherman Act, however, the Court did little more than conclude that a merger bringing 24 percent of the market under one firm's control was not unreasonable.

In determining what constitutes unreasonable restraint, we do not think the dollar volume is in itself of compelling significance; we look rather to the percentage of business controlled, the strength of the remaining competition, whether the action springs from business requirements or purpose to monopolize, the probable development of the industry, consumer demands, and other characteristics of the market.

The *Columbia Steel* decision is remarkable for its absence of coherent theory as well as for its limited impact. It evidences an apparent lack of understanding of how a merger which did not create a monopoly firm could affect market prices and therefore result in a restraint of trade in violation of Sections 1 or 2.[4] The Court failed to formulate a standard by which mergers resulting in a firm of less than monopoly size could be tested. When the largest company in an industry not known for price competition was allowed to purchase its largest steel fabrication competitor, it became evident that the Sherman Act did not forbid a merger unless the merging firms were on the verge of obtaining substantial monopoly power.

Thus, the Sherman Act proved to be an ineffective weapon against mergers which might impair competition. Its rule of reason standard did not forbid mergers unless they were designed to create

4. Among the questions which can be raised about the quoted standard: Why does dollar volume have any significance? Why is not the market share of the remaining competitors a reliable index of their strength (at least prima facie)? Why is intent relevant? Why is the development of consumer demand, etc. significant?

a monopoly and apparently succeeded in doing so.[5] Few mergers would fail under this standard, even though competition might be adversely affected by mergers of lesser size and significance.

B. THE AMENDMENT OF SECTION 7 OF THE CLAYTON ACT

As part of the legislative response to the Supreme Court's newly developed rule of reason standard, Congress in 1914 adopted Section 7 of the Clayton Act in order to limit stock acquisitions. Referred to as the "holding company" section, its aim was to arrest "trusts" in their incipiency.

The statutory provision never had much impact, however. It banned only purchases of stock. Thus all a firm had to do in order to avoid its reach was to acquire the assets of the other firm. (This explains, for example, why U.S. Steel purchased the facilities rather than the stock of Columbia Steel and why that acquisition was tested under Section 1 of the Sherman Act.) In addition, a series of decisions further limited the scope of the original Section 7, first by denying its application even to stock acquisitions if the merger was subse-

5. One possible exception was the singular application of the railroad merger case law to condemnation of bank mergers under Section 1. See United States v. First Nat'l Bank & Trust Co., 376 U.S. 665 (1964) (*Lexington Bank*). However, the Bank Merger Act of 1966, 12 U.S.C.A. § 1828c, closed this door when it established somewhat different procedures and standards for testing bank mergers; it also exempted bank mergers from Section 1 of the Sherman Act and Section 7 of the Clayton Act.

quently transformed into a purchase of assets,[6] and then by requiring that the competitive impact be almost as substantial as that required in Sherman Act cases. See International Shoe Co. v. FTC, 280 U.S. 291, 298 (1930).

The cumulative effect of the foregoing was that between the passage of the Clayton Act in 1914 and the amendment of Section 7 in 1950, only 15 mergers were overturned under the antitrust laws, and 10 of these dissolution orders were based on the Sherman Act. This inactivity, the government's failure in *Columbia Steel,* and a 1948 Report by the Federal Trade Commission (which concluded that unless something was done about the rising tide of economic concentration resulting from mergers, "the giant corporations will ultimately take over the country" [7]) led Congress to amend Section 7.

Thus, in 1950 Congress rewrote Section 7 of the Clayton Act to close the "asset acquisitions" loophole, and the statute now reads (after minor amendment in 1980) as follows:

§ 7: No person engaged in commerce or in any activity affecting commerce shall acquire, directly or indirectly, the whole or any part of the

6. See, e.g., Arrow-Hart & Hegeman Elec. Co. v. FTC, 291 U.S. 587, 596 (1934).

7. FTC, *The Merger Movement: A Summary Report* 68 (1948). The Report was almost immediately subjected to harsh and telling criticism from sophisticated observers because of its numerous unwarranted inferences, but such comments seemed to have no impact on the reception given the Report in Congress.

stock or . . . assets of another person engaged also in commerce or in any activity affecting commerce, where in any line of commerce in any section of the country, the effect of such acquisition may be substantially to lessen competition, or to tend to create a monopoly.

In addition to its concern over economic concentration, Congress wanted to retain local control over industry and to protect small business. The legislative history, according to the Supreme Court, also reflected other values which enter into the application of the statute: the amended Section 7 was to apply to vertical and conglomerate as well as to horizontal mergers (those between actual competitors); Sherman Act standards were considered inapplicable and mergers could be forbidden when the trend toward lessening competition was still in its incipiency; Congress was concerned with competition, not competitors, and therefore the statute could be used to restrain mergers which merely lessened competition; whether a merger had an anticompetitive impact depended upon the functional view of the merger within a particular industry; and finally, by using the word "may" Congress lowered the standard of proof so that only probable anticompetitive effects need be shown. See generally Brown Shoe Co. v. United States, 370 U.S. 294, 311–23 (1962).

C. VERTICAL MERGERS

Vertical mergers generally denote a situation where one firm purchases either a customer or supplier—the former is called a forward vertical integration while the latter, obviously, is labeled a backward integration. Whichever direction the merger takes, the newly acquired firm may now decide to deal only with the acquiring firm, thereby altering competition in three markets: among the acquiring firm's suppliers, customers, or competitors. Suppliers may find that they no longer have a market for their goods, retail outlets may be deprived of supplies, and competitors may find that both supplies and outlets are blocked. The concern, just as in the case of vertical restraints (described in Chapter 8), is that such foreclosures may substantially lessen competition.

On the other hand, a similar market effect may result from the acquiring firm expanding internally through developing its own source of supply or through opening new retail outlets and channeling its purchases or sales through them. Except for the unusual limitations applicable to business activities resulting in monopoly,[8] an internal expansion is generally not challengeable under the antitrust laws. See United States v. Philadelphia Nat'l Bank, 374 U.S. 321, 370 (1963) ("one premise of an antimerger statute such as § 7 is that corporate growth by internal expansion is socially preferable to growth by acquisition"); Brown Shoe Co. v. United States, 370 U.S. 294, 345 n. 72 (1962). Moreover, vertical mergers are somewhat distinctive. The arrangement is more permanent than

8. See United States v. Aluminum Co. of America, 148 F.2d 416, 437–38 (2d Cir.1945) (dicta condemning vertical price squeezes).

contractual franchise, exclusive dealing or tying restraints. For example, it may force other firms to become vertically integrated in order to compete; this in turn may delay entry at the production level and increase the risk premium for the capital which such entrants need.

Thus, antitrust law applications to vertical mergers should be designed so that they generally proscribe only those mergers whose anticompetitive consequences outweigh possible efficiencies (see also pp. 334–36 supra). In addition, they should be consistent with rules governing internal expansion.

Only two significant vertical merger cases have been decided by the Supreme Court under Section 7, and one of these was decided under the original Act. Both are relevant in gaining an understanding of the Clayton Act's application to vertical mergers. They illustrate the difficulties which the Court has encountered in defining and applying the "relevant market" as well as demonstrate its ready reliance on market shares to infer adverse competitive effects. They also establish a strict but not necessarily rigid standard for measuring the legality of vertical mergers under the Clayton Act.

Until United States v. E.I. du Pont de Nemours & Co., 353 U.S. 586 (1957) (*du Pont-GM*), it was generally assumed that the original Section 7 did not apply to vertical mergers. Nevertheless, du Pont's purchase of 23 percent of GM stock before 1920 was held to have foreclosed sales to GM by

other suppliers of automotive paints and fabrics
between 1920 and 1949 (the time of the lawsuit)
and thus to have had an illegal anticompetitive
effect. The decision has continuing significance
because the legal focus on foreclosure to measure
anticompetitive effect has continued. And the
Court's effort to define the product market and its
finding of significant foreclosure were to become
harbingers of difficulties which it would encounter
in applying the antimerger laws to other vertical,
horizontal and conglomerate mergers.

Locating the relevant market is, according to the
Court, a necessary predicate in determining whether the merger will "substantially lessen competition" in violation of the Clayton Act. Only by
examining the effects of the merger in its product
market can its impact on competition be assayed.
Du Pont sold finishes and fabrics to GM, which
used them to paint and upholster its cars. Even
though GM's purchases constituted a negligible
percentage of the total market for these materials,
the Court ruled that "automotive finishes and
fabrics have sufficient peculiar characteristics and
uses" which made them distinctive as a "line of
commerce" under the Clayton Act. This finding,
however, seems contradicted by the record recited
by the Court (and the dissent); du Pont's competitors also produced similar (and interchangeable)
finishes and fabrics which were purchased by GM
and its competitors as well as by nonautomotive
firms. Thus, du Pont's sales to GM did not neces-

sarily constitute a significant foreclosure of sales to du Pont's competitors. Since they sold the same products to other users (including auto companies), there appeared to be no compelling reason to limit the relevant market to automotive sales. See Markham, *The Du Pont-General Motors Decision,* 43 Va.L.Rev. 881, 887 (1957).

Confining the market to automotive finishes and fabrics had the effect of unduly emphasizing the impact of the merger on these sales—and hence upon du Pont's competitors. For example, the foreclosure of paint sales was only 3.5 percent of total industrial finishes but 24 percent of automotive uses. Similarly, GM's purchases of 19 percent of all automotive fabrics from du Pont appears to be a significant foreclosure until it is noted that this represents but 1.6 percent of all uses of this type of fabric.

In deciding whether du Pont's stock acquisition violated Section 7, the Court ruled that two elements had to be established. First, the market affected must be substantial. The antimerger law was not to be applied to consolidations either of minor firms or in insignificant markets. Whatever the appropriate product market, GM's size and du Pont's annual sales of over $26 million to GM easily satisfied this requirement.

Second, the Government had to show a likelihood that competition would be "foreclosed in a substantial share" of the relevant market.[9] The

---

9. Quoting from *Standard Stations,* 337 U.S. 293, 314 (1949), considered at pp. 329–32 supra.

Court relied upon GM's substantial purchases of paints and fabrics from du Pont to infer that du Pont's stock ownership in GM was a decisive factor in the latter's decision to buy du Pont products. It then concluded that the stock acquisition had resulted in a foreclosure of a substantial share of the market to du Pont's competitors and therefore had the necessary anticompetitive effect. This analysis is open to question, however. As the District Court had noted in reaching a contrary opinion: GM's varying purchases from du Pont over the years suggested that such decisions were made because of the commercial merit of du Pont's products and prices. Other facts, such as GM's purchases before the stock acquisition and purchases from du Pont by other auto companies further supported the District Court. (In fact, it would generally be in GM's and du Pont's interests—the latter as a stockholder—for GM to buy finishes and fabrics at the best price, regardless of who supplied them.)

Still the *du Pont-GM* case was sui generis. All other things being equal, GM would of course buy its supplies from stockholders. And in view of each firm's size and the oligopolistic structure of their respective industries, any further interconnection between these two seemed undesirable. The decision can therefore be rationalized as requiring strict scrutiny of vertical mergers involving companies already powerful in their relevant markets, at least when they purchase stock in a leading customer.

The Supreme Court's first opportunity to interpret amended Section 7 came in Brown Shoe Co. v.

United States, 370 U.S. 294 (1962). The case involved both horizontal and vertical integration in
that both Brown and Kinney, the merging firms,
manufactured shoes and distributed them through
their respective retail outlets. The primary impact of the vertical merger, however, was likely to
be in the foreclosure of Kinney's retail outlets to
other shoe manufacturers. Kinney's manufacturing operation was small; its outlets had purchased
80 percent of their shoes from other manufacturers
(excluding Brown). Brown was the fourth largest
manufacturer of shoes in the nation, producing
about 4 percent of the country's footwear; Kinney
was the eighth largest retailer and operated over
350 shoe stores.

An analysis of the effect of this vertical merger
on competition among shoe manufacturers, who
would be adversely affected by a shift of purchases
by Kinney outlets to Brown (Brown's president
having admitted in testimony that "we hoped" to
use the ownership of Kinney to introduce Brown
shoes into Kinney stores) again required an initial
consideration of the product market. Looking into
a variety of factors—the product lines recognized
by the public, the use of separate plants for different types of shoes, the peculiar characteristics
which make one shoe noncompetitive with others,
and distinct customer lines—the Court adopted the
District Court's finding that men's, women's and
children's shoes were separate product markets.
After completing this exercise, however, the Court

ignored these findings and lumped all shoes together in examining the effect of the vertical merger in
the marketplace.

In testing this vertical merger in an unconcentrated market [10] the Court extended the *du Pont-
GM* standard by relying primarily on (1) the potential foreclosure of Kinney outlets to other shoe
manufacturers. This conclusion was buttressed by
the Court's emphasis of (2) Section 7's role in
halting market concentration in its "incipiency,"
(3) the trend toward mergers and market concentration in the shoe manufacturing and retailing
industries, (4) the effect of the merger on shoe
styles and customer preferences, on nonintegrated
manufacturers and retailers, and on middlemen,
and (5) the absence of any justification for the
merger. On close examination, however, much of
this analysis seems misplaced.

The actual and likely foreclosure from the merger was minimal—however measured. Kinney's
350 retail outlets constituted less than one-half of
one percent of all retail outlets selling shoes (of
which there were 70,000) and less than 2 percent of
stores selling shoes only (there were 22,000 of
these). Looking at actual sales, Kinney sold 1.6
percent of all shoes (or 1.2 percent of dollar volume)—and 20 percent of these sales had not been

10. The government identified as the essential issue: "at
what stage in a developing process of industrial concentration
. . . . does Section 7 of the Clayton Act step in to call a halt?"
Brief for Appellee at 84, Brown Shoe Co. v. United States,
supra.

open to other manufacturers since they were supplied from Kinney's plants before the merger. Thus, *the maximum possible foreclosure from the vertical merger was 1.3 percent of shoe sales (80% of 1.6%)* without regard to actual relevant product market figures. And in a deconcentrated market this hardly seemed to portend a substantial lessening of competition.[11]

The Court's other arguments did not add significance to the foreclosure evidence. The fact that Kinney was the largest remaining family-style shoe store chain (whatever that means) neither added nor detracted particularly from these figures since the Court could point to no evidence that shoe store competition extended beyond a store's immediate locality. Nor was the Court's recitation of recent declines in the number of shoe manufacturers or of separate owners of retail shoe outlets important since a vertical merger merely *substitutes* a new owner (here at the retail level). Such substitution has no impact on market concentration—unless, of course, the transaction also results in a horizontal merger.

Seeking to augment the Court's analysis, it has been suggested that vertical integration raises peculiar difficulties where, as in *Brown Shoe,* the merger is "between a manufacturer of branded and nationally advertised shoes, such as Brown, and a

11. In fact, two years after the merger Brown's sales constituted less than 8% of Kinney sales—that is, less than .1% of nationwide shoe sales were actually affected by the merger.

seller of private brand shoes, such as Kinney."
Blake & Jones, *Toward A Three-Dimensional Antitrust Policy,* 65 Colum.L.Rev. 422, 456 (1965). They
contend that vertical integration in this situation
would force independent retailers to compete with
one of their principal suppliers. Moreover, it
would deprive the "make up" manufacturers (those
making shoes to specification) of one of the few
remaining retailers large enough to advertise and
support a competitive brand. This argument is not
supported by the evidence, however, and seems
contrary to other facts in the record and to the
experience of other industries (such as food retailing—see *Topco,* p. 206 supra).

At first glance the Court seemed on more solid
ground in questioning the merger because the defendant could point to no economic or social justification for it. Since a vertical merger might result
in a foreclosure of other manufacturers and therefore might adversely affect competition among
them, Section 7 could reasonably be read as forbidding such mergers between leaders of two industries, albeit relatively small ones. On the other
hand, a closer look suggests that Brown's failure to
claim any efficiencies from the merger was a mis-
take by counsel which also led to a curious statement by the Court, as Professors Blake and Jones
explain:

   The real vice of the *Brown Shoe* case, in our
   view, was the disposition of the issue of economic
   efficiency. The Government had urged that the

Brown-Kinney consolidation was a menace to
competition because the integrated company
would have been more efficient, and would have
been able to sell shoes of equal appearance and
quality at a lower price than its unintegrated
competitors. Brown's counsel, apparently applying the well-known legal principle that every
Government action demands an equal and opposite reaction, found himself in the incomprehen-
sible position of arguing that the merger produced no such economies or likelihood of benefit
to the consumer. In a portion of the opinion
dealing with the effects of the merger on independent retailers, the Court, in a rather summary statement, indicated that it agreed with the
Government both on the facts and the law: that
the merger would result in improved efficiency
and that this improvement supported its finding
that the merger was unlawful. . . . "[T]he
claims of increased efficiency should have been
considered on their merits; if found to be valid
and sufficiently substantial, they should have
resulted in approval of the transaction." (65
Colum.L.Rev. at 456–57.)

In Ford Motor Co. v. United States, 405 U.S. 562
(1972), the Court emphasized heightened barriers
to entry in condemning Ford's attempted acquisition of Autolite, a spark plug manufacturer. The
argument is not persuasive, however, and like the
foreclosure argument, is increasingly challenged.
If the merger is efficient, others will have to match

it to enter, but that is not an economic barrier to entry—and, in any case, is hardly to be condemned. A mere increase in scale is unlikely to deter entry; it does not automatically follow that competing firms must be vertically integrated and, even so, the market for capital is generally competitive.

Lower court decisions have increasingly reflected deep skepticism about the foreclosure and entry barrier arguments. For example, in Freuhauf Corp. v. FTC, 603 F.2d 345 (2d Cir.1979), the Second Circuit overturned an FTC ruling that an acquisition foreclosing 5.8 percent of the market for heavy duty truck wheels did not violate Section 7 when the manufacturer of 25 percent of truck trailers (Freuhauf) bought a firm controlling 15 percent of the market for heavy duty wheels (Kelsey-Hayes). A realignment of sales patterns and possible foreclosure does not necessarily lessen competition, and there was no evidence of likely anticompetitive effect. But see Ash Grove Cement Co. v. FTC, 577 F.2d 1368 (9th Cir.1978), cert. denied, 439 U.S. 982 (1983); Mississippi River Corp. v. FTC, 454 F.2d 1083 (8th Cir.1972).

The 1982 and 1984 Department of Justice Merger Guidelines similarly take a distinctive approach that focuses on the "horizontal effect from nonhorizontal mergers." Starting from the premise that vertical mergers generally do not pose a significant threat to competition, they abandon the foreclosure theory of *Brown Shoe* and limit vertical merger investigations to increased barriers to entry, the facilitation of collusion, and the avoidance of rate regulation. As a practical matter, the government will rarely intervene in vertical mergers; it has filed only on two complaints in the past decade.

D. HORIZONTAL MERGERS

As noted, the fundamental theme of the legislation amending Section 7 in 1950 was a concern with the rising tide of economic concentration in the economy, which the FTC had reported as being due primarily to horizontal mergers. Such concentration was feared because it would facilitate direct and indirect collusion among sellers in a market. Such collusion is often difficult and sometimes even impossible to detect. And if identified, prosecution under the Sherman Act was sometimes uncertain.[12] The Sherman Act, in other words, did not always seem to be an effective restraint on supracompetitive pricing. In addition, concentration was likely to result either in fewer firms or in the smaller firms having a reduced share of the market; mergers could therefore impair felt needs to preserve small businesses and local control over industry.

The Supreme Court's decisions on horizontal mergers have sought to deal with these concerns— but not always with satisfactory results. Again,

12. See the discussion of conscious parallelism and oligopoly pricing at pp. 266–75 supra.

the first decision, and in some respects still the benchmark for horizontal mergers in unconcentrated markets, is *Brown Shoe.* There was no contention that the merger posed a threat to competition among shoe manufacturers, of which there were almost 900; the District Court had held that the merged firm's control of less than 5 percent of shoe manufacturing was economically too insignificant to violate Section 7, and the government did not appeal that finding. The fear, rather, stemmed from the merger of two large retailers. Brown was the third largest shoe retailer (by dollar volume) with 1,230 stores while Kinney ranked eighth; between them they would control some 1,600 shoe stores throughout the nation and would become the second largest shoe retailer having 7.2 percent of all shoe stores and 2.3 percent of total retail shoe outlets.

In deciding whether the Brown-Kinney retail merger violated Section 7, the Supreme Court announced a functional standard for determining whether a merger adversely affected competition. That is, rather than establishing specific tests such as the market shares of the merging firms,[13] the

13. In separate footnotes the Court described the House Report on the bill to amend § 7 as reflecting "a conscious avoidance of exclusively mathematical tests" (footnote 36), and recognized the importance of economic data (footnote 38): "Statistics reflecting the shares of the market controlled by the industry leaders and the parties to a merger are, of course, the primary index of market power; but only a further examination of the particular market—its structure, history and probable future—can provide the appropriate setting for judging the probable anticompetitive effect of the merger."

degree of concentration of the industry, etc., the Court indicated that it would look at the actual and likely effect of the merger.

> [P]roviding no definite quantitative or qualitative tests by which enforcement agencies could gauge the effects of a given merger to determine whether it may "substantially" lessen competition or tend toward monopoly, Congress indicated plainly that a merger had to be functionally viewed, in the context of its particular industry. That is, whether the consolidation was to take place in an industry that was fragmented rather than concentrated, that had seen a recent trend toward domination by a few leaders or had remained fairly consistent in its distribution of market shares among the participating companies, that had experienced easy access to markets by suppliers and easy access to suppliers by buyers or had witnessed foreclosure of business, that had witnessed the ready entry of new competition or the erection of barriers to prospective entrants, all were aspects, varying in importance with the merger under consideration, which would properly be taken into account.

Despite this apparent adoption of an economic impact test for horizontal mergers, the Court spelled out no standard for implementing this approach. And its application of this standard to the facts of the Brown-Kinney merger seemed to betray the announced "rule of reason" approach.

In considering the horizontal effect of the merger the Court first defined the geographic market. It

noted that shoe store customers shopped only within their cities of residence. But it rejected Brown's
further argument for a detailed analysis of buying
patterns in particular cities as impractical and
unwarranted. It therefore concluded that the relevant geographic market where the effect of the
merger could be measured was those cities of over
10,000 in which both Brown and Kinney operated
stores.

In this market it found that the combined share
of shoe sales was often very large—exceeding 20
percent for women's shoes in 32 cities and for
children's shoes in 21 cities and, in a few instances,
exceeding 50 percent in either or both product
lines. Yet most of the cities where Brown and
Kinney had a large percentage of shoe sales were
relatively small and did not constitute large markets. Any impact of the merger as a result was
unlikely to have a significant effect on competition.
Therefore the critical point seemed to be in a
broader market, namely, that "[i]n 118 separate
cities the combined shares of the market of Brown
and Kinney in the sale of one of the relevant lines
of commerce exceeded 5 percent." Aware that a 5
percent national market share did not constitute
impressive evidence of market power, the Court
argued that:

> In an industry as fragmented as shoe retailing,
> the control of substantial shares of the trade in a
> city may have important effects on competition.
> If a merger achieving 5 percent control were now
> approved, we might be required to approve fu-

ture merger efforts by Brown's competitors seeking similar market shares.

Thus, a comparison of what the Court *said* with what it *did* reveals the *Brown Shoe* decision to be a truly schizophrenic case. On the one hand, the Court called for an analysis of the actual and likely impact of the merger in the market place in general and on competition in particular. This would have required a close scrutiny of the functional context of the merger—the ability of the merged firm to restrict output and raise price, the opportunity for collusion, the effect on entry or expansion by others, etc. On the other hand, the Court in fact looked at none of the economic consequences of the merger save one—the structural effect. It found that a merger which created a firm with 5 percent of an atomistic market is, by itself, likely to diminish competition. Not even an expectation of improved market performance (see the discussion of Brown's vertical efficiency, pp. 350–52 supra) would have prevented its invalidation under Section 7.

Aside from this contradiction between the Court's theory and its application of Section 7 in *Brown Shoe*, two other aspects of the opinion warrant attention. First, it seems unlikely that a merger creating the second largest firm (but with only 5 percent of sales) will increase the dangers of collusion among companies in the industry. Although the record does not indicate the degree of concentration at the retail shoe store level, it seems likely that there were at least 20 competing firms in the market and probably many more. And it is generally agreed by economists, whatever their views, that oligopoly or collusive pricing is unlikely in an industry of 20 firms where none is dominant.

The second point worth noting is that the Court's condemnation of a merger controlling 5 percent of the market where the industry is fragmented seems a curious twist on the merger law's concern with concentration. Had the market been concentrated, a merger on the order of Brown-Kinney might be troublesome. But the less concentrated the market, the less significant are the market shares of the merging firms. That is, if a merger resulting in a firm controlling 5 percent is not worrisome, the fact that the market is unconcentrated cannot possibly make that merger more dangerous to competition.

One year later, in United States v. Philadelphia Nat'l Bank, 374 U.S. 321 (1963) (PNB) the Court applied Section 7 to bank mergers (itself a surprising result) and held that a merger creating the largest bank in the Philadelphia area with almost one-third of the market in a highly concentrated industry (the two largest firms would have nearly 60 percent and the top four almost 80 percent) would probably substantially lessen competition. In so doing, the Court outlined a minimum threshold where mergers were presumptively illegal and hence did not require evaluation of their economic impact.

This intense congressional concern with the trend toward concentration warrants dispensing, in certain cases, with elaborate proof of market structure, market behavior, or probable anticompetitive effects. Specifically, we think that a merger which produces a firm controlling an undue percentage share of the relevant market, and results in a significant increase in the concentration of firms in that market is so inherently likely to lessen competition substantially that it must be enjoined in the absence of evidence clearly showing that the merger is not likely to have such anticompetitive effects.

Applied here the test had three elements: (1) the merger created a firm having 30 percent of the relevant market; (2) the concentration among the leading firms is increased by 33 percent (here the combined market shares of the top two firms jumped from 44 to 59 percent); and (3) the evidence (such as on the ease of entry) does not rebut the significance of these market figures and the merger is not otherwise justified (e.g., by evidence that one of the merging companies was "failing" [14]).

Although this legal test is very different from that announced in *Brown Shoe*, *PNB* is not necessarily inconsistent. The first (*Brown Shoe*) applied to deconcentrated industries where the Court at least said that an examination of economic

14. See Citizen Pub'l Co. v. United States, 394 U.S. 131 (1969).

factors was required, whereas the other (*PNB*) set forth an outside limit of presumptive or per se illegality for horizontal mergers in concentrated markets. And if a horizontal merger in a concentrated market does not violate Section 7 under the *PNB* standard, it must still survive the economic impact scrutiny of *Brown Shoe*. On the other hand, *PNB* did not state a rigid per se rule. Its second requirement that a merger involving 30 percent of the market was unlawful if the level of concentration was also significantly raised by the merger was designed to allow large firms in concentrated markets to purchase minor firms without violating Section 7. Although the Court attached a limiting condition—of no contrary evidence—to its standard of presumptive illegality, its rejection of the proffered justifications in *PNB* suggested that few defenses would be upheld. In particular, beneficial effects in another market (here the availability of loans to large borrowers) could not justify mergers with a presumed undesirable impact elsewhere. The Court was unwilling to place itself in the position of having to weigh the relative values resulting from a merger.

Then, in two cases which the Court treated as involving horizontal merger issues (by analytical legerdemain on the market definition issue, see pp. 369–74 infra), the Court further extended the *Brown Shoe-PNB* rule. First in United States v. Aluminum Co. of America, 377 U.S. 271 (1964) (*Alcoa-Rome*), the nation's leading producer of aluminum and aluminum conductor was prohibited from acquiring Rome, one of the largest producers of copper conductor and also a "substantial" manufacturer of aluminum conductor. In the aluminum conductor "market" Alcoa's share was 27.8 percent; Rome accounted for 1.3 percent; and the nine largest firms, which included Alcoa and Rome, produced 95.7 percent. The Court held that the dominant firm in a concentrated industry could not purchase a significant competitive factor (Rome having been a particularly dynamic force) without unlawfully impairing competition.

Similarly, in United States v. Continental Can Co., 378 U.S. 441 (1964), the Court enjoined the merger of the second largest manufacturer of metal containers with the third largest producer of glass containers. In the combined "container" market, Continental ranked second with 21.9 percent; Hazel-Atlas, the acquired firm, had 3.1 percent; and the six largest firms held 70.1 percent of the market. While the Court also emphasized the impact of this merger on future and potential competition, its judgment relied primarily on the total market share (of 25 percent) and the increasing concentration in the industry. Viewed together, these decisions lowered the percentages at which mergers were presumptively illegal; but each also involved a major merger in a concentrated industry. In its apparent concern with structural changes which could facilitate oligopoly pricing, the Court did not substantially alter the aim and effect of merger law as applied in *PNB*.

But then in United States v. Von's Grocery Co., 384 U.S. 270 (1966), the Court appeared to abandon *PNB's* standard of presumptive illegality in favor of an even more stringent rule which would forbid almost all mergers of consequence.[15] Von's, the third largest retail grocery chain in the Los Angeles market, with 4.7 percent of all sales, acquired the sixth largest retailer. Together they accounted for 7.5 percent of all grocery store sales in the area, which was only slightly less than the leader, Safeway. In finding that the merger was contrary to Section 7, the Court emphasized the trend toward mergers and chains as well as toward the decline of independent firms in the market: from 1950 to 1963 the number of owners operating a single grocery store in the Los Angeles retail market decreased from 5,365 to 3,590; the number of food chains with two or more stores increased between 1953 and 1962 from 96 to 150; and between 1949 and 1958 nine of the top 20 chains acquired 126 stores from their smaller competitors. The Court placed primary reliance on the Clayton Act's purpose of preventing powerful combinations from driving out smaller competitors and held that since this merger would further reduce the number of independent firms in the market it violated Section 7.

15. The government, in its argument before the Court, had sought to show that the Los Angeles food retailing market was becoming concentrated and that the merger would further this trend. The difficulty with this contention, however, was that entry was easily and rapidly available; it therefore was highly unlikely that prices could be raised above normal (i.e., competitive) levels. In any case, the Court seemingly ignored the government's theory.

In other words, the Court in *Von's* read the antimerger law as a mandate, wherever possible, to encourage markets composed of small competitors. Even though the market was far from concentrated with over 3,500 independent firms, and with only mixed evidence of increasing concentration (the combined shares of the three, four and five largest firms having declined while that of the 20 largest increased), the Court found that competition might be adversely affected.

> It is enough for us that Congress feared that a market marked at the same time by both a continuous decline in the number of small businesses and a large number of mergers would slowly but inevitably gravitate from a market of many small competitors to one dominated by one or a few giants, and competition would thereby be destroyed.

The Court appeared, in other words, to have made all but the most trivial horizontal mergers illegal per se.[16]

But the durability of the *Alcoa-Rome* through *Von's* rule for horizontal mergers seems doubtful. These decisions, particularly that in *Von's*, appear both inconsistent and economically unsound. *Von's* reliance on the decline of the number of firms in the market, as if this were equivalent to increasing concentration, reveals a lack of insight

---

16. See also United States v. Pabst Brewing Co., 384 U.S. 546 (1966) discussed p. 371 infra; 4 P. Areeda & D. Turner, *Antitrust Law* ¶ 909b (1980) (table of cases listing market shares of merged companies, market structure, and court decision).

and understanding. Concentration refers in general to the market shares held by the four or eight largest firms, not the total number of firms in the market. Here the concern is that when a small group holds a dominant position in the market, express or tacit price-fixing is possible and perhaps likely, and that supracompetitive prices may be charged. But the retail grocery business appeared to be at the opposite pole: entry was easy and rapid; there was a high turnover in the market leadership; price competition seemed intense; the rise of chains and the decline of individual stores was due to a technological (supermarket) revolution; etc. The Court appeared to be returning to the contradictory rule of *Brown Shoe*, namely, condemning the merger because it would lead to lower prices. While voicing concern with concentration, the Court's actions were in fact based upon an approach which would support its worst feature (higher prices).

These and like criticisms appear to have had an effect on the judicial treatment of horizontal mergers under Section 7, and the Supreme Court has backed away from further application of the *Von's* test. Specifically, in United States v. General Dynamics Corp., 415 U.S. 486 (1974), the Court upheld a District Court decision approving a merger of two leading coal producers even though a rapid decline in the number of coal producers had occurred, the merger increased the concentration of the top two firms in the market by over 10 percent, and the

merger resulted in the two largest firms now controlling about half of all sales. Pointing to its
footnote in *Brown Shoe* that market share was
only the beginning place for analyzing a merger's
impact on competition (see pp. 355–58 and n. 13
supra), the Court concluded that the acquired
firm's exhausted coal reserves, combined with long-
term contract commitments, indicated it was no
longer a significant force in the market—and its
disappearance as an independent firm would not
adversely affect competition.

Within the narrow facts of *General Dynamics* the
decision does not itself suggest a new trend. It
involved an unusual situation of an exhaustible
resource rather than a replenishable product, and
for this reason the Court viewed the market as
uncommitted coal reserves rather than, as the government urged, coal production. However, the
Court also indicated that the case involved more
than the correct selection of market shares. Instead it emphasized language in *Brown Shoe,* ignored during the turbulent preceding decade of
Section 7 decisions by the Supreme Court, regarding the limitations of market share analysis as a
conclusive determinant of competitive effect. Subsequent bank merger cases further suggest that the
Court will now more closely examine the meaning
of market share percentages before drawing inferences of likely anticompetitive effect. See, e.g.,
United States v. Marine Bancorporation, 418 U.S
602, 631 (1974); United States v. Citizens & Southern Nat'l Bank, 422 U.S. 86, 120 (1975).

These cases, however, should not be read as illustrating any abandonment of Section 7's goal of protecting competition. For example, in Brunswick v. Pueblo Bowl-O-Mat, 429 U.S. 477 (1977), owners of several small bowling alleys sued a major manufacturer of alleys and alley equipment for having acquired alleys which competed with the plaintiffs'. Brunswick had made the acquisitions after the firms had defaulted on their purchase contracts and could find no other buyers. In a unanimous decision, the Court held that Brunswick's purchases had preserved competition by denying plaintiffs the benefits of increased concentration. Section 7 is designed to prevent a lessening of competition and therefore cannot be used to protect individual competitors from competition.

The Department of Justice issued a new set of rules in 1982 outlining when it would prosecute mergers as a violation of Section 7, and revised them two years later.[17] They substituted the Herfindahl-Hirschman Index (commonly referred to as the HHI) for 4-firm market share measures of concentration. By summing the squares of each firm in the market, the HHI seeks to measure concentration in a way that reflects both the absolute level of concentration and the degree to which larger firms are dominant within the market. Thus, like their 1968 counterpart, the recent

17. U.S. Dep't of Justice, Merger Guidelines, 47 Fed.Reg. 28, 493 (1982); id., 49 Fed.Reg. 26,823 (1984). See Symposium, *1982 Merger Guidelines,* 71 Calif.L.Rev. 281 (1983). They updated and modified rules first issued in 1968.

Guidelines continue to focus on market share data and concentration ratios to create a presumption of illegality (if the HHI is above 1800 and it is increased by 100 points) or legality (if the HHI below 1000, or between 1000–1800 and the increase is less than 50). Their primary aim as before is to prevent acquisitions likely to create monopoly or oligopoly power through collusive practices.

There are numerous differences, however. The threshhold measures of when intervention is appropriate are now considerably higher; the new Guidelines ignore trends toward concentration; but they do emphasize the ease of entry into the market. Here the Guidelines adopt rigorous economic analysis that the only barrier to entry is something that makes it more costly for a new entrant to do business in the market than it costs an established firm. See Demsetz, *Barriers to Entry,* 72 Am.Econ.Rev. 47 (1982). Where entry is so easy that existing competitors could not raise their prices for a significant period of time, there is no reason to challenge a merger; it poses no danger to competition or consumer welfare. Accord United States v. Waste Management, Inc., 743 F.2d 976 (2d Cir.1984) (applying 1984 Guidelines to dismiss complaint brought by the Justice Department against merger of solid waste disposal firms). The 1984 revision of the Guidelines specifically recognized foreign competition and clear and convincing evidence that a merger will achieve economic efficiencies. Fearful that courts will not necessarily follow this lead, the Reagan Administration has proposed a codification of these changes by amending Section 7 of the Clayton Act limiting proscription to mergers with a "significant probability" of anticompetitive effects.

E. DEFINING THE RELEVANT MARKETS

We previously considered the importance of the "market" in understanding the basic concepts of microeconomics (see Chapter 3: the conditions under which goods are exchanged) and in applying the antitrust laws to monopoly (see Chapter 4: identifying the group of sellers, by geography and product, with which a firm competes).

In the merger context, as in monopoly situations, the primary focus is centered on substitutes—namely, will changes in price draw other firms and products into competition—as summarized by the concept of cross-elasticity of demand. When market shares are relied upon to evidence market power and used to infer competitive effects, the drawing of the market's boundaries becomes crucial. The market should include all products that have a high cross-elasticity of demand (i.e., those which could be readily substituted at a slight price increase) with the product of the merging firms.

Under the stress of deciding particular cases, however, the Supreme Court has sometimes lost sight of this standard in establishing product and geographic markets. Thus, in *Alcoa-Rome,* p. 361

supra, the Court followed an inexplicable three-step process in determining that all types of aluminum conductor were a separate submarket in which the merger should be tested. First, it relied on the parties' agreement that *bare* aluminum conductor was a separate market because of its superiority as a conductor of electricity and consumer preference for it in overhead distribution. Second, the Court relied on consumer preference for *insulated* aluminum conductor in overhead distribution as identifying insulated aluminum as a separate market even though it was functionally interchangeable with copper. Then, in a logical tour de force—albeit without apparent rationality—the Court held that if bare and insulated aluminum conductors were separate markets, together they (that is, *all* aluminum conductor) also constituted a separate market. Despite its adoption by the Supreme Court, this market definition has little to commend it. The Court's primary argument that both bare and insulated aluminum are used to conduct electricity is unpersuasive since that would also require the inclusion of copper conductor in this market. Why then did the Court ignore the high cross-elasticity of copper in excluding it from the market and thereby force this contorted market on the case? The only plausible reason appears to be a need to find a market in which the *PNB* test could be applied.[18]

18. Neither the bare nor the insulated market alone would justify finding a violation of Section 7 under the *PNB* framework. Rome was a trivial entrant in the bare aluminum

Nor is *Alcoa-Rome* unique. In United States v. Continental Can Co., 378 U.S. 441 (1964), the Court took a wholly different—and inconsistent—approach. This time metal cans and glass jars were lumped into one container market even though the cross-elasticity of demand among different types of jars or of cans was substantially greater than between jars and cans. By distorting the product market and treating the case as a horizontal merger, the Court in effect overstated the impact of the merger; in fact the merger directly affected only substitute competition. The point is not that the decision forbidding the merger was erroneous, but rather that in making its determination the Court failed to focus on the real issue before it—namely, how to test mergers between firms producing distant substitute products.

Similar difficulties were encountered in the Court's efforts to define geographic markets in merger cases. Perhaps the most significant illustration is United States v. Pabst Brewing Co., 384 U.S. 546 (1966), which examined the legality of the acquisition by Pabst (the nation's tenth largest brewer) of Blatz (the eighteenth largest). The District Court had dismissed the government's complaint because of its failure to show either that Wisconsin or the three-state area of Wisconsin, Illinois and Michigan, were relevant geographic

conductor market with but .3 percent of the market, and the merged company's market share in the insulated aluminum conductor market totaled 16 percent which was only halfway to *PNB's* 30 percent market share standard.

markets.[19] The Supreme Court reversed the decision, apparently holding (contrary to *Brown Shoe*) that all the government needed to show was that the merger had a substantial effect somewhere in the country. The weakness in this approach in *Pabst* is that without first defining a market within which to measure the effect of a merger, any prediction of its impact on competition is meaningless. One is left wondering where the merger will have an adverse effect.

As illustrated by the decision in *General Dynamics,* p. 365 supra, the Court has now required a closer and economically more defensible definition of the relevant market in merger cases. The deliberate character of *General Dynamics,* and its reassertion of the importance of defining the relevant market, is buttressed by two bank merger decisions. First, in United States v. Marine Bancorporation, 418 U.S. 602 (1974), a Seattle bank's acquisition of a Spokane bank in the State of Washington was upheld because state law prohibited the former from establishing a branch in Spokane. The Government's argument that the relevant market was the entire state where the two banks might otherwise have been potential competitors was unpersuasive because the Seattle bank was not a competitor, actual or potential, in the relevant Spokane metropolitan area. Similarly, in

19. And in the nation as a whole, according to the District Court, the government had not demonstrated a probability of lessened competition. The Supreme Court found the requisite anticompetitive effect, however.

United States v. Connecticut Nat'l Bank, 418 U.S.
656 (1974), the Court held that commercial and
savings banks could not be simply aggregated into
a single product market. Careful analysis, the
Court ruled, requires specific evaluation of competition with other credit suppliers as well as more
rigorous examination of the overlap between commercial and savings banks. In doing so, the Court
reiterated its market definition test as being the
localized area in which the acquired bank exper-
iences "significant, direct competition with other
banks, albeit [in potential competition cases] not
[including] the acquiring bank."

The most significant change authored by the
1982/84 Guidelines is their process for defining
product and geographic markets in merger cases.
(For a more complete description, see pp. 113–15
supra.) This change can often be critical because
market definition is the starting point for determining market shares and concentration, the twin
touchstones of merger analysis. Moving beyond
current case law that generally examines only
trade patterns at the current price, the recent
Guidelines seek to define a market capable of being
monopolized by examining all forces that significantly constrain the merging firms and their rivals
in setting prices. That is, the rules ask: which
products or firms are now available to buyers and
where could they turn for supplies if prices increased by five percent? These alternative suppliers and their production must generally be includ-

ed in the market denominator. By casting a larger net and redrawing market boundaries to cover more products and a greater area, the current Merger Guidelines have the potential for finding lower concentration indices and for applying a looser threshhold standard.

F. CONGLOMERATE MERGERS

Conglomerate acquisitions take a variety of forms ranging from short-term joint ventures to permanent mergers. They are generally of three types: (1) product line extensions which add related items to the acquiring firm's existing products (e.g., laundry bleach to a detergent producer); (2) market extensions where the merging firms previously sold the same product but in different geographic areas; and (3) "pure" conglomerates where the partners had no functional business link (e.g., a steel company buying an auto rental or health insurance firm). Whatever the type of conglomerate, the transaction involves firms which are in separate markets, and the merger therefore can have no direct effect on competition. There is no reduction or other change in the number of firms in either the acquiring or acquired firm's market. Foreclosure, at least as we previously examined it in the vertical context, is generally absent except insofar as the merging parties may engage in reciprocal dealing or supply each other's needs. Nor is there any change in the market structure, the firms' market shares, or concentration ratios.

Conglomerate mergers can serve desirable social ends as well as impair competition. For example, they supply a market or "demand" for businesses, thus providing entrepreneurs with liquidity at an open market price. Again, the threat of a take-over may keep management efficient in imperfectly competitive markets. Conglomerate mergers also provide opportunities for firms to achieve pecuniary (capital costs), differential (overhead costs) and promotional (advertising) efficiencies. On the other hand, conglomerate acquisitions are feared because they may lessen future competition through eliminating a potential entrant. Potential competition may also be restricted; a large firm may be converted into a dominant company with a decisive competitive advantage or otherwise have the effect of raising entry barriers. A conglomerate merger may also reduce the number of smaller firms and increase the political power of the merged firm, thereby impairing independent social and political values associated with retaining as many independent decision making centers as possible, guaranteeing small business opportunities, and preserving democratic processes.

The potential competition doctrine, the mainstay of the attack on conglomerate mergers under Section 7, has had a checkered and not wholly satisfactory history. Its first application in connection with conglomerate acquisitions was to a joint venture between two chemical companies in United States v. Penn-Olin Chem. Co., 378 U.S. 158 (1964).

Pennsalt, an Oregon producer of sodium chlorate (a bleaching agent used primarily in the pulp and paper industry) which it sold in the West, joined with Olin Mathieson, an industrial chemical firm which was an intermediate user of sodium chlorate, to build a sodium chlorate plant in Kentucky and to sell that product in the Southeast. Before Penn-Olin's entry into this market, only two firms had plants in the southeastern area, with control of over 90 percent of all sales. The evidence indicated that prior to forming the joint venture both Pennsalt and Olin Mathieson had considered but not completely rejected the possibility of entering the southeastern market independently. The District Court, relying on the competitive value of an additional market entrant, upheld the joint venture. The government had now shown "as a matter of reasonable probability" that both firms would have entered the market if Penn-Olin had not been created. The court reasoned that competition had been enhanced, not lessened; one actual entrant was worth more than two on the sideline.

On review the Supreme Court remanded the case for further findings, however, ruling that if one of the firms probably would have entered with the other remaining "at the edge of the market, continually threatening to enter," the venture should be disapproved.[20] According to the Court the possible

20. Applying these instructions on remand, the District Court determined that independent entry by either of the two firms was improbable and that therefore the "merger" did not violate Section 7. This decision was upheld by the Supreme Court on a second appeal by a divided (4–4) vote. 389 U.S. 308 (1967).

elimination of a potential entrant, even if the evidence failed to show a reasonable probability of entry by the second firm, would be enough to violate Section 7.

The potential competition theory as applied by the Supreme Court in *Penn-Olin* can be questioned on several grounds. First, the Court took no account of the effect of the joint venture's actual entry into the market. This entry increased the number of firms in the Southeast (by 50 percent) and reduced the share of productive capacity held by each of the others; in other words, the likelihood of price collusion was substantially reduced. Yet under the Court's analysis, this evidence of certain entry could be offset by a judicial finding of probable entry by one of the venturers.

Second, the assumption that once one of the venturers enters the market the other is likely to remain a potential entrant relies upon a questionable premise. It ignores the change in the market resulting from the new entrant. The reason that the joint venture (or one of the partners) would enter in the first place is that the price of the product is supranormal, permitting increased profits to be earned. Once an additional firm enters the market, prices should fall with increased output, and the market would no longer be as attractive to new entrants.

Third, even if the market is still attractive to new entrants because prices have not fallen (e.g., demand increased or the new entrant joined in collusive pricing), the significance of the remaining venturer(s) as potential entrant(s) depends on a factor not noted by the Court—namely, the number of other chemical firms with the interests and capabilities of entering the Southeast market. The entry of Penn-Olin and its possible elimination of one venturer as a potential entrant is significant only if there were no other possible entrants.

The Court next considered the legality of a conglomerate merger in FTC v. Procter & Gamble Co., 386 U.S. 568 (1967) (*P & G*). Procter, a large and a diversified manufacturer of detergents and other household products sold in supermarkets, bought Clorox, the largest seller of household liquid bleach. Procter dominated the detergent market, accounting for 54 percent of sales; but it neither made nor sold bleach. Clorox controlled almost 49 percent of the bleach market; its nearest rival Purex accounted for less than 16 percent of bleach sales. In ruling that Procter's acquisition of a producer of complementary products violated Section 7, the Court relied on two somewhat contradictory grounds: first, that the merger would give Clorox—supported by Procter—a decisive competitive advantage in the bleach market, allowing it to discipline competitors and raise new barriers to entry; and second, that Procter was the leading, and perhaps only, potential candidate for entry into the bleach market. Based on these contentions, the Court held that the merger adversely affected actual and potential competition.

Neither basis for its decision is compelling. The
premise of the first ground (that Procter had both
the capability of and interest in driving out competing bleach producers) is no justification for forbidding an acquisition since it could merely post-
pone the inevitable. That is, if the entry is as
desirable to Procter as the Court assumes, Procter
could achieve that end through internal expansion
and then drive Clorox and others from the market.[21] The second ground—that the merger eliminated Procter, the leading and perhaps only potential entrant into the market—is contradicted by
the available evidence. Entry was not impeded by
technical barriers; the market was populated by
many small firms; retail distribution was possible
by any of the large retail chains; large economies
of scale did not bar smaller firms. Nor did the
Court consider whether other large detergent producers could have entered the market. It seems,
in other words, that Procter was probably only one
of several (perhaps many) possible entrants. If so,
its elimination as a potential competitor through
the purchase of Clorox would not have significantly affected current market practices or future competition.

21. In light of Procter's premium payment for Clorox, however, this analysis seems to belie reality. In finding that a
Procter-owned Clorox would have an unfair advantage, the
Court was particularly concerned with Procter's promotional
efficiencies—which, the Court decided, were not socially desirable economic efficiencies and therefore were a reason for disapproving the merger.

Following its success in *P & G,* the Federal Trade Commission sought to extend the potential competition doctrine by applying it to instances where the acquiring firm admittedly was not likely to enter the acquired firm's market by internal expansion (i.e., *de novo*). Thus, in Bendix Corp., 77 F.T.C. 731 (1970), vacated and remanded on other grounds, 450 F.2d 534 (6th Cir.1971), a diversified manufacturer of automotive components and assemblies sought to buy the third largest manufacturer of auto filters (with over 17 percent of the aftermarket). Accepting the administrative law judge's finding that Bendix, the acquiring company, would not have entered the auto filter market *de novo* and therefore was not itself a potential entrant, the Trade Commission ruled that the acquisition nonetheless violated Section 7 because Bendix would have been a likely entrant into the concentrated filter market through acquisition and expansion of a "toehold" firm. The FTC contended that competition within the filter market could have been improved if Bendix had bought a smaller firm and through expansion had become an independent force in the industry, competing with Fram (the acquired firm) as well as with other filter manufacturers.

Despite its imaginative cast, the toehold acquisition theory is not without its critics. First, the theory is not wholly consistent with the language of Section 7—with its requirement of a probable substantial lessening of competition. In *Bendix,* the Commission did not make any finding that either actual or future competition would be impaired. Rather the merger was condemned for not *improving* competition to the degree another merger might have done. Whether the Congress sought to limit, or whether sound policy would have limited, conglomerate mergers to those demonstrably improving the competitive structure in the acquired firm's market seems doubtful.

So far the Supreme Court has specifically declined to decide whether the toehold theory is consistent with Section 7. See United States v. Falstaff Brewing Corp., 410 U.S. 526, 537 (1973); United States v. Marine Bancorporation, 418 U.S. 602, 625, 639 (1974).[22] Indeed, the Court reserved decision on the validity of the "actual potential competition" theory that, but for the merger, the acquiring firm would have entered a concentrated market (de novo or by acquisition of a much smaller firm). However, it did establish two preconditions in *Marine Bancorporation:* (1) the evidence must show that the potential entrant had some way to enter other than by buying the target firm; and, (2) this entry had the substantial likelihood of deconcentrating the target market or of producing other procompetitive effects.

The *Falstaff* decision did expand the meaning of who should be considered a "potential competitor"

---

22. It has, however, acknowledged that "[t]here are traces of this view [that the toehold theory is consistent with § 7] in our cases." United States v. Falstaff Brewing Corp., supra.

by looking beyond the acquiring firm's actual intentions. The District Court had dismissed the government's complaint after finding that the acquiring firm had decided not to enter the market except by acquisition of a significant competitor. (Since Falstaff was therefore not a potential entrant according to the District Court, the merger was merely a substitution of ownership by the acquired firm.) The Supreme Court took a broader view of potential competition. In a decision reminiscent of *Penn-Olin,* the Supreme Court reversed the decision on the ground that Falstaff might still have been "perceived" by the firms in the market as a potential entrant and consequently have forced them to constrain their pricing practices. That is, the Court remanded the case for consideration of whether Falstaff was so positioned on the edge of the market (an "on the fringe potential competitor" who is "waiting in the wings") that it exerted a beneficial influence on it—and therefore that its elimination adversely affected future competition.[23] As in *Penn-Olin,* however, the Court did not reach the ultimate question of whether Falstaff's elimination as a potential competitor would have a significant effect on the market.

Whether courts are equipped to make such complex findings—especially of whether limit-pricing would be profitable and likely or of a reasonable

---

23. Two questions were involved: (1) Was Falstaff perceived as a potential competitor? (2) If it was, would its elimination significantly affect competition or were others similarly situated?

probability of entry by the acquiring firm in the near future—seems questionable. Anomalous results are likely. That is, where barriers are high, the acquiring firm (and all others) may be unlikely entrants; where the barriers are low, the market is competitive and the elimination of a potential entrant is irrelevant. Compare Tenneco, Inc. v. FTC, 689 F.2d 346 (2d Cir.1982) (entry barriers protecting market from competition excluded acquiring company from being a potential entrant) with Yamaha Motor Co. v. FTC, 657 F.2d 971 (8th Cir. 1981), cert. denied, 456 U.S. 915 (1982) (finding both high entry barriers and that acquiring firm was a likely entrant), and Mercantile Texas Corp. v. Board of Governors, 638 F.2d 1255 (5th Cir.1981) (acquiring firm a significant future entrant because entry barriers limited).

CHAPTER X

PATENT LICENSES

"The patent system added the fuel of interest to the fire of genius." A. Lincoln.

Patents are government sanctioned monopolies which grant inventors exclusive rights to their inventions, thus preventing others from using the inventions (unless they pay the inventor for the use) for seventeen years. As such, patents may appear to conflict with the antitrust laws, since the latter endeavor to prevent or destroy the creation of monopoly power. However, this conflict is more illusory than real. The granting of a monopoly right for the use of an invention does not necessarily confer monopoly power; substitutes may be readily available or the invention may have little commercial value. More importantly, the fundamental purpose of both the patent and antitrust laws is to promote innovation and to encourage efficient use of resources. That is, both seek to increase output—with the ensuing overall effect of lowering prices.[1]

1. Even though the patentee receives a monopoly on his invention, it will not be commercially marketable unless it represents an improvement over, or is available at a lower price than, the products for which it is a substitute. This can be illustrated as shown in Figure 12 on the following page:

MC_1 is the cost of producing the nonpatented product. In a competitive market that product will be sold at price p_1. The

A. AN INTRODUCTION TO PATENTS

Under the broad authority of Article I, Section 8 of the Constitution "[t]o promote the progress of science and useful arts, by securing for limited times to authors and inventors the exclusive right to their respective writings and discoveries," Congress adopted a patent code. This code provides that patents can be issued for "any new and useful process, machine, manufacture, or composition of

patented product is commercially valuable because it has a lower production cost (MC_2) and can therefore be sold at a lower price (p_2). Because of the monopoly grant, it will be sold above price p_2, but below the previous price (of p_1), and a greater quantity (i.e., more than q_1) will be produced.

FIGURE 12: MARKETABLE PATENTS

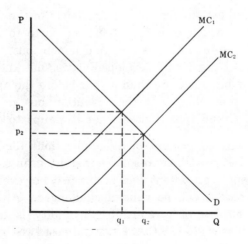

matter, or any new and useful improvement thereof" for a term of seventeen years from the date of issue. 35 U.S.C.A. § 101. In order to satisfy these requirements, the inventor must show that he is the first person to reduce the invention to practice and that the invention is both nonobvious and useful. See Anderson's-Black Rock, Inc. v. Pavement Salvage Co., 396 U.S. 57 (1969); Graham v. John Deere Co. of Kansas City, 383 U.S. 1 (1966); see generally Kitch, *Graham v. John Deere Co.: New Standards for Patents,* 1966 Sup.Ct.Rev. 293. This has led the Court to hold that mathematical formulas or processes cannot be patented (Gottschalk v. Benson, 409 U.S. 63 (1972); Parker v. Flook, 437 U.S. 584 (1978)), but that live, human-made micro-organisms can. Diamond v. Chakrabarty, 447 U.S. 303 (1980).

Applications for patents are made to the Patent Office, which examines them ex parte to insure that the invention is new and nonobvious, that it was not previously developed or was not known to the public for more than a year before the application was filed, that the invention has practical utility, and that it does what it claims to do.

About 60 percent of all applications filed with the Patent Office result in patent grants. The issuance of a patent does not assure, however, that the patent will be valid if challenged. Although the burden of establishing invalidity is on the challenger (35 U.S.C.A. § 282), almost two-thirds of all challenged patents have in recent years been held invalid.[2] Several factors have contributed to this result. First, the ex parte procedure for examining patent applications does not encourage the disclosure of evidence of invalidity to the Patent Office. Courts have, as a result, been skeptical of patent grants and quick to shift the burden of proof back to the patentee. Second, even if a patent is upheld when challenged, that judgment is binding only on the parties. Blonder-Tongue Labs., Inc. v. University of Illinois Foundation, 402 U.S. 313 (1971). Third, the patent's validity can be put in issue in numerous situations: when the patentee sues for infringement or the infringer seeks a declaratory judgment that the patent is invalid; when a licensee challenges it (Lear, Inc. v. Adkins, 395 U.S. 653 (1969) (state law estoppel doctrine inapplicable)); when the government or private plaintiff in an antitrust suit challenges a patent relied on by the defendant (Walker Process Equip., Inc. v. Food Mach. & Chem. Corp., 382 U.S. 172 (1965)) or one which is otherwise involved in the case (United States v. Glaxo Group Ltd., 410 U.S. 52 (1973)).

Patents may be used by the inventor, sold, licensed to others for their use, or not used at all. Most, perhaps up to 90 percent of all patents, are unused because they have no commercial value. Whatever the reason, however, the nonuse of a

2. This has led one court to remark that "a patent is merely a license to bring a lawsuit" and caused the inventors of key radio patents to lament that they were "being litigated to death."

patent has not yet been held to violate either the patent or the antitrust laws. See Continental Paper Bag Co. v. Eastern Paper Bag Co., 210 U.S. 405 (1908); cf. Dawson Chem. Co. v. Rohm & Haas Co., 448 U.S. 176 (1980) ("Compulsory licensing is a rarity in our patent system, and we decline to manufacture such a requirement out of § 271(d).")

Licensing is usually done for a fee (called a royalty), the amount charged being frequently based upon usage. Licensing is often favored because it tends to expand use of the invention, increase competition in its use, and disperse the technology, thereby encouraging improvements. On the other hand, licensing has its drawbacks, such as encouraging the development of intimate relations among competitors (thereby facilitating price-fixing), lessening the likelihood of challenges to invalid patents, and discouraging the invention of more efficient alternatives. But it is the specific provisions of the licenses themselves which have attracted primary antitrust attention and are therefore the focus of our attention.

Before examining basic antitrust applications to patent licenses, the primary rationale for patent monopolies should be noted. In essence the patent grant provides the inventor with a financial incentive to invent—that is, to invest in the research and development which are prerequisite to invention. In fact without some protection for the inventor, others could merely copy his ideas and sell the products thereof at a lower price (since they would have avoided the costs incurred in the development of the invention [3]). The patent laws, then, prevent "free riders" from denying the inventor a return on his investment and ingenuity. This is not to say that without the patent monopoly there would be no inventions. But it is a premise of the patent laws—largely unverified—that without such protection fewer socially valuable inventions would result.[4] In addition, inventors would otherwise seek to keep their inventions secret; whereas one of the conditions inherent in a patent is that the patentee disclose how the invention works with the result that the inventor's knowledge is shared and at the end of 17 years is available for use by anyone.

B. PRICE, TERRITORIAL AND USE RESTRICTIONS

Price-fixing among competing sellers (horizontal) and between supplier and retailer (vertical) is, as previously noted, illegal per se. The legal judgment is that since such arrangements can seldom be justified it would be a waste of time to hear

---

3. And the marginal cost of using an invention, once it has been determined how to copy it, is zero.

4. Whether a 17-year monopoly is necessary to maximize invention and efficient resource allocation is unclear, however. Eminent economists have disputed the degree of protection required for optimal invention and use. For example: Arnold Plant maintains that patents misdirect resources through over-rewarding innovative ideas; Kenneth Arrow concludes that inventive activity is underrewarded by patents; Frank Knight contends that patent rewards are misdirected toward the last-step routinizers at the expense of the true innovators.

their defenses. The application of this rule to horizontal cartel arrangements seems generally unassailable. Whether it should be as rigidly applied to vertical arrangements between firms not competing with one another is less clear. (See the discussion of *Dr. Miles,* p. 282, supra.) This "debate" has carried over into the patent licensing area, but with somewhat different results.

A patentee's right to exclude others from making and selling his invention allows him to keep the business generated by it entirely to himself. He is, like the producer of non-patented goods, also entitled to set whatever price he wishes. And in the case of patented products, it can be assumed that he will charge a monopoly price, if the market permits (see Figure 12, p. 385 supra), in order to maximize his revenues.

Where the patentee's ability to produce the invention is insufficient to satisfy demand, he may wish to license others to manufacture and sell it. The question then arises whether the patentee may control the price at which his licensee sells the patented product.[5] Despite several efforts to overturn it, the Supreme Court has never abandoned the rule first announced in Bement v. Na-

5. Note, the question here is different from that decided in *Dr. Miles* (aside from the fact that a patent was not involved there) in that the patentee has not manufactured and sold the product to the retailer. In fact, in an early case, Bauer & Cie v. O'Donnell, 229 U.S. 1 (1913), it was held that vertically imposed resale price maintenance agreements relating to patented products were unenforceable. The Court distinguished *Bement* on the grounds that it involved licensing, not resale.

tional Harrow Co., 186 U.S. 70 (1902), that a patentee may enforce minimum price clauses in its licensing arrangements. Thus, in *Bement* the Court enjoined one of several competing licenses from selling below the license-prescribed price; the Court reasoned that since the patentee had the right to prohibit others from using the patent— including the licensee—he also had the lesser included right of requiring the licensee to sell the patented article. See also USM Corp. v. SPS Technologies, Inc., 694 F.2d 505 (7th Cir.1982) (Posner, J.) (upholding price discrimination in royalty schedule of a license agreement; review of antitrust liability and doctrine of patent misuse).

A different rationale was relied upon to reaffirm this rule in United States v. General Elec. Co., 272 U.S. 476 (1926) (also considered p. 290 supra). GE had licensed Westinghouse to manufacture and sell lamps under GE's patents. Prices were to be maintained at the same level as GE fixed for its distributors. Upholding the price-fixing condition in GE's licenses, the Court switched its grounds and justified the condition as normally and reasonably adapted to secure for the patentee the pecuniary reward of his lawful monopoly:

One of the valuable elements of the exclusive right of a patentee is to acquire profit by the price at which the article is sold. The higher the price, the greater the profit, unless it is prohibitory. When the patentee licenses another to make and vend, and retains the right to continue

> to make and vend on his own account, the price
> at which his licensee will sell will necessarily
> affect the price at which he can sell his own
> patented goods. It would seem entirely reasona-
> ble that he should say to the licensee, "Yes, you
> may make and sell articles under my patent, but
> not so as to destroy the profit that I wish to
> obtain by making them and selling them my-
> self."

The Court was concerned, in other words, that if
GE could not set the price at which Westinghouse
sold the lamps, Westinghouse might decide to sell
them at a price which would render GE's lamp
manufacture and sales unprofitable. On the other
hand, it could be suggested that if Westinghouse
can make and sell the item much cheaper, it
should be encouraged to do so (and, therefore,
price-fixing should be prohibited). Yet if faced
with this option GE might decide not to license
Westinghouse to manufacture and sell these lamps.
Nor could GE necessarily protect itself through the
level at which it set the royalty: if it overestimated
Westinghouse's costs the royalty rate would be too
low; yet if it set the rate too high it could make
the manufacture and sale of lamps by Westinghouse unprofitable.[6] In other words, the setting of
a minimum price may be the most efficient way to
protect the patentee, to encourage licensing, and,
as the Court said, to assure that GE obtained its
monopoly reward.

6. This point is illustrated by the following figure:

There is another possible explanation for the GE
license to Westinghouse, however. The two firms

FIGURE 13: SETTING THE ROYALTY RATE

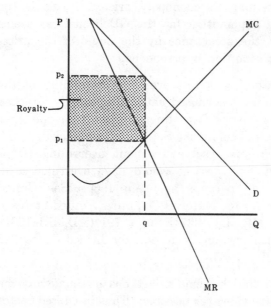

This figure merely repeats the drawing of the monopoly pricing
figure (Figure 7, p. 72 supra). *MC* represents the cost of
producing the invention. In order to obtain his monopoly
reward, the patentee sets his price at such a level that his
output (the quantity demanded) is at the point where his
marginal revenue (*MR*) equals his marginal cost (*MC*). (See
pp. 67–70 supra for an explanation of monopoly pricing.) In
order to assure that he obtains this reward when licensing
others, the patentee will set a royalty rate that equals the
difference between the marginal cost (i.e., competitive price)
and the monopoly price—or the difference between p_1 and p_2 on
the above figure. The total royalties (reflected by the shaded

may have used the price-fixing license as a device
to become participants in a cartel. If GE's patent
was of questionable validity GE, rather than risk a
ruling of invalidity, may have licensed Westinghouse in order to share its market—while still
maintaining its monopoly price. If this is the
actual explanation for the GE license, as seems
likely, the acceptance by the Court of the price-
fixing condition is erroneous.

Continuing doubts over the desirability of the
GE ruling has caused it to be repeatedly attacked
by the Justice Department. Each time the issue
was raised before the Supreme Court, however, the
matter was resolved without overruling *GE* —
though four justices would have overruled it in
1948 and perhaps again in 1965. See United
States v. Line Material Co., infra; United States v.
Huck Mfg. Co., 227 F.Supp. 791 (E.D.Mich.1964),
aff'd per curiam by an equally divided Court, 382
U.S. 197 (1965).

And the Supreme Court has distinguished the
GE rule whenever possible. Thus in United States
v. Masonite Corp., 316 U.S. 265 (1942), the Court
ruled that a patentee could not fix the price at
which its (former) competitors sold the patented
product under a price-limiting license. The Court
viewed the arrangement as a classic horizontal
price-fixing conspiracy. It differentiated the case
from *GE* on the ground that Masonite, unlike GE,

area) will equal the monopoly profits the patentee would have
received had he produced the output himself.

did all the manufacturing for the group. Such a distinction seems artificial. In both cases the patentee sought to use independent business organizations to distribute the invention at a patentee-fixed price. Yet in one case the arrangement was upheld while in the other it was prohibited by the Sherman Act.

Then in United States v. Line Material Co., 333 U.S. 287 (1948), the Court was faced with a cross-licensing agreement whereby separate grantees of a "basic patent" and an "improvement patent" licensed each other in order that each could efficiently exploit both inventions. The cross-license was necessary if the full benefit of these "blocking" inventions were to be made available to the public since the improvement infringed upon the basic patent and therefore could not be made available independently. The cross-license arrangement contained a price limitation, as in *GE,* incorporated in order to assure that each patentee received his monopoly reward without a complicated royalty arrangement. Nevertheless, the Court distinguished *GE* by arguing that two patentees had combined in *Line Material* and held that such license combinations were illegal per se. But, as one commentator has observed: "A more arbitrary and unprincipled per se rule would be difficult to construct." W. Bowman, *Patent and Antitrust Law* 195 (1973). The patents here were not competing; therefore, the price feature could not have been part of a scheme to eliminate noninfringing competition. If *GE* is still the law, then *Line Material* seems illogical. It was, in any case, a victory for accountants.

This decline in the *GE* doctrine has continued. For example, in United States v. New Wrinkle, Inc., 342 U.S. 371 (1952), the Court condemned a price restraint in the license of pooled patents assigned to a holding company—even though the patents did not complement each other (as in *Line Material*). If the pooled patents conflicted, as the parties assumed, the price restricted pool could have had no effect—other than in sharing the monopoly reward among claimants. Thus the Court's distinction of *GE* obscured the fact that the license terms could not have contributed to a price cartel beyond that allowed a patentee by *GE*.

In other words, the *GE* rule of patent licensing containing price control now appears to be limited to cases involving a single licensee.

The antitrust law's per se approach to price-restricted patent licenses has not extended to market or territorial allocations. Section 261 of the Patent Code declares that the patentee may assign his exclusive right "to the whole or any specified part of the United States." 35 U.S.C.A. § 261. And courts have upheld patent licenses assigning licensees particular territories as authorized by Congress. But such restraints are exhausted by the first sale. That is, one purchasing a patented product, even from a restricted licensee, may use or sell it without restraint. Keeler v. Standard

Folding Bed Co., 157 U.S. 659 (1895); see Adams v. Burke, 84 U.S. (17 Wall.) 453 (1873).

Another type of limited license is that defined as the "field of use." In the leading case of General Talking Pictures Corp. v. Western Elec. Co., 305 U.S. 124 (1938), the patentee had divided its licensing of an invention related to sound amplification into two classes: "home" (radio receivers) and "commercial" (e.g., motion picture sound equipment) use. Each was licensed for manufacture by different companies. In upholding the patentee's claim that a purchaser from its home-restricted licensee had infringed upon the patent through commercial use of the device, the Court implied (though it specifically declined to rule) that the use restriction was lawful. As with price restrictions, however, the Supreme Court has not extended or subsequently reaffirmed this rule,[7] though a substantial number of cases have upheld various forms of field-limited licenses relying on *General Talking Pictures.* Compare Robintech, Inc. v. Chemidus Wavin, Ltd., 628 F.2d 142 (D.C.Cir.1980), with United States v. Studiengesellschaft Kohle, 670 F.2d 1122 (D.C.Cir.1981).

It was only recently, however, that the Court ruled that a tie-in aimed at controlling an unpatented product is permitted. Early cases first held that a tie-in barred an infringement suit. Thus in

7. See, e.g., Automatic Radio Mfg. Co. v. Hazeltine Research, Inc., 339 U.S. 827, 834–35 (1950) (licensing of multiple patents under a single license upheld).

Morton Salt Co. v. G.S. Suppiger Co., 314 U.S. 488 (1942), the licensor of a patented salt dispensing machine could not condition its use on the lessee's purchase of nonpatented salt tablets from the patentee-licensor. This constituted a misuse of the patent and the patentee was therefore disqualified from enforcing the patent, even against direct infringers. Two years later the Court extended this doctrine of patent misuse to antitrust law in holding that a contributory infringer could not be sued by a patentee who refused to license a combination invention without purchase of key unpatented components. Mercoid Corp. v. Mid-Continent Inv. Co., 320 U.S. 661 (1944); Mercoid Corp. v. Minneapolis-Honeywell Regulator Co., 320 U.S. 680 (1944). Subsequently, in 1953, Congress codified the law into a Patent Code, adding sections 271(c) and (d) "for the express purpose of reinstating the doctrine of contributory infringement as it had been developed by decisions prior to *Mercoid* . . ." Aro Mfg. Co. v. Convertible Top Replacement Co., 377 U.S. 476, 492 (1964).

Finally, in Dawson Chem. Co. v. Rohm & Haas Co., 448 U.S. 176 (1980), the Court ruled that a contributory infringement suit is not stopped by the patentee's reliance on a tie-in to control the sale of an unpatented product. This arrangement was ruled to be protected by the Code. Here the plaintiff, Rohm & Haas, owned a patent on the only proven method of applying a chemical herbicide to crops. The compound itself was not patented, but it also had no commercial use except as part of the plaintiff's patented process. When the defendant made and sold the compound with instructions detailing its use as a herbicide—knowing that its customers' use of the chemical in accordance with these instructions would directly infringe the patent—Rohm & Haas charged the defendant with contributory infringement. The defendants had sought a license on the patented process alone from the plaintiff—without buying the chemical from Rohm & Haas—but it had refused all such requests. The defendant argued, therefore, that this constituted an illegal tying scheme whereby the plaintiff conditioned the license of its patent on purchase of the unpatented product. Relying on sections 271(c) and (d), however, the Court upheld the suit, concluding that these additions to the Patent Code had, in effect, overruled the *Mercoid* cases. The decision is also important for its recognition of the property rights created by the patent system (and their need for protection) and its finding that a patentee is not required to license his invention. It is further recognition that tying arrangements may serve useful and desirable purposes. See also Aronson v. Quick Point Pencil Co., 440 U.S. 257 (1979) and pp. 313–27 supra.

C. SETTLEMENT AND ACCUMULATION

Because of doubts concerning their validity and coverage, competing patents are frequently disputed and settlements sought. In other areas of the law, settlement is generally urged as socially preferable to litigation, and this position was adopted in Standard Oil Co. (Indiana) v. United States, 283 U.S. 163 (1931) (Brandeis, J.) (*Cracking Case*), where several oil companies held competing patents on a "cracking" process for extracting additional gasoline from petroleum (after the basic amount had been extracted by a "straight run" process). In order to avoid further litigation of their various claims, four oil companies pooled their patents, cross-licensed each other, and agreed to share in some fixed proportion the royalties which they received (primarily from others) under the multiple licenses. The government attacked this arrangement as a pooling of royalties which eliminated competition in royalty rates among the patentees. The agreement to divide royalties was alleged to be a restraint of trade violating Section 1 of the Sherman Act and enabling defendants to maintain royalties at monopoly levels.

Accepting the government's conclusion that the pooled patents were competing, the Court nevertheless upheld the cross-license arrangement and royalty division. It applied a rule of reason standard to the arrangement, observing that settlements which exchange patent rights and permit royalty divisions are often necessary if technical advancement is not to be blocked by litigation. Thus the interchange of patents on reasonable terms to all manufacturers desiring to participate may promote competition. Moreover, royalties cannot, the Court said, fix or adversely affect prices where the patented cracked gasoline constituted only 26 percent of total gas supplies.

The Court's analysis is not without its critics. Settlements are not always preferable in the patent context. The patent law's aim, according to the *GE* rule, is to reward the inventor. But settlement shares the reward among competing claimants, thus indiscriminately rewarding both subsequent infringers and holders of invalid patents— since litigation would have determined the priorities or possibly overruled all claims. And if none of the patents was valid, a settlement which shared royalties would result in higher prices, for without the settlement prices would have been set at a competitive level. That is, the royalty payments act to raise the marginal cost of the patented products. Nor is it clear from the Court's evidence that these "costs" are less than the social costs of litigation except where "blocking" patents are involved (as in *Line Material*).

Moreover, if, as the Court said, the patents being settled were competing, then the ruling seems questionable for an additional reason. That is, the Court's conclusion that the defendants' royalty rates could neither control the supply nor fix the price of cracked gas because their control was limited to one-quarter of available gas supplies is erroneous. A simple diagram shows that the price of gas is determined by the supply of straight run *and* cracked gas combined:

FIGURE 14: SUPPLY OF GASOLINE

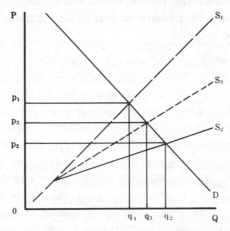

In Figure 14, S_1 is the amount of straight run gas which will be supplied. Quantity q_1 will be made available at price p_1 if the market is competitive. Using the cracking process, additional gas is available (after straight run gas is obtained) as shown by S_2—and quantity q_2 will be supplied at price p_2. If the defendants agree to a shared royalty, the result will be a rise in the "cost" of cracked gas as illustrated by the supply curve S_3—and quantity q_3 will be produced at price p_3. That is, royalty rates cause the cost of gas to rise, thereby reducing supply and raising the price, whether or not the defendants have monopoly power in the total gasoline market.[8] This suggests then that, contrary to

8. The Court's economic analysis was also erroneous when it selected total gasoline as the relevant market (and found that the defendants controlled only 26 percent of it). In fact the market was for patents on "cracked" gas—for which there were

the Court's view in the *Cracking Case,* it would pay for the defendants to have conspired to fix royalty rates—and the Court should have examined their conduct more closely.

The Court has been less charitable in applying the *Cracking Case* rule of reason standard to other patent settlements. For example, in United States v. Singer Mfg. Co., 374 U.S. 174 (1963), a Swiss manufacturer's assignment of its American patent to an American licensee for the purpose of facilitating suit against a Japanese infringer and of excluding Japanese imports into the United States, was held to violate Section 1. It is not reasonable to combine with another to challenge a third person's patent in order to prevent entry into the market.[9]

---

no close substitutes. And here the defendants had monopoly power, controlling 100 percent of the market.

9. Similarly, procuring or enforcing a patent obtained by fraud may violate Section 2, the Sherman Act's prohibition on monopolization. Walker Process Equip., Inc. v. Food Mach. & Chem. Corp., 382 U.S. 172 (1965); see American Cyanamid Co. v. FTC, 363 F.2d 757 (6th Cir.1966). On the other hand, "where a patent has been legally acquired, subsequent conduct permissible under the patent laws cannot trigger any liability under the antitrust laws. SCM Corp. v. Xerox, 645 F.2d 1195 (2d Cir. 1981) (refusal to license Xerox patents not a violation of Section 2 of the Sherman Act).

CHAPTER XI

PRICE DISCRIMINATION AND THE ROBINSON–PATMAN ACT

Section 2 of the Clayton Act was originally (in 1914) aimed at forbidding local price-cutting by monopolistic suppliers seeking to exclude competitors from their markets. This Act, which generally prohibited price discrimination, was amended by the Robinson-Patman Act in 1936. The latter sought to limit the purchasing power of large buyers—particularly of food chain stores. It was adopted in the midst of the Great Depression, as a response to the claims of beleaguered small businesses, with the intention of limiting price concessions granted powerful buyers. It prohibited such price discrimination unless it was supported by cost savings or was proven necessary to meet a competitor's price offer. Section 2 was enforceable against both buyers seeking, as well as sellers offering, "unjustified" price discounts or their equivalents.

In practice the Act has proved to be less than satisfactory. It has been applied primarily against those small sellers who were coerced into granting discounts or into competing against larger sellers, on the one hand, and against firms engaging in vigorous competition, on the other. As a result, the Robinson-Patman Act has been roundly criticized as being anticompetitive and contrary to the general purposes of the antitrust laws. It has been attacked for discouraging price competition and promoting price uniformity. Consequently its significance in antitrust enforcement has faded in recent years. Although it was once the basis for numerous actions by the Federal Trade Commission (to whom the Department of Justice ceded prosecutorial jurisdiction), few government-initiated actions are brought under it today.[1]

One troublesome feature of the Robinson-Patman Act—particularly for the lawyer—is its complex and indeterminate language. The operative sentences are long and convoluted; each phrase seems to contain an exception so that their cumulative effect is an invitation to confusion. Justice Jackson colorfully summarized the statute as "complicated and vague in itself and even more so in its context. Indeed, the Court of Appeals seems to have thought it almost beyond understanding." FTC v. Ruberoid Co., 343 U.S. 470, 483 (1952). Nor have interpretive decisions saved the Act or added rational sense to it. (But see the Supreme Court's most recent decisions in *Gypsum* and *A & P,* discussed pp. 409–11 infra, on the "meeting competition" defense.) Lest these judgments be considered inordinately harsh, the authoritative comments of two astute foreign observers read:

1. For example, twenty years ago the FTC issued over 70 complaints and consents in a single year (1966). In late 1984, there was but one R–P case pending before the Commission, see *Antitrust Advisor* 307 (C.Hills ed. 3d ed. 1985).

There is a real danger that an account of the case-law under the Robinson-Patman Act—particularly an account intended primarily for readers outside the United States—will be met with frank unbelief. The idea that a manufacturer may break the law by granting a wholesaler's discount to a wholesaler who also runs retail shops, or by selling goods direct to retailers at a price higher than one of his wholesalers may be charging, or by beating an offer made to an important customer by a rival manufacturer or even by matching that offer unless he is satisfied that his rival can justify his low price by cost savings—all this may simply seem impossible to square with the purpose of the antitrust policy is to preserve a system of free competition.

(A.D. Neale & D. Goyder, *The Antitrust Laws of the U.S.A.* 245 (3d ed. 1980).)

The Act cannot, nevertheless, be dismissed as unimportant. Its rule influences almost all pricing decisions of every major business in the country. Private treble damage actions are not infrequently founded upon it. Small businesses have retained sufficient political power to prevent its repeal and they may cause its future enforcement to be more vigorous.

Therefore, a summary of its scope and basic application are set forth here. But the discussion which follows can provide only a skeletal outline of the Act. For a comprehensive, but dated analysis, see F. Rowe, *Price Discrimination Under the Robin-*

son-Patman Act (1962, Supp.1964).   See also L.
Sullivan, *Antitrust* ch. 8 (1977).

A. THE STATUTE

The Robinson-Patman Act applies only (1) to
sales (2) of commodities (3) of like grade and quality (4) in commerce.   Each of these jurisdictional
elements must be established, in addition to the
substantive criteria of (5) price discrimination and
(6) injury to competition—or one of the alternative
violations as noted below. A seller does not violate
the Act unless he has sold similar commodities to
two different purchasers; the Act does not apply to
leases or to a seller's refusal to deal.   One of the
sales involved in a price discrimination must have
crossed a state boundary for the "in commerce"
requirement to be satisfied.   Gulf Oil Corp. v. Copp
Paving Co., 419 U.S. 186 (1974).   In addition, the
Act does not apply to sales of services or in-
tangibles such as electricity or advertising since
they are not "commodities." [2]   Nor does it cover
different prices for goods with physical differences
which affect their acceptability to buyers—though

2. Attempts to expand the meaning of these terms have not
met with favor. See, e.g., Ambook Enterprises v. Time Inc., 612
F.2d 604, 610 (2d Cir.1979) (Friendly, J.) (The "FTC's purported
discovery, forty-two years after the event, of a meaning in the
Robinson-Patman Act [that newspaper advertising is a commod-
ity] contrary to the ordinary reading of the language, disavowed
on the floor of the Senate, disclaimed by the statute's principal
author two years after its passage, raising grave problems of
administration, and contrary to a consistent course of judicial
decision on this and related matters, is a discovery of something
that is not there.").

the attachment of a brand name to a product (which affects its consumer "acceptability") does not add sufficient "physical difference."

Once the foregoing elements are satisfied, a prima facie violation of Section 2(a) is established by showing that the seller discriminated in his prices with the effect of lessening competition. Any price difference is a price discrimination; but charging the same price to two customers is never price discrimination under the Act—even though the seller's costs of serving one are much higher than those of serving the other (and therefore charging both customers the identical price constitutes economic price discrimination). Injury to competition includes "primary line" injury to competitors of the seller, "secondary line" injury to competitors of the buyer, and "third line" injury to competitors of the buyer's customers.

The seller charged with discrimination may justify his price differences in two ways. First, through "cost justification." If the difference in two selling prices reflects only a difference in the seller's cost of supplying the different purchasers, regardless of the effect of such price differences upon other sellers or disfavored buyers, the seller's price discrimination is lawful. This proviso found in Section 2(a) has been applied narrowly, however, and has been upheld as the justification of but few price differentials. United States v. Borden Co., 370 U.S. 460, 468–69 (1962).

Second, the seller may affirmatively justify its price discrimination by showing that the lower price was charged "in good faith to meet an equally low price of a competitor." Again, the defense is complete and overrides any showing of competitive injury. Standard Oil Co. v. FTC, 340 U.S. 231, 246 (1951). In general, this defense applies only to defensive pricing which responds to—but does not "beat"—a competitor's lawful price.

However, as the Court held in United States v. United States Gypsum Co., 438 U.S. 422 (1978), also discussed p. 239 supra, defendants cannot justify direct, systematic comparison of prices, sales terms and other services with competitors as being necessary to conform with the meeting competition requirements. All that is required by the Robinson-Patman Act is "[a] good-faith belief, rather than absolute certainty" that another seller has offered the buyer a lower price. In most circumstances a "commercially reasonable belief" that without a price concession the sale will be lost will be established by documentary evidence of competing quotes, corroborating evidence from other buyers or buyer threats to stop making purchases. In any case, the meeting competition defense of the Robinson-Patman Act will not serve to insulate price-fixing or its facilitation from attack under the Sherman Act.

While the focus of the Act is on price discrimination by the seller, other provisions prohibit false brokerage or discriminatory allowances or services.

These complement the price discrimination prohibition by condemning disguised price reductions. They are per se prohibitions in that injury to competition need not be shown and the affirmative defenses (of cost justification and meeting competition) are usually not available to them. FTC v. Simplicity Pattern Co., 360 U.S. 55, 62–71 (1959). In addition, Section 2(f) imposes liability on buyers who "knowingly . . . induce or receive a discrimination in price which is prohibited by this Section." This subsection is the other side of the price discrimination (Section 2(a)) coin. For example, in Automatic Canteen v. FTC, 346 U.S. 61, 74 (1953), the Court ruled that a buyer is not liable under Section 2(f) if the lower price that he "induced" is within one of the seller's defenses such as cost justification or if he reasonably could not know that it was not so protected. See also Kroger Co. v. FTC, 438 F.2d 1372 (6th Cir.), cert. denied, 404 U.S. 871 (1971) (defenses must also fit buyer's perspective). More recently, complementing its decision in *Gypsum,* the Court in Great Atlantic & Pac. Tea Co. v. FTC, 440 U.S. 69, 80–81 (1979), held that a buyer could not be liable for price discrimination under Section 2(f) where the seller made its offer in a reasonable and good faith effort to meet competition. Seeking to reconcile the Robinson-Patman Act with the competitive aims of the Sherman Act, the Court ruled that a buyer does not have an affirmative duty of disclosure of the exact amount by which competing bids undercut the seller with whom he is negotiating. Uncertainty in this circumstance is beneficial to competition, and if it leads to one seller undercutting the other, the buyer should not be "rewarded" with Robinson-Patman Act liability.

Finally, an almost unused section (Section 3) of the Act makes it a criminal offense to discriminate geographically or to sell at "unreasonably low prices" where the purpose of either action is to destroy competition or eliminate a competitor.[3] See United States v. Nat'l Dairy Products Corp., 372 U.S. 29 (1963) (statute upheld against constitutional challenge of void for vagueness).

B. INJURY TO COMPETITION

A description and analysis of basic decisions on the competitive effects requirement under Section 2(a) are central to an understanding of most cases involving charges of price discrimination. They also illustrate the Act's limitations and peculiarities.

1. PRIMARY LINE INJURY

Although it has been held that mere price discrimination which diverts any sales from a competitor supports the inference that competition has been injured, the general rule is that the mere diversion of sales to the discriminating seller from

3. This provision did not amend the Clayton Act. Hence it is not an "antitrust" law under Section 4 of the Clayton Act and is not a subject of private treble damage enforcement. Nashville Milk Co. v. Carnation Co., 355 U.S. 373 (1958).

his competitors is not in itself sufficient to establish an impairment of competition on the primary line level. Compare Samuel H. Moss, Inc. v. FTC, 148 F.2d 378 (2d Cir.1945), with Anheuser-Busch, Inc. v. FTC, 289 F.2d 835 (7th Cir.1961). See also F. Rowe, supra at 162 ("To equate the diversion of business among rival sellers with injury to competition is to indict the competitive process itself.")

On the other hand, price discrimination will be found to have injured the discriminating seller's competitors if it is demonstrated that the purpose or effect of the selective [4] price cut is to drive competitors out of business. The concern is that selective price discrimination could be used to eliminate competitors and give the discriminating seller (or favored buyer) monopoly power, which will then be followed by raising prices to a monopoly level. This scenario will work, however, only if the subsequent monopoly profits exceed the costs of driving out competitors. And this depends generally on the existence of effective barriers to easy market entry by others or to re-entry by those driven out. Because such predatory price discrimination is not likely to be profitable, it is possible—indeed, probable—that the price discriminator is not acting with a predatory intent but rather with a desirable (i.e., competitive) purpose—to increase its sales, market shares, and profits. In other words, the careless or overly vigorous application

4. Note that uniform price cuts do not violate the Act because there is then no price discrimination.

of Section 2(a) may lead to price uniformity and may dampen rather than enhance price competition.[5]

Primary line price discrimination cases generally arise when a national seller charges different prices for the same product in separate geographic areas. The question in such territorial price discrimination cases is whether the seller's price differentiation is competitive and lawful or predatory and unlawful. Two tests have been applied. One looks to evidence of intent to destroy a competitor. It may be shown expressly by internal documents of the defendant (Porto Rican American Tobacco Co. v. American Tobacco Co., 30 F.2d 234 (2d Cir. 1929)) or inferentially from business tactics, below cost pricing, or other unexplained price moves. Utah Pie Co. v. Continental Baking Co., 386 U.S. 685 (1967). (*Utah Pie*). The second approach relies upon a substantial dislocation of market shares which can be attributed to discriminatory prices in support of a finding of competitive injury. For a list of indicia which have been relied upon as refuting or confirming the existence of competitive impairment under this test, see F. Rowe, supra at 160–62.

5. This analysis also suggests that Section 2(a) is redundant in that it repeats the prohibitions of the Sherman Act. That it allows relief on a lesser showing of illegality is no justification, moreover, because (as noted below) the effect of such an enforcement standard is to discourage price competition. But see General Foods Corp., 3 CCH Trade Reg.Rep. ¶ 22,142 (FTC Apr. 6, 1984) (using single economic test to analyze Sherman, FTC and Robinson-Patman Act issues).

The Supreme Court's decision in *Utah Pie*, reveals the rule here established to be exceptionally stringent in its action against aggressive pricing by national sellers and possibly anticompetitive in its impact. Utah Pie controlled some two-thirds of the market for frozen pies in the Salt Lake City area. Apparently attracted by the high profits being earned in this market, Pet Milk (and two other large companies) entered with its own line of pies priced much lower—below, in fact, those Pet Milk charged in nearby California and other markets. When its competitive responses failed to keep out Pet Milk—with Utah Pie's market share lowered to roughly half of the market—Utah Pie sued under the Robinson-Patman Act (i.e., for treble damages under Section 4 of the Clayton Act) charging geographic price discrimination. And the Supreme Court ruled that Utah Pie's evidence adequately supported a jury finding of probable competitive injury, even though the apparent complaint was that a national company had destroyed only Utah Pie's near monopoly of the frozen pie business in Salt Lake City. The result, it would seem, is that under *Utah Pie* a national firm will be inhibited from seeking to enter a market through price-cutting for fear that a competitor who is thereby injured can recover treble damages. See generally Bowman, *Restraint of Trade by the Supreme Court: The Utah Pie Case,* 77 Yale L.J. 70 (1967).[6]

6. For a subsequent account of the demise of the Utah Pie Co., see Elzinga & Hogarty, *Utah Pie Co. and the Consequences of Robinson-Patman,* 21 J.Law & Econ. 427 (1978).

The application of economic evidence to distinguish between predatory and competitive price-cutting—led by the work of Areeda and Turner, discussed pp. 144–46 supra—has caused a substantial doctrinal retreat, although *Utah Pie* has never been overruled. The resulting compromise in some courts of appeal is illustrated by O. Hommel Co. v. Ferro Corp., 659 F.2d 340 (3d Cir.1981), cert. denied, 455 U.S. 1017 (1982). The Third Circuit held that when reviewing selective price cuts within a market "[t]here are two basic means of meeting the competitive injury requirement: (1) actual competitive injury shown by market analysis; and (2) predatory intent from which competitive injury may be inferred." In this case, where actual competitive harm had not been shown, the court concluded that "Robinson-Patman primary line liability cannot be imposed merely upon evidence of below-average cost pricing." Not surprisingly, this dual requirement of predation and primary line injury is seldom satisfied. But see Falls City Indus. Inc. v. Vanco Beverages, Inc., p. 417 infra.

Reflecting new sensitivity to the importance of encouraging price competition and the need to harmonize the Robinson-Patman Act with the antitrust laws, the Federal Trade Commission has limited the reach of primary line injury in three cases. First, the FTC agreed to a settlement modifying its order in Borden, Inc., 102 F.T.C. 1147 (1983); id. 461 U.S. 940 (1983), on remand, 711 F.2d 758 (6th Cir.1983); the consent order prohibited sales of Borden's reconstituted lemon juice which would result in quarterly net revenues below variable cost. Then in General Foods Corp., 103 F.T.C. 204 (1984) the Commission dismissed an attempted monopolization and price discrimination charge against Maxwell House Coffee. After finding that GF had not come dangerously close to achieving monopoly, a divided Commission was "unable to find any prospect of injury to competition" under the Robinson-Patman Act. Finally, in ITT Continental Baking, 104 F.T.C. 280 (1984) the Commission explained that primary line injury can be demonstrated either by a detailed marked analysis identifying how the discrimination actually injured competition or by establishing predatory intent from which the injury is inferred. The former is now next to impossible to prove; the latter can be shown only by "sales at prices below average variable cost for a significant period of time" that are likely "to force equally efficient firms to shut down completely." (Compare the emerging rules of predatory pricing, discussed pp. 144–46 supra.)

2.   SECONDARY LINE INJURY

Protection of buyer-level competition was a principal reason for the 1936 amendment of Section 2 (of the Clayton Act) by the Robinson-Patman Act. Thus, secondary line injury considers the effect of discriminatory prices given one buyer (e.g., chain stores) on their competitors (e.g., small stores) who are unable to obtain the favorable price. There must, of course, be a competitive relationship between the two buyers—that is, between the one buying the commodities at the higher and the other buying at the lower price. Thus different prices can be lawfully charged to customers of different functional classes; wholesale purchasers do not normally compete with retail purchasers. Similarly, customers located in separate geographic markets cannot generally suffer competitive injury.

Once competitive contact exists, however, courts have readily inferred injury from price differentials among competing customers. Thus, in the leading case of FTC v. Morton Salt Co., 334 U.S. 37 (1948), a substantial price differential which could influence resale prices supported a finding of probable adverse effect. Later cases added that for such adverse effect, the price differential cannot be so small as to be inconsequential in its influence on sales and thus on competition, and also that it must have existed for a sufficient period of time to affect competitors. In Falls City Indus., Inc. v. Vanco Beverage, Inc., 460 U.S. 428 (1983), the defendant had sought to avoid the *Morton Salt* presumption of competitive injury from a price difference by arguing that its lower prices had not favored large buyers and that it was not a monopolist. That is, the Act should not apply to conduct which does not give the firm charging discriminatory prices an anticompetitive edge. The Supreme Court rejected this view, repeating its stand that "injury to competition is established prima facie by proof of substantial price discrimination between competing purchasers over time." This inference can be overcome only by "evidence breaking the causal connection between a price differential and lost sales or profits." [7]

This continuing mechanical interpretation of the Act seems at odds with marketplace realities and the usual meaning of competition. A more stringent application of the Robinson-Patman Act where secondary line injury occurs could readily be rationalized on the ground that buying advantages are unrelated to efficiency and are not essential for competition. The real difficulty in the secondary line cases, however, lies in their application to vertically integrated firms who are, as a consequence, prevented from passing on efficiencies to their customers in terms of lower prices. See, e.g., Purolator Prods., Inc. v. FTC, 352 F.2d 874 (7th Cir. 1965).

On the other hand, the Supreme Court has gone so far, in Perkins v. Standard Oil Co. of California, 395 U.S. 642, 648 (1969), as to read the competitive effects requirement as reaching any level in the chain of distribution at which the injured party can show "a causal connection between the price

---

7. The *Morton Salt* presumption is not as significant in private damage actions where the plaintiff must now show both a violation of the Act and actual injury to competition. See J. Truett Payne Co. v. Chrysler Motors Corp., 451 U.S. 557 (1981). The presumption applies only to the first requirement of a showing of violation. And actual injury to competition is unlikely because price competition (i.e., discrimination) is likely to intensify rather than diminish actual marketplace rivalry.

discrimination in violation of the Act and the injury suffered." For a persuasive criticism of extension of competitive effect beyond secondary line injury, see F. Rowe, supra at 195.

C. STATUTORY DEFENSES

Two major defenses to a charge of price discrimination are the meeting competition and cost justification defenses.

1. "MEETING COMPETITION"

The meeting competition proviso makes discriminatory prices lawful when the seller acts "in good faith to meet an equally low price of a competitor." It is an absolute defense—regardless of other injury to competitors or competition—and has been explained as "the primary means of reconciling the Robinson-Patman Act with the more general purposes of the antitrust laws of encouraging competition between sellers." Great Atlantic & Pacific Tea Co. v. FTC, 440 U.S. 69, 83 n. 16 (1979). The test for applying the defense is whether "a reasonable and prudent person . . . [would] believe that the granting of a lower price would, in fact, meet the equally low price of a competitor." United States v. United States Gypsum Co., 438 U.S. 422, 451 (1978).

Thus in *A & P,* after a seller's bid was rejected by a customer as "not even in the ball park," its second bid was upheld even though lower than that of competitors.[8] The seller was not required to verify the competitive price in proving good faith; it was enough that the seller (1) relied on information from a reliable customer "who had personal knowledge of the competing bid," (2) had attempted to investigate by asking the customer for more information, and (3) faced "a credible threat of termination of purchases" if it did not lower its bid. The Supreme Court similarly ruled in *Gypsum* that a seller should not communicate with competitors for price verification; the competitive dangers of such discussions outweighed any need to limit the meeting competition defense.

Finally, in *Vanco,* the Supreme Court settled a long dispute among the circuits by ruling that a genuine price cut in response to prevailing competition may be made on an area-wide rather than individual customer basis. Relying on congressional intent, marketplace realities, the cost of individual customer assessments, and the need to protect vigorous price competition, the court expanded the practicality of the defense. It is, of course, still limited by the "prudent businessman" requirement which seeks to assure that the response is measured and reasonable. The seller cannot rely on a competitive price that is "inherently unlawful" or knowingly undercut a competitive offer. But it

8. In point of fact, *A & P* involved a charge of unlawful inducement of price discrimination by a buyer under Section 2(f). But since the buyer's liability is derivative from the unlawfulness of the seller's conduct, the issue in the case was whether the seller had a valid "meeting competition" defense.

can be used to obtain new customers as long as the lower price does not continue beyond what is necessary (i.e., without checking).

2.   COST JUSTIFICATION

An otherwise unlawful discriminatory price is permitted where the differential "makes only due allowance for differences in the cost of manufacture, sale, or delivery, resulting from the differing methods or quantities" in which the goods are sold. An affirmative defense with the burden on the defendant, it relates only to price discrimination and cannot be used to rebut charges of promotional discrimination (under Section 2(d) or 2(e)).

In practical effect, the defense has been called "largely illusory." *Report of the Attorney General to Study the Antitrust Laws* 171 (1955). To be successful in proving cost justification, the seller must group customers in meaningful functional categories with similar buying characteristics. It is critical that members within each group are reasonably similar with respect to the seller's cost of doing business with them. Thus, in United States v. Borden Co., 370 U.S. 460 (1962), the Court rejected a seller's attempt to differentiate between chain and nonchain retail (grocery) customers whose volume of purchases were often similar. Subsequent cases have focused on whether, when grouping buyers, the seller has in fact properly matched the supposed cost saving with the price difference and the cost saving factor must, of course, be one of those identified in the statute.

Complex questions exist on the measurement and assignment of costs, particularly in times of exaggerated inflation or deflation and multinational firms. With the burden of establishing the cost justification on the defense, it is seldom a useful tool in trial. Often it is better to rely on cost differences as a functional discount and thus as not invoking any price discrimination. In that context, the issue is whether the discount properly compensates the buyer for its distribution services and a precise accounting is unnecessary. Whether a dual-level distributor—a firm selling wholesale and retail—can take advantage of the functional discount exception remains unclear. See Boise-Cascade Corp., 3 CCH Trade Reg.Rep. ¶ 22,330 (FTC 1986) (finding violation of section 2(f) for receiving wholesale discounts on all purchases where only half were resold to retailers and the remainder were sold directly to ultimate customers).

CHAPTER XII

THE CHANGING BALANCE
IN ANTITRUST

Antitrust has always been asked to serve diverse objectives as well as respond to conflicting policy pulls. It has been argued, for example, that antitrust's assigned goal is to serve economic efficiency, thus improving consumer welfare. Others assert with equal force that the antitrust laws are designed solely to control private economic power and nurture many small sellers, even at the sacrifice of economic efficiency. These contradictory views are reflected in the inconsistency of antitrust decisions, their ambivalence between the per se and rule of reason approaches, and the courts' willingness to accept rapid and sharp doctrinal shifts.

At the heart of this debate over the interpretation of the antitrust laws are distinctive positive and normative positions. Those focusing on economic efficiency emphasize the costs of antitrust intervention, the evidence that substantial transaction economies are available from private restraints, and the independent value of economic freedom as well as its importance for innovation and rivalry. Confident of the predictive powers of economic analysis, they conclude that neither economic nor political freedom is threatened by firm size or by freeing firms from close antitrust oversight.

On the other hand, proponents of more vigorous use of the antitrust laws to limit private arrangements stress the contribution that smaller enterprises make to innovation, the need for retaining individual opportunity, and the protections assured by economic pluralism. They would use the antitrust laws to preserve smaller firms for their own sake as well as to protect political democracy from abusive private economic power. They are skeptical of theoretical but difficult to measure economic benefits from private restraints. Antitrust intervention may be imperfect, but defenders of an active policy assert that the likely benefits far outweigh the costs.

The economic evidence is, of course, never complete and seldom wholly one-sided; every conclusion is qualified. New data and new theories continue to emerge, upsetting conventional views. But current evidence strongly favors those who would concentrate on economic efficiency. The past decade, for example, has seen the emergence of the importance of price theory to antitrust analysis, the development of transaction cost economics, and the articulation of contestable market theories. As a result, even antitrust populists now generally concede the relevance (but not the primacy) of economic analysis to antitrust.

Among the primary questions now asked in evaluating almost every restraint are: who will be most directly affected (i.e., what is the market), how will it affect output and price decisions, can it reduce transaction costs or produce other identifiable efficiencies, are there significant barriers to entry or is the market vulnerable to outside influence (if prices are raised), and so forth. Answers to these questions are used to determine whether the restraints are likely to limit output, raise price, or otherwise adversely affect consumer welfare.

Earlier notions once common to antitrust economics no longer hold sway. For example, it was widely believed that economic power in one product or service was readily leveraged to another— that power, like amoeba, is self-generating. While vestiges of these views still limit antitrust doctrine (e.g., *Hyde* (tie-ins), p. 326 supra; *Northwest Wholesale Stationers* (boycotts), p. 224 supra), few press the issue seriously, and those decisions that have not explicitly rejected the leverage theory acknowledge its flaws. Once popular arguments that antitrust should be used primarily for social or political (i.e., noneconomic) objectives have now moved to the periphery; the issue is whether these purposes are ever legitimate and can make a useful contribution.

What has happened, in other words, is that the starting blocks in antitrust have been moved. Not only does antitrust begin with economic analysis, that economic understanding is frequently controlling. Concepts such as "efficiency," "transaction costs," and "output effects" are dominant rather than claims of "fairness" or "individual freedom to trade." Clearly the most significant decision reflecting this shift in antitrust analysis continues to be Justice Powell's opinion in *Sylvania,* pp. 302–05 supra. His sophisticated understanding of price theory and in particular of the free rider effect ushered in a new period of antitrust with the Supreme Court and enforcement agencies increasingly focused on the new economic learning.

Several decisions of recent years supporting this conclusion were examined more closely in chapter 5. This shift is even reflected in the "defeats" for economic analysis, as illustrated by the Supreme Court's decision in *Aspen Skiing,* discussed p. 148 supra. That decision was sharply criticized for freezing the distribution system established by a firm with monopoly power; ironically, the Court seemingly required a firm with monopoly power to collaborate with its competitors and possibly to fix prices with them. One explanation for this result (which garnered the unanimous vote of the participating justices) was the absence of an efficiency justification for the monopoly firm's conduct. The Court's opinion emphasized efficiency justifications for its decision with copious citations to Judge Bork's treatise. See Malina, *Supreme Court Update—1985,* 54 Antitr.L.J. 289, 295 (1985).

The primary doctrinal impact of this emphasis on economics and economic efficiency in antitrust law is the return to the rule of reason as the principal tool of antitrust analysis. It is now the acknowledged measure for nonprice vertical restraints, including most tie-in arrangements. Increasingly, the reasonableness standard applies to many horizontal restraints. If a persuasive business reason for the restriction can be developed—especially to show that the arrangement will save on transaction costs (e.g., *BMI*, p. 189 supra)—a close examination of the economic effects is warranted. Thus, it is no longer accurate to say that the per se rule applies with full force to price fixing, boycotts, or market divisions; a "partial" (post-justification) per se rule is more often the actual standard that will be applied.

For lawyers, law students, courts, and businesses, this return to a rule of reason in antitrust creates uncertainty and often dissatisfaction. Businesses threatened by treble damage litigation find scant comfort in the likelihood of ultimate justification after a rule of reason trial. The rule itself is uncertain, and there is little guidance as to what evidence is relevant or decisive. For example, in applying the rule to vertical restraints, the *Sylvania* Court indicated that interbrand benefits should be weighed against intrabrand costs. But the two effects are not comparable; antitrust is generally only concerned with interbrand effects. The impact of an effective vertical restraint on intrabrand competition is likely to be total—yet that fact has no economic significance. And as long as competition is present, the market will

impose its own cost-benefit check on a manufacturer enforcing nonprice vertical restraints.

The fear of private market power is sufficiently
strong that the courts are reluctant to identify
areas for per se legality, as is sometimes suggested.
See, e.g., Posner, *The Next Step in the Antitrust
Treatment of Restricted Distribution: Per Se Legality,* 48 U.Chi.L.Rev. 6 (1981). At best the Department of Justice, through its Merger and Vertical
Restraint Guidelines, has identified safe harbors
where it is unlikely to prosecute. Mergers with
HHI concentrations below 1000 (and probably, below 1800) will not be pursued as violations of
Section 7 of the Clayton Act unless unusual circumstances are present. But once again this interpretation of the appropriate understanding of the
Clayton Act does not necessarily insulate the merging parties from costly private treble damage litigation.

Facing these concerns, it seems likely that the
courts will cut back further on the role of the per
se rule. Four members of the Supreme Court were
willing to overturn the partial per se test applicable to tie-ins and adopt a rule of reason standard in
Hyde. Similar movement seems apparent in the
antitrust doctrine applied to boycotts. Wholesale
abandonment of the per se test is not on the
immediate horizon, however. The pull of history is
strong and the Supreme Court is usually reluctant
to overturn precedent, even when the rationale for
the old rule no longer seems persuasive. The costs

of change are believed to be important and the opportunity to rely on artful distinctions is ever present.

If antitrust doctrine is likely to evolve in this direction, the strongest unmet need will continue to be for further clarification of the reasonableness rule. Despite numerous opportunities, the Supreme Court has not provided much leadership on the meaning of the rule. The Department of Justice has occasionally sought to suggest approaches for a structured rule of reason approach in its briefs to the Court with only marginal success. See also Easterbrook, *The Limits of Antitrust,* 63 Tex.L.Rev. 1 (1984). Thus, the critical factor increasingly is: who must bear the burden of proof to show that the conduct violates the antitrust laws because its effects are anticompetitive—or that it should be permitted because it enhances efficiency. Under a rule of reason approach, the burden of showing anticompetitive effects is on the plaintiff; under the partial per se approach, the burden is on the defendant to show the efficiency justification. With the underlying economic evidence unclear or at least debatable, this burden may be decisive.

It is obviously distressing to many that the per se benchmarks once used to guide business conduct, explain prosecutorial discretion, and rationalize judicial decisions are becoming blurred. However, decisions overturning clear per se requirements generally reflect a better understanding of the underlying economic issues and have led to more rational antitrust policy. They have also redirected the focus of antitrust analysis away from efforts to characterize conduct as horizontal or vertical, or as simply involving price fixing, tie-ins or boycotts. The uncertainty resulting from the wider adoption of the rule of reason seems a necessary price for an antitrust policy moving to a new and possibly higher ground.

APPENDIX

SHERMAN ACT [1]

15 U.S.C.A. §§ 1–7

§ 1. Every contract, combination in the form of trust or otherwise, or conspiracy, in restraint of trade or commerce among the several States, or with foreign nations, is declared to be illegal. Every person who shall make any contract or engage in any combination or conspiracy declared to be illegal shall be deemed guilty of a felony, and, on conviction thereof, shall be punished by fine not exceeding one million dollars if a corporation, or, if any other person, one hundred thousand dollars, or by imprisonment not exceeding three years, or by both said punishments, in the discretion of the court.

§ 2. Every person who shall monopolize, or attempt to monopolize, or combine or conspire with any other person or persons, to monopolize any part of the trade or commerce among the several States, or with foreign nations, shall be deemed guilty of a felony, and, on conviction thereof, shall be punished by fine not exceeding one million dollars if a corporation, or, if any other person, one hundred thousand dollars, or by imprisonment not

1. 26 Stat. 209 (1890) as amended.

exceeding three years, or by both said punishments, in the discretion of the court.

§ 3. Every contract, combination in form of trust or otherwise, or conspiracy, in restraint of trade or commerce in any Territory of the United States or of the District of Columbia, or in restraint of trade or commerce between any such Territory and another, or between any such Territory or Territories and any State or States or the District of Columbia, or with foreign nations, or between the District of Columbia and any State or States or foreign nations, is declared illegal. Every person who shall make any such contract or engage in any such combination or conspiracy, shall be deemed guilty of a felony, and, on conviction thereof, shall be punished by fine not exceeding one million dollars if a corporation, or, if any other person, one hundred thousand dollars, or by imprisonment not exceeding three years, or by both said punishments, in the discretion of the court.

§ 4. The several district courts of the United States are invested with jurisdiction to prevent and restrain violations of this act; and it shall be the duty of the several United States attorneys, in their respective districts, under the direction of the Attorney General, to institute proceedings in equity to prevent and restrain such violations. Such proceedings may be by way of petition setting forth the case and praying that such violation shall be enjoined or otherwise prohibited. When the parties complained of shall have been duly notified of such petition the court shall proceed, as soon as may be, to the hearing and determination of the case; and pending such petition and before final decree, the court may at any time make such temporary restraining order or prohibition as shall be deemed just in the premises.

§ 5. Whenever it shall appear to the court before which any proceeding under section four of this act may be pending, that the ends of justice require that other parties shall be brought before the court, the court may cause them to be summoned, whether they reside in the district in which the court is held or not; and subpoenas to that end may be served in any district by the marshal thereof.

§ 6. Any property owned under any contract or by any combination, or pursuant to any conspiracy (and being the subject thereof) mentioned in section one of this act, and being in the course of transportation from one State to another, or to a foreign country, shall be forfeited to the United States, and may be seized and condemned by like proceedings as those provided by law for the forfeiture, seizure, and condemnation of property imported into the United States contrary to law.

§ 7.[2] This Act shall not apply to conduct involving trade or commerce (other than import trade or import commerce) with foreign nations unless—

2. This section was added by the Export Trading Company Act, Pub.L. No. 97–2920, 96 Stat. 1246, (October 8, 1982).

Gellhorn-Antitrust Law & Econ. 3rd Ed.—16

(1) such conduct has a direct, substantial, and reasonably foreseeable effect—

(A) on trade or commerce which is not trade or commerce with foreign nations, or on import trade or import commerce with foreign nations; or

(B) on export trade or export commerce with foreign nations, of a person engaged in such trade or commerce in the United States; and

(2) such effect gives rise to a claim under the provisions of this Act, other than this section.

If this Act applies to such conduct only because of the operation of paragraph (1)(B), then this Act shall apply to such conduct only for injury to export business in the United States.

§ 8. That the word "person," or "persons," wherever used in this act shall be deemed to include corporations and associations existing under or authorized by the laws of either the United States, the laws of any of the Territories, the laws of any State, or the laws of any foreign country.

CLAYTON ACT [3]

15 U.S.C.A. §§ 12–27

§ 1. [Defining the "[a]ntitrust laws" by reference to the relevant Acts and sections; and defining "commerce" generally as trade "among the several States" and defining "persons"—omitted.]

3. 38 Stat. 730 (1914), as amended. The numbering here follows the original Act. Only selected sections are reprinted.

§ 2.[4]   (a) It shall be unlawful for any person engaged in commerce, in the course of such commerce, either directly or indirectly, to discriminate in price between different purchasers of commodities of like grade and quality, where either or any of the purchases involved in such discrimination are in commerce, where such commodities are sold for use, consumption, or resale within the United States or any Territory thereof or the District of Columbia or any insular possession or other place under the jurisdiction of the United States, and where the effect of such discrimination may be substantially to lessen competition or tend to create a monopoly in any line of commerce, or to injure, destroy, or prevent competition with any person who either grants or knowingly receives the benefit of such discrimination, or with customers of either of them: *Provided,* That nothing herein contained shall prevent differentials which make only due allowance for differences in the cost of manufacture, sale, or delivery resulting from the differing methods or quantities in which such commodities are to such purchasers sold or delivered: *Provided, however,* That the Federal Trade Commission may, after due investigation and hearing to all interested parties, fix and establish quantity limits, and revise the same as it finds necessary, as to particular commodities or classes of commodities, where it finds that available purchasers in greater quantities are so few as to render differen-

4.   As amended by the Robinson-Patman Act.   49 Stat. 1526 (1936).

tials on account thereof unjustly discriminatory or
promotive of monopoly in any line of commerce;
and the foregoing shall then not be construed to
permit differentials based on differences in quantities greater than those so fixed and established:
And provided further, That nothing herein contained shall prevent persons engaged in selling
goods, wares, or merchandise in commerce from
selecting their own customers in bona fide transactions and not in restraint of trade: *And provided
further,* That nothing herein contained shall prevent price changes from time to time where in
response to changing conditions affecting the market for or the marketability of the goods concerned,
such as but not limited to actual or imminent
deterioration of perishable goods, obsolescence of
seasonal goods, distress sales under court process,
or sales in good faith in discontinuance of business
in the goods concerned.

(b) Upon proof being made, at any hearing on a
complaint under this section, that there has been
discrimination in price or services or facilities furnished, the burden of rebutting the prima facie
case thus made by showing justification shall be
upon the person charged with a violation of this
section, and unless justification shall be affirmatively shown, the Commission is authorized to issue
an order terminating the discrimination: *Provided,
however,* That nothing herein contained shall prevent a seller rebutting the prima facie case thus
made by showing that his lower price or the fur-

nishing of services or facilities to any purchaser or purchasers was made in good faith to meet an equally low price of a competitor, or the services or facilities furnished by a competitor.

(c) It shall be unlawful for any person engaged in commerce, in the course of such commerce, to pay or grant, or to receive or accept, anything of value as a commission, brokerage, or other compensation, or any allowance or discount in lieu thereof, except for services rendered in connection with the sale or purchase of goods, wares, or merchandise, either to the other party to such transaction or to an agent, representative, or other intermediary therein where such intermediary is acting in fact for or in behalf, or is subject to the direct or indirect control, of any party to such transaction other than the person by whom such compensation is so granted or paid.

(d) It shall be unlawful for any person engaged in commerce to pay or contract for the payment of anything of value to or for the benefit of a customer of such person in the course of such commerce as compensation or in consideration for any services or facilities furnished by or through such customer in connection with the processing, handling, sale, or offering for sale of any products or commodities manufactured, sold, or offered for sale by such person, unless such payment or consideration is available on proportionally equal terms to all other customers competing in the distribution of such products or commodities.

(e) It shall be unlawful for any person to discriminate in favor of one purchaser against another purchaser or purchasers of a commodity bought for resale, with or without processing, by contracting to furnish or furnishing, or by contributing to the furnishing of, any services or facilities connected with the processing, handling, sale, or offering for sale of such commodity so purchased upon terms not accorded to all purchasers on proportionally equal terms.

(f) It shall be unlawful for any person engaged in commerce, in the course of such commerce, knowingly to induce or receive a discrimination in price which is prohibited by this section.[5]

§ 3. It shall be unlawful for any person engaged in commerce, in the course of such com-

5. The Robinson-Patman Act has other provisions, including § 3, 15 U.S.C.A. § 13a:

It shall be unlawful for any person engaged in commerce, in the course of such commerce, to be a party to, or assist in, any transaction of sale, or contract to sell, which discriminates to his knowledge against competitors of the purchaser, in that, any discount, rebate, allowance, or advertising service charge is granted to the purchaser over and above any discount, rebate, allowance, or advertising service charge available at the time of such transaction to said competitors in respect of a sale of goods of like grade, quality, and quantity; to sell, or contract to sell, goods in any part in the United States at prices lower than those exacted by said person elsewhere in the United States for the purpose of destroying competitors, or eliminating a competition in such part of the United States; or, to sell or contract to sell, goods at unreasonably low prices for the purpose of destroying competition or eliminating a competitor.

Any person violating any of the provisions of this section shall, upon conviction thereof, be fined not more than $5,000 or imprisoned not more than one year, or both.

merce, to lease or make a sale or contract for sale
of goods, wares, merchandise, machinery, supplies,
or other commodities, whether patented or unpatented, for use, consumption, or resale within the
United States or any Territory thereof or the District of Columbia or any insular possession or other
place under the jurisdiction of the United States,
or fix a price charged therefor, or discount from, or
rebate upon, such price, on the condition, agreement, or understanding that the lessee or purchaser thereof shall not use or deal in the goods, wares,
merchandise, machinery, supplies, or other commodities of a competitor or competitors of the
lessor or seller, where the effect of such lease, sale,
or contract for sale or such condition, agreement,
or understanding may be to substantially lessen
competition or tend to create a monopoly in any
line of commerce.

§ 4. Any person who shall be injured in his
business or property by reason of anything forbidden in the antitrust laws may sue therefor in any
district court of the United States in the district in
which the defendant resides or is found or has an
agent, without respect to the amount in controversy, and shall recover threefold the damages by him
sustained, and the cost of suit, including a reasonable attorney's fee. The court may award under
this section, pursuant to a motion by such person
promptly made, simple interest on actual damages
for the period beginning on the date of service of
such person's pleading setting forth a claim under

the antitrust laws and ending on the date of judgment, or for any shorter period therein, if the court
finds that the award of such interest for such
period is just in the circumstances. In determining whether an award of interest under this section
for any period is just in the circumstances, the
court shall consider only—

(1) whether such person or the opposing party,
or either party's representative, made motions or
asserted claims or defenses so lacking in merit as
to show that such party or representative acted
intentionally for delay, or otherwise acted in bad
faith;

(2) whether, in the course of the action involved,
such person or the opposing party, or either party's
representative, violated any applicable rule, statute, or court order providing for sanctions for dilatory behavior or otherwise providing for expeditious proceedings; and

(3) whether such person or the opposing party,
or either party's representative, engaged in conduct primarily for the purpose of delaying the
litigation or increasing the cost thereof.

§ 4A. Whenever the United States is hereafter
injured in its business or property by reason of
anything forbidden in the antitrust laws it may sue
therefor in the United States district court for the
district in which the defendant resides or is found
or has an agent, without respect to the amount in
controversy, and shall recover actual damages by it
sustained and the cost of suit. The court may

award under this section, pursuant to a motion by the United States promptly made, simple interest on actual damages for the period beginning on the date of service of the pleading of the United States setting forth a claim under the antitrust laws and ending on the date of judgment, or for any shorter period therein, if the court finds that the award of such interest for such period is just in the circumstances. In determining whether an award of interest under this section for any period is just in the circumstances, the court shall consider only—

(1) whether the United States or the opposing party, or either party's representative, made motions or asserted claims or defenses so lacking in merit as to show that such party or representative acted intentionally for delay or otherwise acted in bad faith;

(2) whether, in the course of the action involved, the United States or the opposing party, or either party's representative, violated any applicable rule, statute, or court order providing for sanctions for dilatory behavior or otherwise providing for expeditious proceedings;

(3) whether the United States or the opposing party, or either party's representative, engaged in conduct primarily for the purpose of delaying the litigation or increasing the cost thereof; and

(4) whether the award of such interest is necessary to compensate the United States adequately for the injury sustained by the United States.

§ 4B. Any action to enforce any cause of action under sections 4, 4A, or 4C, shall be forever barred unless commenced within four years after the cause of action accrued. No cause of action barred under existing law on the effective date of this Act shall be revived by this Act.

§ 4C. (a)(1) Any attorney general of a State may bring a civil action in the name of such State, as parens patriae on behalf of natural persons residing in such State, in any district court of the United States having jurisdiction of the defendant, to secure monetary relief as provided in this section for injury sustained by such natural persons to their property by reason of any violation of the Sherman Act. The court shall exclude from the amount of monetary relief awarded in such action any amount of monetary relief (A) which duplicates amounts which have been awarded for the same injury, or (B) which is properly allocable to (i) natural persons who have excluded their claims pursuant to subsection (b)(2) of this section, and (ii) any business entity.

(2) The court shall award the State as monetary relief threefold the total damage sustained as described in paragraph (1) of this subsection, and the cost of suit, including a reasonable attorney's fee. The court may award under this paragraph, pursuant to a motion by such State promptly made, simple interest on the total damage for the period beginning on the date of service of such State's pleading setting forth a claim under the antitrust

laws and ending on the date of judgment, or for any shorter period therein, if the court finds that the award of such interest for such period is just in the circumstances. In determining whether an award of interest under this paragraph for any period is just in the circumstances, the court shall consider only—

(A) whether such State or the opposing party, or either party's representative, made motions or asserted claims or defenses so lacking in merit as to show that such party or representative acted intentionally for delay or otherwise acted in bad faith;

(B) whether, in the course of the action involved, such State or the opposing party, or either party's representative, violated any applicable rule, statute, or court order providing for sanctions for dilatory behavior or otherwise providing for expeditious proceedings; and

(C) whether such State or the opposing party, or either party's representative, engaged in conduct primarily for the purpose of delaying the litigation or increasing the cost thereof.

(b)(1) In any action brought under subsection (a)(1) of this section, the State attorney general shall, at such times, in such manner, and with such content as the court may direct, cause notice thereof to be given by publication. If the court finds that notice given solely by publication would deny due process of law to any person or persons, the court may direct further notice to such person or persons according to the circumstances of the case.

(2) Any person on whose behalf an action is brought under subsection (a)(1) may elect to exclude from adjudication the portion of the State claim for monetary relief attributable to him by filing notice of such election with the court within such time as specified in the notice given pursuant to paragraph (1) of this subsection.

(3) The final judgment in an action under subsection (a)(1) shall be res judicata as to any claim under section 4 of this Act by any person on behalf of whom such action was brought and who fails to give such notice within the period specified in the notice given pursuant to paragraph (1) of this subsection.

(c) An action under subsection (a)(1) shall not be dismissed or compromised without the approval of the court, and notice of any proposed dismissal or compromise shall be given in such manner as the court directs.

(d) In any action under subsection (a)—

(1) the amount of the plaintiffs' attorney's fee, if any, shall be determined by the court; and

(2) the court may, in its discretion, award a reasonable attorney's fee to a prevailing defendant upon a finding that the State attorney general has acted in bad faith, vexatiously, wantonly, or for oppressive reasons.

§ 4D. In any action under section 4C(a)(1), in which there has been a determination that a defendant agreed to fix prices in violation of the Sherman Act, damages may be proved and assessed in the aggregate by statistical or sampling methods, by the computation of illegal overcharges, or by such other reasonable system of estimating aggregate damages as the court in its discretion may permit without the necessity of separately proving the individual claim of, or amount of damage to, persons on whose behalf the suit was brought.

§ 4E. Monetary relief recovered in an action under section 4C(a)(1) shall—

(1) be distributed in such manner as the district court in its discretion may authorize; or

(2) be deemed a civil penalty by the court and deposited with the State as general revenues;

subject in either case to the requirement that any distribution procedure adopted afford each person a reasonable opportunity to secure his appropriate portion of the net monetary relief.

§ 4F. (a) Whenever the Attorney General of the United States has brought an action under the antitrust laws, and he has reason to believe that any State attorney general would be entitled to bring an action under this Act based substantially on the same alleged violation of the antitrust laws, he shall promptly give written notification thereof to such State attorney general.

(b) To assist a State attorney general in evaluating the notice or in bringing any action under this Act, the Attorney General of the United States shall, upon request by such State attorney general, make available to him, to the extent permitted by law, any investigative files or other materials which are or may be relevant or material to the actual or potential cause of action under this Act.

§ 4G. For the purposes of sections 4C, 4D, 4E, and 4F of this Act:

(1) The term "State attorney general" means the chief legal officer of a State, or any other person authorized by State law to bring actions under section 4C of this Act, and includes the Corporation Counsel of the District of Columbia, except that such term does not include any person employed or retained on—

(A) a contingency fee based on a percentage of the monetary relief awarded under this section; or

(B) any other contingency fee basis, unless the amount of the award of a reasonable attorney's fee to a prevailing plaintiff is determined by the court under section 4C(d)(1).

(2) The term "State" means a State, the District of Columbia, the Commonwealth of Puerto Rico, and any other territory or possession of the United States.

(3) The term "natural persons" does not include proprietorships or partnerships.

§ 4H. Sections 4C, 4D, 4E, 4F, and 4G shall apply in any State, unless such State provides by law for its nonapplicability in such State.

§ 5. (a) A final judgment or decree heretofore or hereafter rendered in any civil or criminal proceeding brought by or on behalf of the United States under the antitrust laws to the effect that a defendant has violated said laws shall be prima facie evidence against such defendant in any action or proceeding brought by any other party against such defendant under said laws as to all matters respecting which said judgment or decree would be an estoppel as between the parties thereto: *Provided*, That this section shall not apply to consent judgments or decrees entered before any testimony has been taken. Nothing contained in this section shall be construed to impose any limitation on the application of collateral estoppel except that, in any action or proceeding brought under the antitrust laws, collateral estoppel effect shall not be given to any finding made by the Federal Trade Commission under the antitrust laws or under section 5 of the Federal Trade Commission Act which could give rise to a claim for relief under the antitrust laws.

§ 5. (b)–(h) [Consent decree procedures added by the 1975 amendments, 88 Stat. 1706, are omitted.]

(i) Whenever any civil or criminal proceeding is instituted by the United States to prevent, restrain, or punish violations of any of the antitrust laws, but not including an action under section 4A, the running of the statute of limitations in respect of every private or State right of action arising under said laws and based in whole or in part on any matter complained of in said proceeding shall be suspended during the pendency thereof and for one year thereafter: *Provided, however,* That whenever the running of the statute of limitations in respect of a cause of action arising under sections 4 or 4C is suspended hereunder, any action to enforce such cause of action shall be forever barred unless commenced either within the period of suspension or within four years after the cause of action accrued.

§ 6. The labor of a human being is not a commodity or article of commerce. Nothing contained in the antitrust laws shall be construed to forbid the existence and operation of labor, agricultural, or horticultural organizations, instituted for the purposes of mutual help, and not having capital stock or conducted for profit, or to forbid or restrain individual members of such organizations from lawfully carrying out the legitimate objects thereof; nor shall such organizations, or the members thereof, be held or construed to be illegal combinations or conspiracies in restraint of trade, under the antitrust laws.

§ 7. No person engaged in commerce or in any activity affecting commerce shall acquire, directly or indirectly, the whole or any part of the stock or other share capital and no person subject to the jurisdiction of the Federal Trade Commission shall acquire the whole or any part of the assets of another person engaged also in commerce or in any activity affecting commerce where in any line of commerce in any section of the country, the effect of such acquisition may be substantially to lessen competition, or to tend to create a monopoly.

No person shall acquire, directly or indirectly, the whole or any part of the stock or other share capital and no person subject to the jurisdiction of the Federal Trade Commission shall acquire the whole or any part of the assets of one or more persons engaged in commerce or in any activity affecting commerce where in any line of commerce in any section of the country, the effect of such acquisition, of such stocks or assets, or of the use of such stock by the voting or granting of proxies or otherwise, may be substantially to lessen competition, or to tend to create a monopoly.

This section shall not apply to persons purchasing such stock solely for investment and not using the same by voting or otherwise to bring about, or in attempting to bring about, the substantial lessening of competition. Nor shall anything contained in this section prevent a corporation engaged in commerce or in any activity affecting commerce from causing the formation of subsidiary corporations for the actual carrying on of their immediate lawful business, or the natural and legitimate branches or extensions thereof, or from owning and holding all or a part of the stock of such subsidiary corporations, when the effect of such formation is not to substantially lessen competition.

Nor shall anything herein contained be construed to prohibit any common carrier subject to the laws to regulate commerce from aiding in the construction of branches or short lines so located as to become feeders to the main line of the company so aiding in such construction or from acquiring or owning all or any part of the stock of such branch lines, nor to prevent any such common carrier from acquiring and owning all or any part of the stock of a branch or short line constructed by an independent company where there is no substantial competition between the company owning the branch line so constructed and the company owning the main line acquiring the property or an interest therein, nor to prevent such common carrier from extending any of its lines through the medium of the acquisition of stock or otherwise of any other common carrier where there is no substantial competition between the company extending its lines and the company whose stock, property, or an interest therein is so acquired.

Nothing contained in this section shall be held to affect or impair any right heretofore legally acquired: *Provided,* That nothing in this section shall be held or construed to authorize or make lawful anything heretofore prohibited or made illegal by the antitrust laws, nor to exempt any person from the penal provisions thereof or the civil remedies therein provided.

Nothing contained in this section shall apply to transactions duly consummated pursuant to authority given by the Civil Aeronautics Board, Federal Communications Commission, Federal Power Commission, Interstate Commerce Commission, the Securities and Exchange Commission in the exercise of its jurisdiction under section 10 of the Public Utility Holding Company Act of 1935, the United States Maritime Commission, or the Secretary of Agriculture under any statutory provision vesting such power in such Commission, Secretary, or Board.

§ 7A. (a) Except as exempted pursuant to subsection (c), no person shall acquire, directly or indirectly, any voting securities or assets of any other person, unless both persons (or in the case of a tender offer, the acquiring person) file notification pursuant to rules under subsection (d)(1) and the waiting period described in subsection (b)(1) has expired, if—

(1) the acquiring person, or the person whose voting securities or assets are being acquired, is engaged in commerce or in any activity affecting commerce;

(2)(A) any voting securities or assets of a person engaged in manufacturing which has annual net sales or total assets of $10,000,000 or more are being acquired by any person which has total assets or annual net sales of $100,000,000 or more;

(B) any voting securities or assets of a person not engaged in manufacturing which has total assets of $10,000,000 or more are being acquired by any person which has total assets or annual net sales of $100,000,000 or more; or

(C) any voting securities or assets of a person with annual net sales or total assets of $100,000,000 or more are being acquired by any person with total assets or annual net sales of $10,000,000 or more; and

(3) as a result of such acquisition, the acquiring person would hold—

(A) 15 per centum or more of the voting securities or assets of the acquired person, or

(B) an aggregate total amount of the voting securities and assets of the acquired person in excess of $15,000,000.

In the case of a tender offer, the person whose voting securities are sought to be acquired by a person required to file notification under this subsection shall file notification pursuant to rules under subsection (d).

(b)(1) The waiting period required under subsection (a) shall—

(A) begin on the date of the receipt by the Federal Trade Commission and the Assistant Attorney General in charge of the Antitrust Division of the Department of Justice (hereinafter referred to in this section as the "Assistant Attorney General") of—

(i) the completed notification required under subsection (a), or

(ii) if such notification is not completed, the notification to the extent completed and a statement of the reasons for such noncompliance, from both persons, or, in the case of a tender offer, the acquiring person; and

(B) end on the thirtieth day after the date of such receipt (or in the case of a cash tender offer, the fifteenth day), or on such later date as may be set under subsection (e)(2) or (g)(2).

(2) The Federal Trade Commission and the Assistant Attorney General may, in individual cases, terminate the waiting period specified in paragraph (1) and allow any person to proceed with any acquisition subject to this section, and promptly shall cause to be published in the Federal Register a notice that neither intends to take any action within such period with respect to such acquisition.

(3) As used in this section—

(A) The term "voting securities" means any securities which at present or upon conversion entitle the owner or holder thereof to vote for the election of directors of the issuer or, with respect to unincorporated issuers, persons exercising similar functions.

(B) The amount or percentage of voting securities or assets of a person which are acquired or held by another person shall be determined by aggregating the amount or percentage of such voting securities or assets held or acquired by such other person and each affiliate thereof.

(c) The following classes of transactions are exempt from the requirements of this section—

(1) acquisitions of goods or realty transferred in the ordinary course of business;

(2) acquisitions of bonds, mortgages, deeds of trust, or other obligations which are not voting securities;

(3) acquisitions of voting securities of an issuer at least 50 per centum of the voting securities of which are owned by the acquiring person prior to such acquisition;

(4) transfers to or from a Federal agency or a State or political subdivision thereof;

(5) transactions specifically exempted from the antitrust laws by Federal statute;

(6) transactions specifically exempted from the antitrust laws by Federal statute if approved by a Federal agency, if copies of all information and documentary material filed with such agency are contemporaneously filed with the Federal Trade Commission and the Assistant Attorney General;

(7) transactions which require agency approval under section 18(c) of the Federal Deposit Insurance Act (12 U.S.C.A. § 1828(c)), or section 3 of the Bank Holding Company Act of 1956 (12 U.S.C.A. § 1842);

(8) transactions which require agency approval under section 4 of the Bank Holding Company Act of 1956 (12 U.S.C.A. § 1843), section 403 or 408(e) of the National Housing Act (12 U.S.C.A. §§ 1726

and 1730a), or section 5 of the Home Owners' Loan
Act of 1933 (12 U.S.C.A. § 1464), if copies of all
information and documentary material filed with
any such agency are contemporaneously filed with
the Federal Trade Commission and the Assistant
Attorney General at least 30 days prior to consummation of the proposed transaction;

(9) acquisitions, solely for the purpose of investment, of voting securities, if, as a result of such
acquisition, the securities acquired or held do not
exceed 10 per centum of the outstanding voting
securities of the issuer;

(10) acquisitions of voting securities, if, as a result of such acquisition, the voting securities acquired do not increase, directly or indirectly, the
acquiring person's per centum share of outstanding
voting securities of the issuer;

(11) acquisitions, solely for the purpose of investment, by any bank, banking association, trust company, investment company, or insurance company,
of (A) voting securities pursuant to a plan of reorganization or dissolution; or (B) assets in the ordinary course of its business; and

(12) such other acquisitions, transfers, or transactions, as may be exempted under subsection (d)(2)
(B).

(d) The Federal Trade Commission, with the concurrence of the Assistant Attorney General and by
rule in accordance with section 553 of title 5,

United States Code, consistent with the purposes of this section—

(1) shall require that the notification required under subsection (a) be in such form and contain such documentary material and information relevant to a proposed acquisition as is necessary and appropriate to enable the Federal Trade Commission and the Assistant Attorney General to determine whether such acquisition may, if consummated, violate the antitrust laws; and

(2) may—

(A) define the terms used in this section;

(B) exempt, from the requirements of this section, classes of persons, acquisitions, transfers, or transactions which are not likely to violate the antitrust laws; and

(C) prescribe such other rules as may be necessary and appropriate to carry out the purposes of this section.

(e)(1) The Federal Trade Commission or the Assistant Attorney General may, prior to the expiration of the 30-day waiting period (or in the case of a cash tender offer, the 15-day waiting period) specified in subsection (b)(1) of this section, require the submission of additional information or documentary material relevant to the proposed acquisition, from a person required to file notification with respect to such acquisition under subsection (a) of this section prior to the expiration of the waiting period specified in subsection (b)(1) of this section, or from any officer, director, partner, agent, or employee of such person.

(2) The Federal Trade Commission or the Assistant Attorney General, in its or his discretion, may extend the 30-day waiting period (or in the case of a cash tender offer, the 15-day waiting period) specified in subsection (b)(1) of this section for an additional period of not more than 20 days (or in the case of a cash tender offer, 10 days) after the date on which the Federal Trade Commission or the Assistant Attorney General, as the case may be, receives from any person to whom a request is made under paragraph (1), or in the case of tender offers, the acquiring person, (A) all the information and documentary material required to be submitted pursuant to such a request, or (B) if such request is not fully complied with, the information and documentary material submitted and a statement of the reasons for such noncompliance. Such additional period may be further extended only by the United States district court, upon an application by the Federal Trade Commission or the Assistant Attorney General pursuant to subsection (g) (2).

(f) If a proceeding is instituted or an action is filed by the Federal Trade Commission, alleging that a proposed acquisition violates section 7 of this Act or section 5 of the Federal Trade Commission Act, or an action is filed by the United States, alleging that a proposed acquisition violates such section 7 or section 1 or 2 of the Sherman Act, and the Federal Trade Commission or the Assistant Attorney General (1) files a motion for a preliminary injunction against consummation of such acquisition pendente lite, and (2) certifies to the United States district court for the judicial district within which the respondent resides or carries on business, or in which the action is brought, that it or he believes that the public interest requires relief pendente lite pursuant to this subsection—

(A) upon the filing of such motion and certification, the chief judge of such district court shall immediately notify the chief judge of the United States court of appeals for the circuit in which such district court is located, who shall designate a United States district judge to whom such action shall be assigned for all purposes; and

(B) the motion for a preliminary injunction shall be set down for hearing by the district judge so designated at the earliest practicable time, shall take precedence over all matters except older matters of the same character and trials pursuant to section 3161 of title 18, United States Code, and shall be in every way expedited.

(g)(1) Any person, or any officer, director, or partner thereof, who fails to comply with any provision of this section shall be liable to the United States for a civil penalty of not more than $10,000 for each day during which such person is in violation of this section. Such penalty may be recovered in a civil action brought by the United States.

(2) If any person, or any officer, director, partner, agent, or employee thereof, fails substantially to comply with the notification requirement under subsection (a) or any request for the submission of additional information or documentary material under subsection (e)(1) of this section within the waiting period specified in subsection (b)(1), and as may be extended under subsection (e)(2), the United States district court—

(A) may order compliance;

(B) shall extend the waiting period specified in subsection (b)(1) and as may have been extended under subsection (e)(2) until there has been substantial compliance, except that, in the case of a tender offer, the court may not extend such waiting period on the basis of a failure, by the person whose stock is sought to be acquired, to comply substantially with such notification requirement or any such request; and

(C) may grant such other equitable relief as the court in its discretion determines necessary or appropriate,

upon application of the Federal Trade Commission or the Assistant Attorney General.

(h) Any information or documentary material filed with the Assistant Attorney General or the Federal Trade Commission pursuant to this section shall be exempt from disclosure under section 552 of title 5, United States Code, and no such information or documentary material may be made public, except as may be relevant to any administrative or judicial action or proceeding. Nothing in this section is intended to prevent disclosure to either body of Congress or to any duly authorized committee or subcommittee of the Congress.

(i)(1) Any action taken by the Federal Trade Commission or the Assistant Attorney General or any failure of the Federal Trade Commission or the Assistant Attorney General to take any action under this section shall not bar any proceeding or any action with respect to such acquisition at any time under any other section of this Act or any other provision of law.

(2) Nothing contained in this section shall limit the authority of the Assistant Attorney General or the Federal Trade Commission to secure at any time from any person documentary material, oral testimony, or other information under the Antitrust Civil Process Act, the Federal Trade Commission Act, or any other provision of law.

(j) Beginning not later than January 1, 1978, the Federal Trade Commission, with the concurrence of the Assistant Attorney General, shall annually report to the Congress on the operation of this section. Such report shall include an assessment of the effects of this section, of the effects, purpose, and need for any rules promulgated pursuant thereto, and any recommendations for revisions of this section.

§ 8. [Provisions relating to banks and their officers, employees and directors are omitted.]

That from and after two years from the date of the approval of this Act no person at the same time shall be a director in any two or more corporations, any one of which has capital, surplus, and undivided profits aggregating more than $1,000,000, engaged in whole or in part in commerce, other than banks, banking associations, trust companies, and common carriers subject to the Act to regulate commerce, approved February fourth, eighteen hundred and eighty-seven, if such corporations are or shall have been theretofore, by virtue of their business and location of operation, competitors, so that the elimination of competition by agreement between them would constitute a violation of any of the provisions of any of the antitrust laws. The eligibility of a director under the foregoing provisions shall be determined by the aggregate amount of the capital, surplus, and undivided profits, exclusive of dividends declared but not paid to stockholders, at the end of the fiscal year of said corporation next preceding the election of directors, and when a director has been elected in accordance with the provisions of this Act it shall be lawful for him to continue as such for one year thereafter.

. . .

FEDERAL TRADE COMMISSION ACT [6]

15 U.S.C.A. §§ 41–58

§ 1. A Commission is created and established, to be known as the Federal Trade Commission

6. 38 Stat. 717 (1914), as amended, 15 U.S.C.A. §§ 41–58; only selected provisions are reprinted.

(hereinafter referred to as the Commission), which shall be composed of five Commissioners, who shall be appointed [for a term of seven years] by the President, by and with the advice and consent of the Senate. . . .

§ 4. The words defined in this section shall have the following meaning when found in this Act, to wit:

"Commerce" means commerce among the several States or with foreign nations, or in any Territory of the United States or in the District of Columbia, or between any such Territory and another, or between any such Territory and any States or foreign nation, or between the District of Columbia and any State or Territory or foreign nation.

"Corporation" shall be deemed to include any company, trust, so-called Massachusetts trust, or association, incorporated or unincorporated, which is organized to carry on business for its own profit or that of its members, and has shares of capital or capital stock or certificates of interest, and any company, trust, so-called Massachusetts trust, or association, incorporated or unincorporated, without shares of capital or capital stock or certificates of interest, except partnerships, which is organized to carry on business for its own profit or that of its members.

"Documentary evidence" includes all documents, papers, correspondence, books of account, and financial and corporate records.

"Acts to regulate commerce" means the Act entitled "An Act to regulate commerce," approved February 14, 1887 [the Interstate Commerce Act], and all Acts amendatory thereof and supplementary thereto and the Communications Act of 1934 and all Acts amendatory thereof and supplementary thereto.

"Antitrust Acts" [is defined as in Clayton Act § 1].

§ 5. (a)(1) Unfair methods of competition in or affecting commerce, and unfair or deceptive acts or practices in or affecting commerce, are declared unlawful.

(2) The Commission is hereby empowered and directed to prevent persons, partnerships, or corporations, except banks, savings & loan institutions described in section 18(f)(3), common carriers subject to the Acts to regulate commerce, air carriers and foreign air carriers subject to the Federal Aviation Act of 1958, and persons, partnerships, or corporations insofar as they are subject to the Packers and Stockyards Act, 1921, as amended, except as provided in section 406(b) of said Act, from using unfair methods of competition in or affecting commerce and unfair or deceptive acts or practices in or affecting commerce.

(3) This subsection shall not apply to unfair methods of competition involving commerce with foreign nations (other than import commerce) unless—

(A) such methods of competition have a direct, substantial, and reasonably foreseeable effect—

(i) on commerce which is not commerce with foreign nations, or on import commerce with foreign nations; or

(ii) on export commerce with foreign nations, of a person engaged in such commerce in the United States; and

(B) such effect gives rise to a claim under the provisions of this subsection, other than this paragraph.

If this subsection applies to such methods of competition only because of the operation of subparagraph (A)(ii), this subsection shall apply to such conduct only for injury to export business in the United States.

INDEX

References are to Pages

465

RULE OF REASON—Continued
Standard of, 248–50
Standard Oil (N.J.), 125, 169–70

SHERMAN ACT
    Generally, 19–27, 31–44
Conspiracy, 257–65
Early interpretations, 24–27
Mergers, 336–40

SYLVANIA CASE
Generally, 302–07

TRADE ASSOCIATIONS
    Generally, 230–47
Price verification, 239–44
Purposes, 230–34
Rule of reason, application of, 234, 238–39, 243–44

TYING
    Generally, 313–27
Patents, and, 398–99

VERTICAL RESTRAINTS
    Generally, 278–333
Clayton Act, 315–18
Distribution restrictions, 282–307
    Agents, 290–94
    Customer, 294–307
Exclusive Dealing, 328–33
Non price, 294–308
Per Se Rule, 324–27
Refusal to deal, 308–13
Resale price maintenance, 282–89
Rule of reason, 298–307
Sherman Act, 320–23
Supplier restrictions, 308–33
Sylvania case, 302–07
Territorial, 294–307
Tying, 313–27

†